Beagles For Dummies®

Cheat Sheet

Choosing a Breeder

When you look for a Beagle breeder, look for one who (see Chapter 3 for more details):

- ✔ Belongs to the National Beagle Club of America and exhibits her dogs in conformation, obedience, or other events
- ✔ Screens the dogs she breeds for hip problems and eye diseases, and can show you the results of such screenings
- ✔ Owns the mother dog (the dam) but not the father dog (the sire)
- ✔ Doesn't breed any female dog under 2 years of age and never breeds any female more than once a year
- ✔ Raises the puppies inside her home
- ✔ Begins socializing the puppies as soon as possible after birth
- ✔ Takes the puppies to her veterinarian for checkups and their initial shots
- ✔ Refuses to sell a puppy who's less than 7 weeks of age
- ✔ Investigates prospective buyers
- ✔ Guarantees the puppy's health and temperament in writing
- ✔ Stays in touch after the sale

Selecting a Puppy

Here's what to look for to make sure that you choose a healthy Beagle puppy (get the details from Chapter 4):

- ✔ A clean, healthy, friendly mother
- ✔ Easy movement without limping or apparent pain
- ✔ Bright, clear eyes
- ✔ Dry, odor-free ears
- ✔ Clean skin and full coat with no bald spots
- ✔ Healthy stools
- ✔ A friendly but not hyperactive personality

Logging On to Helpful Web Sites

- ✔ American Kennel Club: www.akc.org
- ✔ American Society for the Prevention of Cruelty to Animals: www.aspca.org
- ✔ The Humane Society of the United States: www.hsus.org
- ✔ American Veterinary Medical Association: www.avma.org
- ✔ Association of Pet Dog Trainers: www.apdt.com

For Dummies: Bestselling Book Series for Beginners

Beagles For Dummies®

Buying the Basics

Pick up these supplies now, and your Beagle's homecoming will go much more smoothly (Chapter 5 offers more details):

- Crate
- Baby gates and/or exercise pen
- Dog dishes
- Dog food
- Collar and leash
- Plastic bags to pick up poop
- Grooming gear including a brush, nail clippers, doggy toothbrush and toothpaste, and doggy shampoo
- Pet-stain cleaner
- A first-aid kit (Chapter 11 tells you what items to include)

Beagle-Proofing

Make sure that your home and yard are safe places for your Beagle before she joins your family. Consider doing the following (refer to Part II for additional advice):

- Install an escape-proof fence around your yard
- Put away all loose and hazardous items inside and outside
- Fasten electrical cords to the floor or wall with duct tape
- Block staircases with baby gates
- Install door guards for kitchen cabinets
- Move houseplants out of reach
- Move wastebaskets out of reach
- Put the toilet seat down!

Emergency Phone Numbers

Keep these phone numbers on your fridge or near your phone. For extra insurance, enter them into your cell phone's auto-dial.

Vet's Office	
Emergency Care Clinic	
Breeder	
Pet Sitter/Dog Walker	
Animal Poison Control	888-426-4435 ($55 consultation fee)

For Dummies: Bestselling Book Series for Beginners

Beagles

FOR

DUMMIES®

by Susan McCullough

BICENTENNIAL
1807
WILEY
2007
BICENTENNIAL

Wiley Publishing, Inc.

Beagles For Dummies®

Published by
Wiley Publishing, Inc.
111 River St.
Hoboken, NJ 07030-5774
www.wiley.com

Copyright © 2007 by Wiley Publishing, Inc., Indianapolis, Indiana

Published by Wiley Publishing, Inc., Indianapolis, Indiana

Published simultaneously in Canada

For general information on our other products and services, please contact our Customer Care Department within the U.S. at 800-762-2974, outside the U.S. at 317-572-3993, or fax 317-572-4002.

For technical support, please visit www.wiley.com/techsupport.

Wiley also publishes its books in a variety of electronic formats. Some content that appears in print may not be available in electronic books.

Library of Congress Control Number: 2006934823

ISBN-13: 978-0-470-03961-8

ISBN-10: 0-470-03961-2

Manufactured in the United States of America

10 9 8 7 6 5 4 3 2 1

1B/RT/RR/QW/IN

About the Author

Susan McCullough writes about all things dog for media outlets all over the United States. She is the family life columnist for *Dog Fancy,* the nation's most widely read dog magazine, and also has published articles in *Family Circle, The Washington Post, AKC Gazette, AKC Family Dog, Your Dog,* and *Popular Dogs.* She also is the author of several dog-care books, including *Housetraining For Dummies* (Wiley, 2002) and *Senior Dogs For Dummies* (Wiley, 2004).

Susan belongs to the Dog Writers Association of America (DWAA) and the American Society of Journalists and Authors. She is a three-time winner of the DWAA Maxwell Award for excellence in writing about dogs, and won the 2001 Eukanuba Canine Health Award for outstanding writing about canine health.

When she's not writing or hanging out with friends and family (both two-legged and four-legged), Susan counsels puzzled people on how to deal with the quandaries that inevitably arise when dogs join human households. She lives in Vienna, Virginia, with her husband, Stan Chappell; their daughter, Julie Chappell; and their Golden Retriever, Allie.

Dedication

For Beagles everywhere

Author's Acknowledgments

The author is just one member of a team that produces a book like this one. I want to thank everyone else who also made this book a reality, including

- Tracy Boggier, acquisitions editor at Wiley, who asked me to take on this project.

- Alissa Schwipps, senior project editor, who made our second book project together even more fun than the first.

- Nancy Fox, DVM, veterinarian and Beagle devotee, who made sure that the manuscript contains the best available info for those who love Snoopy-dogs.

- Stan Chappell, my husband, for reasons too numerous to elaborate on here.

- Julie Chappell, my daughter, for being exactly who she is.

- Windy Run's Allie McChappell CGC, who reminds me every day that life is always better when shared with at least one canine companion.

Publisher's Acknowledgments

We're proud of this book; please send us your comments through our Dummies online registration form located at www.dummies.com/register/.

Some of the people who helped bring this book to market include the following:

Acquisitions, Editorial, and Media Development

Senior Project Editor: Alissa Schwipps

Acquisitions Editor: Tracy Boggier

Copy Editors: Vicki Adang, Darren Meiss

Editorial Program Coordinator: Hanna K. Scott

Technical Editor: Nancy Fox, DVM

Senior Editorial Manager: Jennifer Ehrlich

Editorial Assistants: Erin Calligan, David Lutton

Cover Photos: © Ausloos, Henry/ Animals Animals Earth Scenes

Cartoons: Rich Tennant (www.the5thwave.com)

Composition Services

Project Coordinators: Heather Kolter and Jennifer Theriot

Layout and Graphics: Joyce Haughey, Stephanie D. Jumper, Barry Offringa, Brent Savage, Erin Zeltner

Special Art: Illustrations by Lisa S. Reed

Anniversary Logo Design: Richard Pacifico

Proofreaders: John Greenough, Charles Spencer, Techbooks

Indexer: Sherry Massey

Special Help
Carmen Krikorian

Publishing and Editorial for Consumer Dummies

Diane Graves Steele, Vice President and Publisher, Consumer Dummies

Joyce Pepple, Acquisitions Director, Consumer Dummies

Kristin A. Cocks, Product Development Director, Consumer Dummies

Michael Spring, Vice President and Publisher, Travel

Kelly Regan, Editorial Director, Travel

Publishing for Technology Dummies

Andy Cummings, Vice President and Publisher, Dummies Technology/General User

Composition Services

Gerry Fahey, Vice President of Production Services

Debbie Stailey, Director of Composition Services

Contents at a Glance

Table of Contents

Introduction

*A*sk any prospective dog owner what breeds she has in mind, and almost without fail, she'll include a Beagle on her list of possibilities. Her reasons aren't hard to figure out. Beagles have so much going for them: They're cute, they have easygoing personalities, they're small, they require relatively little grooming, and they're fun. And did I mention that they're cute? (I did? Well, no matter. Their cuteness is an attribute worth emphasizing.)

But inevitably, even a package that appears as perfect as a Beagle seems to be also contains some imperfections. After all, as my father says, "Dogs are only human." We humans are capable of wondrous achievements and considerable kindness — but alas, we are not perfect. We have enough flaws to make us interesting and then some. So, too, does the wonder-dog we call the Beagle.

Like any dog, a Beagle needs time and attention if he is to become the dream dog you're seeking. Feeding, training, and multiple walks to the pooch potty are among the many tasks you'll need to perform to raise a Beagle well. But Beagles also may pose some breed-specific challenges. If you're not prepared to deal with all of those challenges — general and breed-specific alike — you may find yourself gritting your teeth at your Snoopy-dog instead of delighting in his company.

I've written *Beagles For Dummies* so you won't have to grit your teeth — at least not very often. Instead, you'll not only lose your heart to one of these incredibly adorable creatures, you'll also come to appreciate the many wonderful qualities that Beagles bring to their people.

About This Book

Beagles For Dummies has two reasons for being: first, to be a people-friendly guide that tells you everything you must know about this breed; and second, to give you enough information to decide whether Beagles are, in fact, the breed for you. Between this book's covers, you find answers to questions like:

- ✔ What are Beagles supposed to look like and how are they supposed to behave?
- ✔ Should I choose a puppy or an adult dog? Male or female?

✔ How do I know that a Beagle breeder is a reputable breeder?

✔ What do I need to do to survive my Beagle's first few days at home? Heck, how do I survive, much less enjoy, his entire puppyhood?

✔ How and when should I feed my Beagle?

✔ What should I teach my Beagle to do? How do I teach him? What if I can't teach him anything?

✔ What health problems is my Beagle likely to have when he's young? How about when he grows up — or gets old?

This book answers all of those questions and a whole lot more. The great thing about this book is that you can find the answers to those questions and any others in any way you want. If you want to know everything about living with a Beagle, you may want to begin reading here and continue to the end. But if you have a specific concern, such as how to keep your Beagle out of the clothes hamper or why he tends to wander, feel free to skip the preliminaries. Instead, just scan the Table of Contents or Index and, from there, head to the pages that tell you exactly what you want to know.

Conventions Used in This Book

To help you navigate, this book, and all *For Dummies* books, include the following conventions:

✔ *Italics* emphasize and highlight new words or terms.

✔ **Boldfaced** text indicates the action parts of numbered steps.

✔ Monofont indicates a Web address.

As a writer who specializes in dog topics, I've added some conventions of my own. For example, most editors like to refer to dogs in gender-neutral terms. In other words, unless you're talking about a specific dog such as Prince or Princess, you're supposed to refer to members of the canine species as *it*. In this book, I break that rule.

Any dog, even when spayed or neutered, is clearly male or female and deserves the dignity of being referred to in that manner. For that reason, I refer to any dog as *he, she, him,* and *her*. I alternate between male and female pronouns in each chapter, using roughly an equal mix of each pronoun throughout the book. Either way, any of those pronouns apply to both genders unless I state otherwise. I also use the word *who*, not *that* or *which*, to refer to our four-legged friends.

I also like to write the way most people talk, even when the talk refers to a dog's bodily wastes. Consequently, I talk about when dogs *poop* and *pee,* not when they do *number one* and *number two,* or *tinkle* or *urinate* or *defecate.* Sometimes I also use the term *potty* to refer to bathroom matters. I also don't favor euphemisms when discussing important subjects. That's why I refer to the decision to end a dog's life as *euthanasia,* not *putting the dog to sleep.*

What You're Not to Read

This book is full of important, even essential, information to the would-be or actual Beagle owner, and I've assembled that information so you can find it easily and understand it the first time you read it. That said, not all of what you read fits the category of essential or even important; some falls under the interesting-but-you-really-don't-need-to-know-it category. To help you distinguish between what you must know and what you can do without, I've made the latter easy to recognize. The material in the following list may be interesting — but if you skip it, you won't be a deficient Beagle owner. Promise!

  ✓ **Text in sidebars:** The sidebars are shaded boxes that appear here and there throughout the book. They contain interesting tidbits that make you an even better Beagle owner — but if you skip them, you still know everything you need to know.

  ✓ **Anything highlighted with a Technical Stuff icon:** The information in these paragraphs is also interesting, but essential only if you're looking to go way, way beyond the basics of Beagle ownership.

  ✓ **The stuff on the copyright page:** The material on this page isn't even interesting, except to the publisher's legal department. Feel free to skip this page unless you're really into publishing or copyright law — and in that case, I'm sure you'll get more information on the subject somewhere else!

Foolish Assumptions

Every book is aimed at a certain type of reader, and this book is no exception. In writing this book, I've assumed that:

  ✓ You're thinking about adding a Beagle to your family, and you want to find out more about the breed before making your final decision.

✔ You can't decide whether to get a male or female Beagle, or whether to adopt a young puppy, an older puppy, or an adult dog.

✔ Your Beagle will arrive home soon, and you want to know how to get ready for his homecoming.

✔ You've either never had a Beagle before, or you had one in the distant past — and, either way, you need to find out as much as possible about Beagle care in the shortest possible time.

✔ You already own a Beagle and want some help schooling him in basics such as housetraining, coming when called, and sitting when told.

✔ You're having trouble training your Beagle, and you need some guidance to surmount his (and your) learning curve.

How This Book Is Organized

If you read any part of *Beagles For Dummies,* no matter how small, you'll add to your knowledge of how to raise and care for these wonderful dogs. Here's how I organized the book to help you live happily ever after with a Beagle and to deal with any challenges that come your way.

Part I: Getting to Know Beagles

A decision to open your heart and home to a Beagle shouldn't be made in haste. This part tells you what you need to know to choose your dream dog. You discover the breed's origins and about how a healthy Beagle should look and act. You also discover good places to look for a Beagle and how to evaluate the puppies or dogs you see when you get there.

Part II: Starting Life with Your Beagle

Now that you've selected the Beagle of your dreams, what do you do? Part II answers that question by guiding you through the whole process of preparing for your new dog's arrival: bringing your Beagle home and not only surviving, but thriving, during the days that follow the homecoming; puppy-proofing your house before your Beagle arrives; figuring out where your new dog should eat, sleep, poop, and play; coping with the hectic first day and night; and starting to bond with your Beagle. It's all here.

Part III: Caring for Your Beagle

This part covers the nuts and bolts of Beagle care: what and how to feed your dog; common health issues and how to deal with them; and how to take great care of your Beagle whether you're tending the home fires or out seeing the world. Here you get some ideas on how to sift through the dizzying array of feeding options for your dog; how to work with your vet to keep your Beagle healthy; and what to do when, inevitably, something goes wrong. Here, too, is where you find information on health conditions that are common to Beagles.

Part IV: Training Your Beagle

Charlie Brown may have said, "Happiness is a warm puppy," but when that puppy is a Beagle, happiness also is a trained Beagle. You are your Beagle's first and best teacher, and in this part you find the information and direction you need to mold your four-legged friend into a model citizen. You find out how to teach your Beagle proper potty protocol, which is a crucial component to living happily ever after with one of these dogs. You also discover how to teach basic commands and what you can do if your Beagle proves to be a challenging student. Also included are pointers on how to work with experts such as dog trainers and animal behaviorists.

Part V: The Part of Tens

Here's where you find information that provides extra hints on how to keep your Beagle healthy and happy and describes common mistakes that Beagle owners make. In addition, a final chapter lists some interesting facts about how Beagles — canine and otherwise — affect our lives.

Finally, if you want additional resources that provide more information about Beagles, I've included an appendix chock full of information and ideas at the very end of the book.

Icons Used in This Book

To help you find particular kinds of information as you read this book, keep your eyes peeled for the following icons:

This icon appears whenever an idea or item can save you time, money, or stress when taking care of your Beagle.

Any time you see this icon, you know the information that follows is so important that it's worth reading more than once.

This icon flags information that highlights dangers to your Beagle's health or well-being.

This icon appears next to information that's interesting but not essential. Don't be afraid to skip these paragraphs.

Where to Go from Here

You can read this book any way you choose. If you want to jump-start your knowledge of all things Beagle, start at the beginning and continue through to the end. On the other hand, if you need to read up on just a couple of specific issues, mosey on over to the Table of Contents or to the Index to determine exactly where to find the information you need. For example, if you already have your Beagle and need to teach him to do his business outside rather than inside, head to Chapter 14. On the other hand, if you're still trying to decide whether to get a Beagle, check out Chapters 1 and 2.

Finally, this book is meant to be a reference manual and guide, but it doesn't replace the advice that veterinarians, trainers, and behaviorists can give in person after they work with you and your one-of-a-kind dog. If the suggestions here don't work for you or your Beagle, or if you can't find an answer to a particular question in this book, don't hesitate to consult any of these professionals.

Part I
Getting to Know Beagles

"Like a lot of Beagles, he's pretty domesticated, but there's still some of the hunter in him."

In this part . . .

So you're thinking of adding a Beagle to your life? Good for you! Life with these little hounds can lead to years of merriment, entertainment, and love — if you do your homework beforehand. Part I gives you all the information you need to make sure that the Beagle is the right breed for you and advice on choosing your own very special Beagle soul mate.

Chapter 1

Beagles and You: Made for Each Other?

*W*ho can resist a Beagle? Those floppy ears, soulful eyes, and irrepressible good spirits can melt the heart of the most stone-cold human being on the planet. Even better, they're low maintenance — as least when you compare them to long-haired breeds, such as Afghan Hounds, Golden Retrievers, and Collies. But despite their many great qualities, Beagles aren't necessarily for everyone. To determine whether the Beagle is your dream dog, you need to know much more about the breed. This chapter summarizes the many advantages that Beagles offer to the wannabe dog owner, and also describes what Beagles need to live happily ever after with you.

Ain't Nothin' but a Hound Dog

The American Kennel Club (AKC), which is the number-one arbiter of dog breeds in the United States, recognizes more than 150 breeds. To make more sense of these various manifestations of *Canis familiaris,* the AKC has developed seven breed classifications, or *groups.* The breeds within each group generally have similar origins and talents, although they may not all look very much like each other.

The Beagle belongs to the AKC Hound Group. That's because although any dog of any breed has a far better sense of smell than any human, the hound breeds have the best sniffers of all. Those noses enable hounds to be excellent hunters, and they can do their hunting without getting very much direction from their human partners. Many hounds, such as Greyhounds and Scottish Deerhounds, have great eyesight, too.

Physically and temperamentally, hounds are a pretty diverse group. Some breeds are sweet and mellow, others are feisty, and still others are somewhat aloof. Some, like the Afghan Hound, are quite large. Others, like the Dachshund, are notably short in stature. Coat types range from short and hard to long and soft, with a lot of variation in between. Still, most hounds are happy to curl up with you and share the love if they've had sufficient exercise and attention. And unlike some breeds that act as though they're the canine embodiments of Velcro, hounds are relatively independent. Occasionally they need their space — and if you sometimes need your space, they understand and give it to you.

Within the Hound kingdom, the Beagle is the court jester. He's a merry little dog who keeps everyone in stitches. He's a sociable fellow who enjoys company without getting neurotic. And he can be plenty mischievous, not to mention sufficiently independent to get into that mischief from beyond your immediate purview.

Other hound breeds

Beagles have plenty of company in the Hound group. Other breeds lumped into this category include:

Afghan Hound	Ibizan Hound
American Foxhound	Irish Wolfhound
Basenji	Norwegian Elkhound
Basset Hound	Otterhound
Black and Tan Coonhound	Petit Basset Griffon Vendéen
Bloodhound	Pharaoh Hound
Borzoi	Rhodesian Ridgeback
Dachshund	Saluki
English Foxhound	Scottish Deerhound
Greyhound	Whippet
Harrier	

The Beagle's Bill of Rights

Just like the American colonists back at the time of the Revolutionary War, every Beagle has certain inalienable rights — needs that must be fulfilled in order to have a happy life with you. Most of these needs are pretty basic, and no less than what you'd want for yourself. In other words, a little empathy from you should result in a lot of comfort and joy for your Snoopy-dog. That empathy should help you realize that Beagles and all other dogs need and deserve the things described in the following sections.

Lots of love

Beagles are relatively independent dogs, but they're also very social creatures. That means that a Beagle may have his own agenda, but that agenda almost always includes hanging out with his people as often as possible. He's not necessarily a stick-to-your-side dog, but he certainly wants to be part of any action that's going on within his household. If you're looking for an aloof pooch who prefers solitude to companionship, the Beagle is not for you.

Safe shelter

As Chapter 2 explains, Beagles were originally bred to hunt rabbits, but the typical pet Beagle doesn't get much opportunity to chase down bunnies (probably much to the bunnies' relief!). For that reason, today's Beagle isn't meant to live a life in a yard, a dog-house, or an outdoor kennel. He should live in your house with you, and be part of your family.

That said, keeping your Beagle in your house can be a challenging enterprise. The little hound's sense of humor may not always be to your liking; he has an uncanny ability to ferret out stuff that you don't want him to have (lingerie, anyone?). Chapter 5 contains lots of suggestions on how to make your home a great place for a Beagle and also limit his ability to make mischief.

Food, glorious food

Beagles are relatively small, so you don't need to worry about your canine companion running up a humongous food bill. Still your little hound does need enough nutritious food to keep his skin pink, his coat healthy, and his physique sleek. Chapter 8 explains not only what to feed your Beagle, but also how to feed him so he reaps the maximum possible benefit from every meal.

Room to run (preferably with you)

Like other dogs that were bred to hunt, the Beagle has a prodigious amount of energy — even though he's pretty small for a hunting dog. Unless you're giving your dog regular chances to chase down rabbits, you need to provide him with other opportunities to exercise. A couple of brisk, 20-minute walks each day can keep his muscles toned (not to mention what such strolls may do for your own health!), but don't limit yourself to twice-daily turns around your block. Head on over to Chapter 9 to find ways to be active that both you and your little hound will love.

A touch of class (es)

All dogs need some training, and the Beagle is no exception. For one thing, the trained Beagle is probably a lot happier than his untrained counterpart. The unschooled dog makes lots of mistakes, such as messing in the house, jumping up on people, and trashing household goods, but doesn't understand why his people are always angry at him. How would you feel if someone you depended on was angry at you, and you had no idea why? Probably pretty miserable. The same is true of the clueless, untrained Beagle.

By contrast, the trained Beagle has a much better time of fitting in with his family. Because he knows that he's not supposed to take a whiz on the white Berber carpet in the living room, he'll never get scolded for doing so. Because he understands that he's not supposed to become a canine pogo stick and jump all over his people, those people are happy to get down to his level and interact with him. The Beagle is a born extrovert, so all this positive interaction can't help but make him happy.

And he's not the only one who's happy — the people in the trained Beagle's life are happy, too. They have a family member who's a pleasure to be around and who doesn't cause undue stress. They don't have to worry about their Snoopy-dog growling at strangers, snapping at anyone who comes near his favorite toy, or finding an unwelcome little deposit atop their favorite easy chair. People with trained dogs are free to truly enjoy their dogs. A trained dog is a true companion, a friend in the best sense of the word.

Finally, the trained Beagle also is more likely to be safe than his untrained counterpart. That's because a Beagle with basic obedience training will know how to come when he's called, stop doing something when told to do so, and perform other maneuvers that can help keep him out of trouble.

Part IV gives you the scoop on how to transform your clueless little hound into a well-mannered Beagle, and how to deal with a dog who's got one or more challenging behavioral issues. Also included is information not only on how to train your Beagle yourself, but also on how to choose an obedience instructor and to choose among training options.

Great health care

Beagles generally are very healthy dogs — but like all dogs (and, for that matter, people), they need good medical care to stay that way. Providing such care is a two-pronged effort that consists of:

- ✔ **Preventing illness:** You and your veterinarian work together to keep all of your Beagle's systems functioning at optimal levels. Such care includes regular checkups, immunizations when necessary, determining your Beagle's reproductive future, and getting a handle on how your Beagle looks and acts when he's healthy. Chapter 11 addresses all these issues and more.

- ✔ **Treating illness or injury:** You and your vet work in partnership to help your Beagle recover from any illness or injury he sustains. Chapter 12 outlines symptoms that require an emergency visit to your veterinarian or emergency clinic, those that require a phone call to your vet, and which ones shouldn't cause you any worry. Chapter 11 gives you the lowdown on how to care for your dog after the visit to the vet, including a primer on dispensing any medication the vet prescribes.

Although Beagles generally enjoy good health, they are more vulnerable to certain conditions than other dogs are. Chapter 12 outlines those conditions and describes how you and your vet can resolve them.

Good grooming

Unlike other dogs, especially those with long hair, Beagles need relatively little grooming. However, "little grooming" does not mean the same thing as "no grooming"! The Beagle does require certain sprucing-up rituals to look and feel his best. Among those rituals: daily tooth brushing, weekly coat brushing, a monthly bath, periodic ear cleaning and nail trims, and ongoing efforts to keep his coat free from parasites such as fleas and ticks. Chapter 10 offers a primer on how to groom your Beagle.

Why Beagles Are Wonderful

Beagles don't win the breed popularity contest, but they come darn close. The American Kennel Club reports that in 2005, the most recent year for which figures are available, Beagles were the fifth-most popular of the AKC's 154 recognized breeds. Only Labrador Retrievers, Golden Retrievers, Yorkshire Terriers, and German Shepherd Dogs drew more registrations than the Beagle did. The little hound has been consistently popular over several decades — in fact, the breed was number one in registrations from 1953 through 1959.

What's behind the Beagle's appeal? Probably several factors: For starters, they're cute; they're small; and they're easy to groom. Other pluses are that most Beagles are multitalented, supersociable, and get along well with children.

Hop on over to Chapter 2 to get more info on why so many people choose to share their lives with one or more Beagles. You'll also discover the Beagle's European ancestry and get the lowdown on what a Snoopy-dog is supposed to look like.

Buyer's Remorse: Why a Beagle May Not Be Your Dream Dog

As wonderful as Beagles are, they're not for everybody. In the interest of objectivity, it's only fair that I outline some of the challenges of trying to live happily ever after with one of these little hounds.

Among the Beagle's less-than-sterling attributes is his occasional stubbornness — in fact, without training, the Beagle can be downright ornery if his priorities conflict with yours. Part IV helps you counteract this independence — or at least channel it in another direction — by giving you detailed suggestions on how to civilize your little hound. I pay special attention to a frequent complaint from Beagle owners — that their dogs frequently flunk potty training — by devoting an entire chapter (Chapter 14) to housetraining.

Another possible problem that Beagle ownership may pose is that the dog's short, hard coat is practically guaranteed to worsen any airborne allergies that a person has. If dog hair makes you sneeze, a Beagle's presence may turn you into a sneezing machine.

Another possible downside is the breed's, well, mouthiness. Beagles are vocal creatures, and are not shy about expressing themselves in a regular dog bark or in that unique form of song known as howling. They are hounds, after all, and hounds do howl.

Chapter 2 explains what you may not like about Beagles, so you can make an objective decision about whether this breed is the right one for you and your family.

What to Ask Yourself

The best way to determine whether you're ready to welcome a Beagle into your life is to ask yourself questions that help you assess your needs and the dog's needs, and determine whether those two sets of priorities are compatible. This section offers points to ponder as you make this crucial decision.

Why do I want a Beagle?

Be sure that the reasons you want a Beagle result from your knowledge of the breed and yourself, not from misconceptions or will-o-the-wisp whims. Think about the issues in the following sections.

What do I like about Beagles?

Maybe you're interested in Snoopy-dogs because you grew up with one, and your memories of that dog are warm, fuzzy, and soft-focus. But it's important to remember that childhood memories don't tell the whole story of life with an individual dog.

That Beagle you loved also may have driven your mother crazy, perhaps because the dog never learned basic bathroom manners. And even if that Beagle was housetrained (to your mom's understandable relief), that dog was a unique individual. You probably will never find a Beagle who's quite like him — nor should you try to.

Or maybe you've met your neighbor's Beagle and adore that dog's friendly, outgoing personality. However, that dog not only has his own one-of-a-kind temperament, but also probably has had more than a little training and positive exposure to people. To help your Beagle be as sociable as your neighbor's, you'll need to put in *lots* of time to teach him basic manners and help him learn that the world can be a friendly place.

Chapter 2 tells you more about Beagle traits, and Chapter 7 explains how to socialize your Beagle. Part IV discusses how to make your Beagle a good canine citizen.

Who is this dog for?

Only two answers to this question are okay: "for me" or "for me and my family." In other words, no Beagle or other dog should be a gift — and please don't bestow a Beagle on another person as a surprise. Chances are, that surprise or gift will not be welcome. Unless you know that the recipient is dying to have a dog and is prepared to care for one, give an inanimate gift, such as a plush Beagle or other stuffed animal, instead.

And please don't get a Beagle "for the kids" unless you, the parent, are prepared to take full responsibility for the dog's care. Little kids generally are too young and irresponsible to care for a dog properly. Older kids and teens may have the necessary maturity, but they don't have the necessary time. I'm lucky if my own teenage daughter has the time to walk our dog one night a week. Fortunately, I adore our dog and am his main caregiver — so my daughter's lack of time to help out isn't an issue.

Have I recently lost a dog?

Living with a dog, no matter how wonderful he is, carries a major downside: He will probably die before you do. And when he does, the loss leaves a huge hole in your life — and in your heart. The same is true if your dog is simply lost and hasn't returned, or if you had to relinquish the dog to a shelter or somewhere else because you could no longer live with the dog. At such times, it's natural to want to fill those holes with a new canine companion. By doing so, you hope to staunch the flow of grief that's flowing from your soul.

But unless you've come to terms with your loss, hold off on adding a new dog to your life. If you're still angry or grieving over the dog who's no longer here, you'll have a hard time forming a bond with the dog who's arrived. Any dog deserves to have a person who loves him without qualification. If you're still coping with the loss of an earlier canine companion, bonding with a new dog can be all but impossible.

No animal can replace another. Each dog, whether he's a Beagle or any other breed, is a unique individual and deserves to be appreciated as such. If you're still processing the loss of your previous pooch, you're not going to appreciate the special qualities a new dog will bring to your life. For both your sake and the new dog's, hold off on bringing that dog into your life until your sadness and anger over the loss of the previous dog give way to happy memories. I promise you that change will happen — in time.

If you had to relinquish a dog to a shelter or rescue group because the dog had behavioral problems, or if you had problems that made dog ownership impossible, make sure all such issues are resolved before you bring a new dog into your life. Otherwise, the issues that doomed your relationship with Dog No. 1 are likely to recur with Dog No. 2.

Do I have commitment issues?

A Beagle has a pretty good life expectancy for a dog: 10 to 14 years on average, and in some cases, even longer. If you add a puppy to your household, you're looking at more than a decade of care; with an older dog, your time together will be shorter, but the care you need to give will be the same. A Beagle from a shelter or rescue group may need even more care. Such dogs may have behavioral problems because they were mistreated or abandoned.

In any case, before you take any dog into your heart and home, you need to be sure that you can commit yourself to the animal for his entire lifetime. Consider the following questions:

Have I been thinking about getting a dog for a while?

You shouldn't add a dog to your life on impulse. If you've suddenly seen a dog whom you want to adopt immediately, slow down. Unless you've pondered whether you're ready for a dog and whether you can care for that dog properly, you need to wait. No dog deserves to be stuck with a person who's made a hasty decision that she regrets — or, worse, to be abandoned or relinquished to a shelter because that impulsive person decided that she didn't want a dog after all.

Have I thought about how a dog will change my life?

When you welcome a dog into your home, your life changes. Gone are the days when you can leave the office at 5 or later and head over to the local watering hole to schmooze with friends or colleagues — not when you have a dog who's sitting at home waiting to be fed, taken out, and played with after being home alone all day. Gone, too, are the days when you can sleep in on Saturday morning or stay inside on a rainy evening — not when you have a pooch who needs to potty outside at those times.

Your dog will need your care and attention every single day of his life — if not from you directly, then from someone trustworthy when you can't be there. From now on, any plans you make must take into account not just what you want, but also what your dog needs.

Am I willing to put a dog's needs ahead of my own desires?

A dog depends on you not only for basic care, but also for love and companionship — and you need to put that dependent individual's needs ahead of what you may want. Ignore those needs and you're likely to have a very neurotic dog.

I learned this lesson one long-ago summer when, as a single, dog-owning woman living in a city, I rented a share in a beach house that was located several hours' drive from my home. Every other weekend, I'd head to the beach house and board my dog in a local kennel. Within a month or so, Molly had become very skittish and would start freaking out whenever I was out of her sight, even when I went to the bathroom. (She'd cry outside the closed bathroom door.) I realized that between my being at work all day and being away on the weekends, Molly was literally crying for my attention. Her need for me was clear, so I ended my beach weekends. Molly was much happier — and, in the end, so was I.

Is my home good for a Beagle?

The Beagle is a highly adaptable fellow, but not even a Snoopy-dog is suitable for each and every home. To determine whether your home is Beagle-friendly or even Beagle-neutral, consider the following:

Do I already have a dog?

Neither a "yes" nor a "no" automatically means that your domicile isn't suitable for a Beagle. But if you do have a dog, and that dog is large, you may have a problem. That's because in the inevitable jockeying for top-dog position that will ensue when your Beagle hits the scene — a jockeying that could include growls, snarls, and wrestling matches that rival the WWE's *SmackDown* — a larger dog is likely to win, no matter how feisty your Beagle is. The best your Beagle can hope for is to escape uninjured.

In general, you're better off if both dogs are of the same approximate size and of opposite genders. Even then, however, you need to supervise the introductions and make sure the two dogs learn to get along. Chapter 6 describes how to introduce your new Beagle to any other canine members of your household.

What about my kids?

Beagles usually get along well with kids, assuming that the kids know how to treat a dog properly. But in too many families, that isn't the case. If your children are under the age of 6, think twice about getting a Beagle or any other dog. Hop on over to Chapter 6 for suggestions on how to help your Beagle and your kids become best friends.

Do I live in an apartment?

A Beagle will not endear you to your neighbors if he gives in to his urge to howl. Think twice about bringing a Beagle into such close quarters. Your neighbors will be grateful.

Do I spend much time at home?

No one says that your Beagle needs to have you around 24/7, but this very social pooch will be much happier if you or someone else is around for at least part of the day. If you're the sort who's on the go outside your home from the break of dawn until the dead of night, you may have a hard time fitting a Beagle — or any other dog — into your life.

Can I afford a Beagle?

Dog ownership doesn't come cheap. Beyond the upfront cost of buying or adopting the dog, you take on plenty of other expenses when you welcome a dog into your family. Here's what you can expect to pay for over your Beagle's lifetime:

- **The dog:** No matter where you get your Beagle — from a shelter, a rescue group, or a reputable breeder — you'll have to part with some cash to bring that dog home. In mid-2006, the Beagle rescue group in my area charged a $200 adoption fee to cover the cost of that Beagle's care in a foster home, spaying or neutering, and a microchip implant, among other expenses. A nearby animal shelter charged $100 to $300 to adopt a dog, depending on the animal's size. A reputable breeder is likely to charge several hundred dollars for a puppy, particularly if the pup is a show prospect. Chapter 3 outlines where you should look for the Beagle of your dreams — and where you shouldn't look, too.

- **Supplies:** You'll need to lay in some Beagle equipment before you acquire your Beagle: for starters, a crate, dishes, grooming gear, collar, leash, food, and toys. Chapter 5 tells you everything you need to buy for Beagle before he comes home.

- **Medical care:** Every Beagle needs a yearly wellness exam, as well as periodic immunizations against various diseases. And unless you plan to breed your Beagle, you'll also have to pay for the dog to be spayed or neutered — unless you adopt a rescue or shelter dog who's already been fixed. Additional expenses will result when your Beagle gets sick and needs expert attention. Chapters 7 and 11 describe how you can work with your vet to keep your Beagle in the pink, and Chapter 12 discusses how to cope if your dog becomes ill or injured.

✔ **Travel expenses:** If you travel, you need to consider the costs of taking your Beagle with you or leaving him home. Chapter 13 covers the pro's and con's of either option.

A Final Thought

If you've thought carefully about why you want a Beagle, concluded that your domicile would be perfect for a little hound, determined that you will be a great parent and companion to a Snoopy-dog, and know that you can deal with the challenges this breed presents, congratulations! You've decided to add a wonderful dog to your life.

However, your decision-making is far from over. Now you need to determine whether you want a male or female Beagle; whether you want a puppy, young adult, or senior pooch; and where you want to start looking for your future companion. You also need to arm yourself with info on what to look for when evaluating the Beagles you meet. The rest of Part I will give you the scoop on how to find the Beagle who's just right for you.

Chapter 2

The Incredible, Lovable Beagle

*N*o question about it: If we were to rate the various dog breeds for cuteness and adorability on a scale of 1 to 10, the Beagle would probably score a 15. The dog's huge and winsome eyes, soft and floppy ears, and snuggle-able size appeal enormously to humans of all ages.

But the Beagle is much more than a saucer-eyed canine love object. Like so many other breeds, the Beagle originated to work with people to perform one or more specific tasks for the benefit of human beings. In this chapter, I discuss what those tasks were, how the Beagle helped to accomplish them, and how the Beagle's history affects the breed today.

Mommy, Where Do Beagles Come From?

Determining the Beagle's origins is a tricky proposition — mainly because historians don't agree as to when the very first Beagles appeared. Some claim that the ancient Greeks bred small hounds for the purpose of hunting rabbits many hundreds of years before the birth of Christ. Others maintain that the breed's ancestry dates from around 200 A.D.

What's in the name?

The origin of the term *Beagle* is as mysterious as the origin of the breed itself. Some dictionaries credit the French with coining the term *be'guele* to denote an open mouth — perhaps a reference to the breed's ability to howl. Other sources suggest that the breed's name derived from the French term *begle,* Celtic term *beag,* or the Old English *begele.* All three terms mean small — which is appropriate, considering the breed's small size.

But while scholars may disagree as to when the little hound first appeared on the scene, those who study Beagle history do seem to agree that the ancestors of the Beagles we know today developed in England as early as the 1300s to hunt hares. In fact, in the prologue to *The Canterbury Tales,* the 13th century author Geoffrey Chaucer describes a prioress, or nun, who had "small houndes . . . that she fed with roasted flesh, and milk, and wastel bread."

However, the breed name didn't appear in print until at least a century later. The known debut of the name *Beagle* in the English language was in 1475, in a story called *The Squire of Low Degree.* The author, who is unknown, wrote, "With theyr begles in that place and seven-score raches [small French hounds] at his rechase . . ."

By the time Elizabeth I ascended the British throne in 1558, many British nobles liked to hunt rabbits with the help of *pocket Beagles*: very small hunting hounds that measured only 9 inches tall at the shoulder. (By comparison, today's Beagles are supposed to measure between 13 and 15 inches.)

Although these diminutive hounds pursued their long-eared quarry with great enthusiasm, the rise of fox hunting — which most nobles found far more exciting than hunting rabbits or hares — required hounds that were bigger and faster than the pocket Beagle. Consequently, by the mid-1700s, the popularity of Beagles among the English nobility declined in favor of a dog that is the ancestor of today's *Foxhound,* a dog that is considerably larger than any Beagle, pocket-sized or otherwise.

But in the 1800s, the British began to regain their interest in hunting with Beagles. Under the leadership of the Reverend Philip Honeywood, among others, the British began to develop fine hunting packs of Beagles. At the same time, many dog fanciers in England began to show their canine stock in events designed to build interest in breeding the dogs being shown. These events were the first *conformation dog shows,* which live today in such well-known gatherings as England's Crufts show and the American Westminster Kennel Club dog show. To provide a vehicle for showing Beagles, a group of British enthusiasts formed The Beagle Club in 1890.

Meanwhile, across the Atlantic Ocean, Beagles were earning their keep in American households by hunting game and thus helping to put food on American tables. But by the mid-19th century, Americans were becoming just as interested in dog shows as their counterparts on the other side of the pond.

Some Americans began importing high-quality British Beagles, and by 1884 — the same year that the American Kennel Club (AKC) formed (see the "Just what is the AKC, anyway?" sidebar) — these enthusiasts had formed the American-English Beagle Club to exhibit their dogs in conformation shows. At the same time, though, another group of enthusiasts formed the National Beagle Club (NBC) of America to not only improve the Beagle's looks but also its ability to hunt game. By the end of the 19th century, the two clubs had merged into one organization dedicated to improving the breed's performance in the show ring and in the field.

Although some of today's Beagles have earned accolades as both conformation champions and field champions, many continue to excel in either one venue or the other. As I explain in Chapter 4, these differences are crucial considerations in what sort of Beagle companion you should search for and select.

Just what is the AKC, anyway?

The American Kennel Club (AKC), headquartered in New York City and Raleigh, North Carolina, records data and statistics for the 154 dog breeds — including the Beagle — that the club considers to be purebred. Among the info the club gathers are births of litters, registrations of individual dogs, and titles that dogs earn in events such as dog shows, agility trials, and competitive obedience.

But the AKC is more than just a registry. The organization also sponsors all kinds of events at which dogs earn those titles. These events include not only the three types listed above, but also such varied activities as tracking competitions, herding tests, and hunting trials. Although the AKC serves as a sponsor, the actual events are held by clubs that belong to the AKC, such as the National Beagle Club of America.

The AKC also tries to promote responsible dog breeding and ownership through education programs targeted to breeders and owners. The organization tries to spread the word on good breeding practices, but it doesn't have any enforcement or endorsement powers. A puppy with AKC papers is simply a puppy registered with the AKC. The papers don't guarantee a dog's health or temperament.

The Official Beagle Blueprint

Although Beagles have been around in one form or another for quite awhile, the Snoopy-dog that most people are familiar with is only a little more than a century old. That dog's adorable face, tenacious personality, awesome scent-sniffing ability, and obsession with bunnies didn't happen by accident — trust me, no hot doggy love and subsequent surprise puppies occurred here! Today's best Beagles, like all high-quality purebred dogs, result from breedings that are carefully planned by human beings.

Why all the care in planning? Because human beings want Beagles to have a certain look and temperament. In fact, the National Beagle Club of America developed a multipage set of specifications that describe in precise detail what a perfect Beagle should look and act like. (Likewise, all other national breed clubs produce similar specifications for their respective breeds.) This blueprint for a Beagle, which is called the *breed standard,* outlines what reputable breeders should try to produce in their Beagle puppies and what judges should look for when they assess Beagles in the conformation show ring. The breed standard puts into words what a picture such as Figure 2-1 shows: the ideal Beagle.

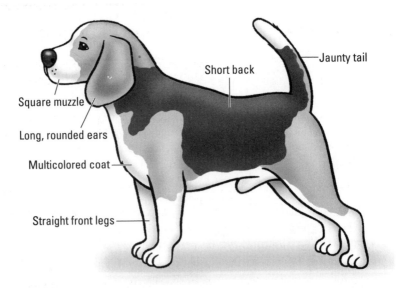

Jaunty tail

Short back

Square muzzle

Long, rounded ears

Multicolored coat

Straight front legs

Figure 2-1: Highlights of the Beagle breed standard.

The following sections describe the breed standard developed by the National Beagle Club and recognized by the AKC.

General appearance

The AKC standard specifies that a Beagle should resemble a minia-ture Foxhound that is solid and big for his inches, with the wear-and-tear look of a hound that can last in the chase and follow his quarry to the death. In other words, the ideal Beagle can look cute, but he shouldn't look frail or delicate. He should embody the look of a solid dog who will chase a rabbit or other quarry until the quarry gives up, wears out, and/or gets caught.

The standard also notes that Beagles come in two sizes: the 13-inch Beagle and the 15-inch Beagle. The 13-incher is supposed to be no taller than 13 inches at the front shoulder. Similarly, the 15-inch Beagle should not exceed 15 inches in height at the front shoulder.

Specific parts

Of course, the standard does much more than offer a big-picture description of what a Beagle should look like. The standard places far more emphasis on exactly how specific parts of the Beagle's body should appear.

Decoding the breed standard

If you decide to read the actual breed standard approved by the National Beagle Club of America, you may encounter some puzzling terms. Here are definitions of the terms that are most likely to cause confusion:

- **Cow hocks:** A condition in which the hind legs turn in on each other. Cow hocks and the opposite condition, divergent hocks, may affect the dog's ability to move properly.

- **Forelegs:** The front legs.

- **Loin:** The area on each side of the backbone between the ribs and the hips.

- **Occipital:** The bone at the back of the top of the skull. In some dogs, this bone is quite prominent, even triangular-looking.

- **Rib spring:** The width of the chest.

- **Stop:** An indentation at the midpoint of the face. A *definite stop* refers to a clear, distinct indentation between the top half and bottom half of the face.

- **Withers:** The shoulders. Most measurements of a dog's height are from the floor to the top of the withers.

If you plan on showing your Beagle, log onto the AKC Web site at www.akc.org/breeds/beagle, where you can find a copy of the actual breed standard.

Head

A Beagle's skull should be fairly long, with a slight dome at the back part of the head. The skull as a whole should be relatively broad and full, not elongated. Those long, silky ears should reach almost to the end of the nose if drawn out straight, and they should be rounded at the tips. The eyes should be hazel or brown in color and should be large, set far apart, and have a gentle, pleading expression. The muzzle should have a square shape, and the profile should show a clear distinction between the bottom of the face and top of the face.

Body

Wrinkles are OK for Chinese Shar-pei but not for Beagles! The standard stipulates that the neck and throat should not exhibit any skin folds. The shoulders should not be upright; rather, they should slope downward. The dog's chest should be deep and broad but not out of proportion to the rest of the body. The Beagle's back should be relatively short (no channeling of Dachshunds here!).

Legs, feet, and tail

The wiener dog takes another hit when the Beagle breed standard addresses legs, feet, and tails. The standard stipulates that a Beagle's front legs should be straight, not crooked or — yes, the standard gets this specific — resembling the front legs of a Dachshund. The hips and thighs should be strong and muscular. The tail needs to be fairly high on the rump and carried in a jaunty fashion, but it should not curve over the back.

Coat and color

The Beagle should have a medium-length, easy-to-groom coat that lies close to the body and is hard to the touch. Silky tresses are a definite no-no.

As for coat color, the standard is vague, saying only that any recognized hound color is OK. The most common color is the black, white, and tan *tri-color,* but other colors common to hounds such as red and white, chocolate tri-color (solid chocolate brown instead of black), and shaded tri-color (varied shades of brown instead of black) are OK, too. So, too, is *ticking*: tiny spots of brown or black in white fur.

Defects

The standard also discusses how judges should rate the less-than-perfect Beagle. Among the defects that would cause a judge to disqualify a dog from or deduct points in the show ring are the following:

- ✔ Height exceeding 15 inches
- ✔ A narrow skull
- ✔ A cranium that's too high
- ✔ Small eyes
- ✔ Protruding eyes
- ✔ Excessively short ears
- ✔ Ears set too high on the head
- ✔ Ears that rise from their point of origin before falling
- ✔ Excessive skin folding at the throat
- ✔ Straight shoulders
- ✔ Excessively deep or shallow chest
- ✔ Swayed or excessively long back
- ✔ Cow hocks
- ✔ Excessively long tail
- ✔ A tail curved forward or over the dog's back
- ✔ Lack of feathering at the end of the tail
- ✔ Soft coat
- ✔ Thin coat

Few, if any, Beagles meet all the standard's criteria for perfection. Some deficiencies are no big deal in the show ring, while others are considered so serious that the dog can't be shown. Still, disqualification from the show ring certainly doesn't mean that the affected Beagle won't be a wonderful, healthy pet or participant in other dog activities. Plenty of Beagles who don't make the grade in conformation can earn straight A's as lively, loving companions — and more. Chapter 3 describes in greater detail how wannabe pet owners can find the Beagle of their dreams by buying or adopting the Snoopy-dog who would never make Westminster.

Fashion tips for the owner

The Beagle breed standard, unlike many other standards, also describes proper attire for the fashion-conscious owner. The recommended ensemble applies only to those owners who participate in formal hunts with packs of Beagles. Among the suggested clothes are green coats and white breeches or knickerbockers for men. Women should substitute white skirts for the breeches. Both sexes should accessorize their ensembles with a black velvet cap, white tie, green or black stockings, white spats, and black or dark brown shoes. Vest and gloves are optional.

Why the World Loves Beagles

Every year, the AKC tallies up the number of dogs registered for each of the breeds the organization currently recognizes — and each year, Beagles pups and litters are among the breeds that garner the most registrations. For example, in 2005 — the last year for which registration stats were available at the time I was writing this book — the Beagle bagged the number 5 position out of 154 breeds. Only Yorkshire Terriers, German Shepherd Dogs, Golden Retrievers, and Labrador Retrievers drew more registrations. That's not a fluke, either; the Beagle has held its own among the big dogs (and the Yorkie, too) for many years.

And it's easy to see why. Beagles offer something for almost everyone, including the following:

- ✔ **They're adorable.** Few people can resist the winsome eyes, soft muzzle, and all-around cuteness of a Beagle. Just one soulful gaze from this sweet-looking little hound is enough to render almost any dog lover totally smitten. And just one day with this happy-go-lucky little dog (the eyes may look sad, but the rest of the dog is happy, happy, happy) may well hook you for life.

- ✔ **They're low-maintenance.** With a Beagle, you don't have to worry about untangling the coat, creating a canine top-knot, or booking an appointment with the local groomer. Beagles do need bathing and brushing, as well as ear tending, puppy pedicures, and tooth care, but you can easily perform all those functions yourself — especially with the help of the tips included in Chapter 10.

✔ **They're small.** The pocket Beagle may have been a Renaissance fad, but today's Beagle is still pretty compact. That small size makes this breed ideal for people who can't or don't want to deal with the logistics of caring for larger dogs. (Believe me: Getting an 80-pound canine to get into the bathtub or out of the car when that dog would rather do something else can be, um, challenging.) And if your leashed Beagle decides to make like a sled dog and pull you down the street while the two of you are walking, your size advantage can put a quick stop to such behavior. That said, Chapter 15 includes pointers on teaching your Beagle good walking manners, and using brute strength isn't one of my recommendations.

✔ **They're versatile.** Beagles are truly multitalented individuals. As Chapter 9 shows, they not only can excel in the conformation ring but also in activities such as competitive obedience, agility, and flyball. Their superb noses make them natural trackers — and of course, they can write the book on hunting small game. But the Beagle's potential doesn't stop with these traditional dog activities. Hop on over to Chapter 19 to discover how Beagles serve on the front lines of the war on terror and also are first-class detectors of hidden mold and termites.

✔ **They're sociable.** Simply put, Beagles enjoy the company of human beings. They relish meeting and greeting just about any person. Beagles not only fit well into human families but also can employ their friendliness in another pursuit: as therapy dogs. These canine healers visit sick people in hospitals and elderly people who are confined to nursing homes. In fact, one of the best known therapy dogs of recent years was a Beagle. Her name was Dani, and she not only gave lots of canine TLC to pediatric cancer patients but also provided a lesson in courage to those patients when she was diagnosed with cancer herself. Fortunately, Dani survived her bout with the big C and continued her therapy duties. You may not want to perform therapy work with your dog, but Chapter 7 offers tips for bringing out the extrovert in any Beagle.

✔ **They're kid-friendly.** Some breeds do better with children than others — and the Beagle is among those canines that can be wonderful companions for kids. The Beagle is small enough to be able to romp with children without knocking them over, but large and sturdy enough to interact with sometimes-clumsy kids with relative safety. Still, to minimize the likelihood of either kid or canine getting hurt when getting together, Chapter 7 provides information on how to help Beagles and children live happily ever after.

A place just for Beagles

Unlike many American breed clubs, the National Beagle Club (NBC) of America has its very own farm: a 508-acre tract called The Institute Farm in Aldie, Virginia, which is south of Washington, DC.

Five members of the club formed a corporation dubbed The Institute Corporation for the express purpose of buying the land and administering the property for the NBC. In 1916, the group bought the land — although the name of the seller remains an open question. Records indicate that the corporation bought the land from the estate of one Isabella Skinner Turner. However, one of the corporation's founders said that the land had been part of the estate of a gentleman who'd planned to use the tract for a hunt club. The gentleman, whose name is not known, sailed to England to buy a pack of hounds. To his great misfortune and that of the hounds, they sailed back to America on the RMS Titanic and perished when that ship struck an iceberg and sank in April 1912. Historians speculate that the gentleman had contracted to buy the property but had not completed the purchase before he and his hounds met their deaths.

Today, The Institute Farm serves not only as the site for NBC-sponsored events to test Beagles' hunting prowess (called *field trials* by show folk) and specialty shows, but it also has hosted seminars and events for other dog-related organizations. Among the non-Beagle events held at the farm in recent years has been a seminar for a "Bloodhound Training School" for law enforcement officers who work with Bloodhounds in search-and-rescue.

. . . But Nobody's Perfect

Alas, as wonderful and appealing as the Beagle can be, the breed also has its dark side. Consider the following possible disadvantages of living with Snoopy-dogs:

- ✔ **They are vocal.** All dogs bark, but the Beagle adds a little something extra to his vocal repertoire: the howl. A Snoopy-dog who lifts his head in Beagle-song will certainly get the attention of the people around him — and, if he lives in an apartment, will almost certainly draw the ire of his human neighbors. Chapter 16 addresses ways to alleviate a clash between a vocal Beagle and human sanity.

- ✔ **They may have bathroom issues.** The Beagle has a reputation for being more difficult to housetrain than other breeds. Some experts theorize that Beagle bathroom issues arise because the dog's nose is so sensitive that he can smell the tiniest vestige of left-behind accidents. Patience, consistency, and a commitment to total cleanup of bathroom indiscretions are the keys to teaching your Beagle proper potty protocol. Chapter 14 gives you the scoop on how to housetrain your four-legged friend.

✔ **They follow their noses.** Humorist Dave Barry makes his living by being funny — but when he described the Beagle as a nose with four legs, he wasn't kidding. A dog with a nose sensitive enough to detect one piece of contraband fruit in a pile of luggage is likely to be far more tuned in to the world of smells than a human being would be. Such is the case with the Beagle, who — like the hound that he is — lives to follow the scent. This devotion to odor can get the Beagle into trouble — such as going through the garbage can indoors, wandering off the owner's property outdoors and not looking back, and attempting to eat anything and everything, whether an item is meant to be eaten or not — if his owner isn't vigilant. Chapter 5 describes ways that owners can make their homes impervious to Beagle explorations, and Chapter 15 lists steps owners can take to keep their odor-driven companions from wandering away from hearth and home.

✔ **They won't help your hay fever.** No one can guarantee that any breed of dog will never trigger allergic reactions in people. However, some curly-coated dogs such as the Standard Poodle or Portuguese Water Dogs are less likely than most breeds to prompt the people in their lives to sneeze, sniffle, or suffer from watery eyes. On the other hand, the relatively short, straight hairs on the Beagle's coat could make an allergy-prone person's life a living hell — particularly during seasons when the dog sheds. And it's not just the hair that can trigger allergy attacks: The Beagle's love of the outdoors means he's likely to carry other allergens, such as dirt, grass, and leaves, into your home.

✔ **They have their own agendas.** Beagles are very intelligent dogs, but they're not necessarily as eager to please their people as some other breeds such as Shetland Sheepdogs or Golden Retrievers are. The apparent result may be a dog who seems difficult to school in basic canine good manners, much less teach advanced maneuvers to. Chapter 7 outlines ways to build the bond between you and your Beagle from your very first days together, and Chapters 15 and 16 outline strategies for countering any stubbornness you encounter when you try to train your four-legged friend.

These less-than-sterling qualities should give you pause if you're still debating whether to add a Beagle to your life. That said, none of these apparent deficiencies has to mean that the Beagle makes a bad pet. No dog is perfect — but a Beagle could well be your dream dog despite any physical and behavioral challenges he might pose. The keys to success are knowing what you're getting into and having the patience to raise and train your new friend to be the best, not the worst, he can be.

Chapter 3

Gonna Find Me a Beagle

* *

In This Chapter

▶ Figuring out where to look for a Beagle

▶ Finding a good Beagle breeder

▶ Exploring animal shelters

▶ Understanding Beagle rescue

▶ Knowing where not to look

▶ Finding a Beagle online: yay or nay?

▶ Pondering pet stores

* *

*I*f the Snoopy-dog's big-eyed stare, happy-go-lucky personality, low-maintenance coat, and awesome versatility have you hooked, congratulations! Now you're ready to start the next step toward finding the dog of your dreams: figuring out where to look for your new Beagle.

Fortunately, you can search for your new hound in several great places — at least three, in fact. Unfortunately, though, Beagles may abound at a couple of other types of places you should avoid. This chapter gives you the scoop on where to look for your Beagle — and where *not* to look as well.

Good Places to Look

You can find a Beagle from plenty of places, but some places are decidedly better than others. The three sources I describe in this section deserve unqualified endorsements.

A matter of breeding

If you're looking for a puppy, your best chances for finding a happy, healthy baby Beagle reside with a reputable breeder. That said, not all breeders are created equal. Some breeders produce

Beagles strictly for monetary profit, sacrificing quality to enhance their financial bottom lines. Others, however, breed these little hounds because they want to improve the Beagle as a breed. These breeders put puppies ahead of profits — and if you want a puppy, you should put these types of breeders at the top of your list of places to contact.

Why work with a breeder?

A good breeder offers many advantages to the person who wants to raise a Beagle from puppyhood. First, your puppy won't surprise you when she reaches adulthood; in other words, you'll have a pretty good idea of what kind of adult your puppy will grow up to be. That's because a breeder can show you the pedigree of the puppy you're interested in, and also the pedigrees of the puppy's parents. You'll also be able to meet the puppy's mom — and if you like the mom, you'll probably like her pups, too.

A good breeder also makes sure that a puppy's parents are certi-fied as being free of health problems that are inherited in their breed, such as the following:

- ✔ **Joint problems:** Many Beagle breeders have their dogs' hips and elbows rated by the Orthopedic Foundation for Animals (OFA) to ensure that the joints have developed properly. The ratings are self-explanatory; for example, hips rated "excellent" are just that. If the joints haven't developed correctly, the affected dog may eventually suffer from *hip dysplasia* or *elbow dysplasia,* both of which are painful conditions that can lead to irreversible arthritis. Other breeders opt for another procedure called PennHIP — otherwise known as the University of Pennsylvania Hip Improvement Program. This procedure uses multiple X-rays to analyze a dog's hips, and many vets consider it to be more accurate than an OFA analysis.

- ✔ **Eye diseases:** Good breeders also screen their Beagles for eye diseases and obtain certification by the Canine Eye Registry Foundation (CERF).

These certifications are called *clearances,* and they're all performed by veterinary specialists such as orthopedists or ophthalmologists, although vets can also perform the OFA or PennHIP procedures.

A reputable breeder also will try to learn a lot about you. She's likely to ask you lots of questions about your lifestyle, previous dogs you've owned, and other members of your family. Her ques-tions have two purposes: to ensure that your home is suitable for a Beagle, and to learn enough about you to help you choose exactly the right Beagle puppy. (See also the "What the breeder will ask you" section in this chapter.)

And after you get your Beagle puppy, the reputable breeder won't disappear. Instead, she's ready and willing to serve as an expert resource who will help you solve any problems you encounter after bringing your baby Beagle home — even years later.

That said, working with a reputable breeder has some disadvantages. For one thing, a high-quality Beagle puppy doesn't come cheap. Expect to part with several hundred dollars if you opt to buy a puppy from a good breeder and plan on having that puppy be strictly a pet. If you want a show-quality Beagle, you'll probably pay even more. Chapter 4 tells you more about choosing a show-quality Beagle, a pet-quality Beagle, or a Beagle who's been bred to hunt.

Another possible problem in working with a good breeder is that you may have to wait a long time to buy a puppy. That's because reputable Beagle breeders generally have only a few dogs and may raise only two or three litters each year. Consequently, the demand for healthy Beagle puppies generally far outstrips the supply of such dogs, and buyers may have to wait many months before a puppy is available.

No option is perfect. But if you've set your heart on raising your Beagle from puppyhood, the reputable breeder is the way to go.

Finding a good breeder

How do you find these paragons of Beagle breeding? One place to start is the American Kennel Club (AKC), which you can find on the Web by logging onto www.akc.org/breederinfo/breeder_ search.cfm. There you'll find a list of *breeder referral contacts:* volunteers from different breed clubs who help prospective buyers find nearby breeders. (Simply locate the "Breed Contacts" heading, click "Breeder Referral," and scroll down the alphabetical listing of volunteers until you find the Beagle entry.) E-mail the breeder referral contact for the National Beagle Club (NBC) of America, and she'll respond promptly with some names of local Beagle breeders for you to contact.

In fact, the NBC has a list of breeders on its own Web site; just mosey on over to http://clubs.akc.org/NBC/breeders_list. There you'll find a state-by-state list of NBC members who have puppies for sale, at least occasionally.

Another way to find reputable breeders is to attend a dog show. To find a dog show near you that will include Beagles, log onto the AKC's Web site at www.akc.org/events/search. Here you can ferret out shows that feature Beagles as much as a year in advance in up to three states per search. After you find a show, drive to the event, buy a *catalog* (a program that lists when and in which rings the various breeds will be shown), and take a look around the show site. Soon you'll find the Beagle breeders, most of whom will be happy to give you a business card and talk with you briefly about their dogs in particular, and Beagles in general.

Don't try to chat up a breeder when she's about to take her dog into the ring. At that point, she's understandably nervous and is far more interested in getting her dog ready than in talking to prospective buyers. Wait till she's done and then introduce yourself.

Asking the right questions

Still not sure whether the breeder you've contacted is truly committed to raising healthy Beagle puppies? Just ask some questions — either on the phone when you initially contact the breeder, or at the breeder's home after you've made an appointment to visit. The answers to the following questions can either set your mind at rest or prompt you to look elsewhere.

- ✔ **Do the dogs you breed have health clearances?** The right answer here is, "Yes — I have my dogs' hips, elbows, and eyes checked. Would you like to see the certificates (or clearances)?"

  If a breeder tells you, "My dogs don't have any health problems," don't walk away — run!

- ✔ **What are your breeding practices?** Learning about a breeder's methods show whether she cares more about puppies than profits. Ask questions such as how old the parents are and how often the *dam* (or mama Beagle) gives birth. Using the same dam more than once a year is a no-no, as is breeding dogs that are under 2 years of age. Ask, too, whether the breeder owns both the dam and the *sire* (or papa Beagle). The best answer here is, "No," which means that the breeder is willing to pay for a healthy sire who's likely to exemplify the best in Beagle health and temperament.

- ✔ **Where do you raise your puppies?** The best answer to this question is "In my house." Home-raised puppies get exposure to normal household noises and activity, which helps them adjust better to their new homes than puppies raised in kennels outside the breeder's domicile. In addition, most puppies should remain with their littermates and dam until they are least 8 weeks old.

- ✔ **What guarantees do you offer?** A reputable breeder will stand behind the health of any puppy she sells for the animal's entire life, and she will take back a problem pup at any time (though not necessarily for a refund). Most breeders will guarantee in writing that the puppy won't develop hereditary problems for a year or two. They'll also allow you to have a few days to have your new puppy checked by your own veterinarian. This guarantee is very important in case the vet finds that the puppy has a major health problem — the breeder should be willing to either refund your money or replace the puppy. Chapter 4 explores purchase and adoption contracts in detail.

✔ **Do you belong to the National Beagle Club of America?** Membership in the NBC shows that the breeder is committed to producing better Beagles in each generation. And check to see whether any of the breeder's dogs have earned their breed championships (also known as *conformation titles*); a breeder with plenty of champions to brag about is a person who not only wants to breed great Beagles but has succeeded in doing so. An answer in the negative is a reason for caution; the breeder may have the best of intentions, but without the club membership or titles, you can't be sure that she's committed to breeding better Beagles, let alone any good at doing so.

✔ **Do you have references?** A good breeder will point you to satisfied puppy buyers to help you confirm that she is, indeed, reputable. If she refers you to her veterinarian, that's even better.

✔ **What do you want to know about me?** A breeder who doesn't respond to this question with lots of questions of her own may be a breeder to avoid. Her lack of interest in you may reflect a lack of interest in where her puppy ends up.

What the breeder will ask you

After you've put a few questions to the breeder, she's likely to want to query you in return. Don't be offended by her questions or feel that she's trying to be nosy. Her first concern is for the welfare of her puppies. To that end, she's likely to ask you the following questions:

✔ **Why do you want a dog?** A breeder asks this question to be sure that you're ready to commit yourself fully to raising her puppy for that puppy's entire life, and that you've done some research before you've set off in search of a new canine companion. Good answers to this question include wanting to give and receive unconditional love; wanting someone to nurture; and wanting company. A breeder's likely to raise her eyebrows if you respond that you want to teach your kids to be responsible (they shouldn't be practicing on a Beagle) and looking for protection (if you've done your homework, you should know that Beagles aren't meant to be watchdogs or protection dogs).

✔ **Why do you want a Beagle?** A breeder asks this to see whether you know something about the breed. Chapter 2 can give you a head start on developing the right answers in advance.

✔ **Who will be primarily responsible for the puppy or dog?** A breeder asks this question because she wants to be sure that a responsible adult will be the main caregiver for the puppy or dog. The right answer here is "me," "my spouse," "my partner,"

"Mom," or "Dad." The wrong answer is "my kids." No child, no matter what her age, should be the primary canine caregiver.

✔ **Have you ever owned a dog?** No wrong answer here. Knowing whether you're an experienced dog owner gives a breeder important information that helps her determine which of her puppies is best for you.

✔ **How will you exercise this dog?** Good answers include walking your Beagle three or four times a day on a leash and/or letting the dog run in your securely fenced yard.

✔ **Do you have children — and if so, how old are they?** Having kids doesn't necessarily mean that you can't have a Beagle puppy. However, some breeders may hesitate to sell a puppy to families with children under school age.

✔ **Does anyone in your household have allergies?** As Chapter 2 explains, Beagles do nothing to improve a person's allergies. If your family includes allergy sufferers, a breeder might ask whether you're willing to make adjustments such as cleaning and vacuuming your house frequently and keeping the puppy out of the allergic person's bedroom.

✔ **Does your living situation permit a dog?** Only one right answer here: yes. And be prepared to back up your answer in the form of a lease clearly stating that pets are permitted, or documents showing that you own your home.

✔ **How do you feel about taking your dog for training and obedience classes?** Once again, only one right answer: fine. Although you can start your Beagle's training by employing the info in Chapter 15, the two of you are more likely to live together happily ever after if you also avail yourself of professional guidance.

✔ **Will someone be home during the day to care for the dog?** The ideal answer is "yes," but the minimally acceptable answer is that someone can come home several times a day to care for the puppy. If neither option is possible for you, show that you can arrange for a petsitter to come and care for the puppy. Chapter 13 discusses how to find a good petsitter or dog walker.

✔ **Do you have a veterinarian, or do you know of one?** Either way, a yes shows that you can get professional care for the puppy you're considering. See Chapter 5 for additional advice on choosing a vet.

Gimme shelter

If you're OK with getting an older puppy or adult dog, you may well find the Beagle of your dreams at your local animal shelter.

Maybe you thought that animal shelters carry only mixed-breed dogs, and that you're not likely to find a purebred dog like a Beagle. Actually, though, a substantial number of animal shelter dogs are purebreds; in fact, the Humane Society of the United States (HSUS) estimates that a full one-third of the canine guests in most shelters are purebred. And with the Beagle being among the five most popular dogs in the United States, the chances of finding a Snoopy-dog in a shelter are reasonably good — especially if you're patient.

You may have thought, too, that animal shelters are bleak, depressing places that look as though they've come straight out of a Charles Dickens novel. Think again. More and more cities, such as Richmond, Virginia, and San Francisco, California, are turning their shelters into state-of-the-art animal palaces. At these top-of-the-line establishments, canine and feline guests stay in luxuriously appointed animal apartments complete with soft beds and oodles of toys to chew and play with.

Even those shelters offering more spartan accommodations are doing more to attend to the emotional needs of their guests. I know of one municipal shelter that's located in a very grim section of a major metropolitan city — but the shelter itself offers soft blankets and towels for its doggy guests, a daily ration of rawhide chews, daily runs in an adjoining field, volunteers to teach the dogs basic good manners, and even a doggy agility course with A-frames, a tunnel, and a tire ring to jump through.

Why adopt from a shelter?

Adopting a Beagle from an animal shelter carries two major advantages over getting one from a reputable breeder:

- ✔ The shelter dog costs much less — generally, no more than $100 to cover the cost of the dog's care in the shelter.
- ✔ The adopter gets the enormous satisfaction of knowing that she's saved a dog's life.

That's not to say that a shelter Beagle doesn't offer some challenges over the puppy purchased from a reputable breeder. Some shelter dogs have behavioral problems — and those problems may not show up right away. For example, you may realize that your Beagle has no idea where he's supposed to potty until after you've had him with you for a couple of days.

And while they make every effort to give tender loving care to every animal who needs it, shelter personnel often don't know much about many of those animals. Those who come to the shelter as strays, of course, have no known histories at all — but even those surrendered by owners may come with very little information. In fact, such owners often give reasons for surrendering their dogs that have little or nothing to do with the real factors behind their decisions.

That said, many dogs find themselves in shelters through no fault of their own. More often than not, they've been the victims of irresponsible owners who haven't taken the time to train and care for them properly. Others are victims of life changes such as the death of an owner or some other change in a family's circumstances.

Understanding the adoption process

In some ways, the process of adopting a dog from an animal shelter doesn't differ all that much from buying a puppy from a breeder. Both sources want to be sure that you offer a suitable home for a Beagle. Both will ask you a lot of questions to determine whether, in fact, you make the grade.

Adopting a pet from a shelter usually isn't a one-day event. Generally, after you decide on a Beagle at an animal shelter, you'll need to fill out an application that's likely to include an extensive questionnaire. The questions will focus on your history with dogs, your family, your work schedule, and your living situation. If you rent your home, be prepared to give the shelter your landlord's telephone number; many shelters will call to make sure that your landlord allows you to keep a pet. Be prepared, too, for a shelter volunteer to come visit your home to make sure that it's suitable for your Beagle. After your application is approved, the shelter will arrange for your Beagle to be spayed or neutered, if that operation hasn't taken place already. After the dog has a couple of days to recover from the surgery, you'll get the all-clear to take your new friend home.

You can find more information about shelter adoptions from *Successful Dog Adoption* by Sue Sternberg (Howell Book House) and from another For Dummies title, *Adopting a Pet For Dummies* by Eve Adamson.

Finding a shelter in your area

You just may find your very own special Beagle at a nearby animal shelter. Begin your search by checking your local print or online telephone directory to uncover shelters located near you. Then, log onto the shelter's Web site (they all are on the Web now, it seems!) and check their list of available dogs. If you see a Beagle, pay the shelter a visit. But plan on being tough-minded; don't fall for the first pair of winsome Beagle eyes you see.

Rescue me!

If you like the idea of saving a dog's life, are comfortable with adopting an adult dog, but don't want to wait too long to find a

Beagle, your best bet might be to adopt a dog through a breed rescue group. Read on to find out why the rescue route may be the way to go — and what to keep in mind if you choose this option.

Defining breed rescue

Beagle breed rescue is a multifaceted enterprise that aims to place homeless Beagles into permanent adoptive homes.

The first part is the actual rescue. Beagle rescuers — all of whom are volunteers — look for Beagles who need help; for example, a dog who's due to be euthanized at an overcrowded animal shelter. In fact, a shelter often will ask Beagle rescuers or other purebred rescue groups to take in a purebred dog so the shelter can make room for new arrivals.

Other ways that Beagles enter rescue is via their original owners. A change in life circumstances, the death of an owner, or an owner's inability to properly care for a dog are all reasons that a person may surrender a dog to rescue. And all too often, Beagle rescuers take in dogs that have been cruelly treated or otherwise neglected.

After the Beagle enters rescue, the group assigns the dog to a temporary home — or what rescuers call a *foster home*. The *foster-care provider* takes charge of the Beagle's everyday care. She takes him to a veterinarian for an initial examination to uncover any health problems the dog may have and gives the dog any medical care he needs. She also observes the dog carefully to determine whether he has any training deficiencies or behavioral problems and then takes steps to deal with those issues. The Beagle who pees in the house begins housetraining; the shy Snoopy-dog receives gentle encouragement to engage with the world.

As the Beagle's rehabilitation progresses, the foster-care provider — with the help of other volunteers — begins to look for a permanent home for the dog. The group's aim is to find a happy ending for each rescued Beagle: placement in a loving forever home.

Considering rescue pro's and con's

Working with a rescue group to find the Beagle of your dreams carries many advantages. For one thing, by adopting a rescued Beagle you know that you're giving him a second chance to live in a happy, permanent home. Many people reap tremendous satisfaction from knowing that they've changed the lives of down-on-their luck dogs. That satisfaction increases when the rescued dogs heap love and devotion onto their new human companions. Many adopters of rescued Beagles and other dogs believe that their new canine buddies somehow know that they've gotten second chances and that they're grateful.

Another plus to getting your Beagle through a rescue group is that the volunteer foster "parents" usually get to know their foster "kids" very well. The foster-care provider can provide you with a detailed description of how a fostered dog behaves in a household and will give you a heads-up on possible challenges a particular dog may pose. Such knowledge not only helps you determine whether a dog is right for you and your lifestyle, but also enables the rescue group to place each of its Beagles in the best possible homes. For example, the group may discover that Beagle A isn't crazy about children (which would be very unusual, but it can happen) and would take care to place that dog in a child-free home.

Still another reason to consider adopting a rescued Beagle is the relatively low price tag. For example, Beagle Rescue, Education, and Welfare (BREW) charges an adoption fee of just $200. That's really a pittance considering what that fee covers: spaying or neutering, any immunizations needed, deworming (if necessary), heartworm testing, microchip implanting, and any other medical treatment the Beagle may need. However, other rescue groups may charge a different amount or provide fewer services — so make sure that you know exactly what your fee is paying for.

However, a rescued Beagle is not necessarily a problem-free Beagle. Many Beagles find themselves in rescue because of behavioral problems. Before you adopt any Beagle (or any dog, for that matter) from a rescue group, make sure you find out whether that dog has any emotional baggage. Ask whether the dog has any fears, phobias, or other behavioral challenges. Then, after you find out what the Beagle's issues are, figure out how you'll deal with those issues — and make a rock-solid commitment to do so. You may need simply to spend more time with your new dog than you anticipated. (But then, Beagles are so cute you'd probably do that anyway!) On the other hand, the Beagle's issues may be so complicated that you need to work one on one with a trainer or animal behaviorist to solve the dog's special problems. Chapter 15 can help you deal with many of those challenges, either on your own or with the help of a professional.

Understanding the rescue adoption process

Rescue groups have one overriding goal: to place the Beagles in their care into forever homes. Unlike many animal shelters, which may need to euthanize dogs who aren't adopted within a certain time period, good rescue groups will hold onto adoptable dogs for as long as necessary until those dogs find permanent homes. Such a policy means you or any other wannabe adopter won't get to take home a Beagle until the rescue group decides that you are Beagle-ready.

To that end, many rescue groups post on their Web sites a list of requirements that prospective adopters must meet before they

can even fill out an application. For example, BREW requires that
an adopter agree to give his Beagle at least 30 days to adjust to life
in a new household. Other groups may require adopters to have
fenced yards to thwart the Beagle's all-too-well-known penchant
for wandering.

If you meet those requirements, you can fill out an adoption application. Be prepared to answer a lot of questions about your living
situation, the members of your family, your work situation, your
landlord's telephone number (if you rent your home), and your
knowledge of dogs in general and Beagles in particular. Don't be
offended; the rescue group's not trying to play Big Brother. The
group just wants to be sure that any Beagle you take into your
home will stay in your home; in other words, that you can give a
rescued Beagle the second chance he deserves.

After you send in your application, a rescue volunteer will check out
your references and visit your home to make sure it's as good as you
say it is. Assuming it is, you'll get the rescue group's approval. With
that thumbs-up, feel free to log onto the rescue group's Web site to
see if you can find a Beagle you want — and hop on over to Chapter
4 for pointers on picking the right Beagle for you.

If you want to find out more about purebred dog rescue, take a look
at *Purebred Dog Rescue: Rewards and Realities* by Liz Palika (Howell
Book House) and *Adopting a Pet For Dummies* by Eve Adamson.

Finding a rescue group near you

Don't know where to start looking for a Beagle breed rescue group?
Boot up your computer, check out these groups — and if you see a
Beagle you like, follow the contact instructions provided on the
Web site:

- **National Beagle Club of America:** The club's Web site
  includes a page of links to Beagle rescue groups from all over
  the United States. Log onto `http://clubs.akc.org/NBC/
  beagle_rescue`.

- **Beagle Rescue Foundation of America:** This organization
  raises money to assist Beagle rescue groups throughout the
  country. The foundation's Web site contains a page of links to
  local rescue groups, including some that aren't listed on the
  National Beagle Club of America's Web site. Log onto `http://
  brfoa.tripod.com/brfoaorg.html`.

- **Petfinder:** This national online database of pets who need
  homes lists Beagle and other breed rescue groups from coast
  to coast. The Petfinder Web site also allows you to search
  directly for a Beagle by zip code — although most of the hits
  you'll get will be Beagle mixes. Log onto `www.petfinder.com`.

No rescue Beagles nearby? Not to worry. Some rescue groups can help you find a dog who lives outside your local area and arrange to have the animal transported to you. If you're interested in this possibility, ask the rescue coordinator about whether the group operates a "Canine Underground Railroad," or whether she can help you find out more about rescue dogs who live beyond your local area.

Just Say No: Poor Places to Look

In the where-not-to-look category are three sources that may help you find a Beagle now, but lead to heartbreak later. If you want to maximize your chances of getting a healthy, happy dog, avoid the quick-and-easy route the following three sources appear to offer.

Classified newspaper ads

If you scan the classified advertising of your local newspaper — particularly if that paper is a big metropolitan daily — you're likely to see a couple of pages that list puppies and dogs for sale, at least a few of which probably will be Beagles. After each listing is a phone number to call. For you, a busy Beagle searcher, the classifieds may seem like a shortcut to finding your dream dog. Unfortunately, that's not usually the case.

Reputable breeders generally don't need to advertise their litters anywhere. The high quality and good health of their puppies gives these breeders all the advertising they need. Such breeders have far more potential customers than they have puppies to sell. They keep waiting lists of people who want to acquire Beagle pups. When such breeders do have a litter available (which may be true only a couple of times a year), they contact those on their waiting lists to give them a chance to buy a puppy.

So, who does need to advertise? Generally, a breeder who advertises in the classifieds hasn't taken the time or doesn't know how to produce the healthiest Beagles possible. She probably hasn't done the research necessary to find the best *sire* (father dog) to breed to her *dam* (mama dog). She almost certainly hasn't taken the time or spent the money necessary to ensure that the sire and dam don't have any serious health problems they could pass on to the puppies. And she may know little or nothing about the best environment in which to raise a litter after that litter is born. In short, the classified ads are probably one of the worst places to look for the Beagle of your dreams.

Although newspaper classifieds generally should be among the last places you go to look for a Beagle puppy from a breeder, sometimes breed rescue groups seek permanent domiciles for homeless adult Beagles by placing ads. If you see a Beagle rescue group's ad for one or more adult dogs, give it a look — and check out the sections on rescue that appear elsewhere in this chapter for pointers on how to adopt a dog from a rescue group.

Backyard breeders

What wonderful timing! Just as you've decided that yes, the Beagle is the right breed for you, your neighbor down the street tells you that she's breeding her Beagles, Sammy and Sally. What's more, she'll let you have first pick of the little Sammies and Sallies she expects to result from this most fortuitous union. Do you take her up on her offer?

In a word, no.

Unless your neighbor is an experienced breeder who has entered her Beagles in dog shows and won multiple titles, she brings even less to the breeding process than the breeder who advertises in the newspaper. She may be a great neighbor whose ethics are above reproach. But ethics and neighborliness aren't nearly enough to maximize the odds that the Beagle puppies she produces will be physically and emotionally healthy. Instead of loving your neighbor (at least in this particular instance), read this chapter to discover how to find the experienced breeder you need.

Pet stores

For the most part, pet stores — especially the kind that used to be ubiquitous in shopping malls and shopping centers — are the last places you should look for a Beagle puppy or adult. The reason: Many of the Beagles and other dogs in these stores come from puppy mills, which are notorious for breeding dogs under horrendous conditions.

Unlike legitimate breeders, compassionate rescue groups, and all-breed animal shelters, proprietors of many pet stores and just about all puppy mills have one overriding motive: monetary profit. Consequently, mill operators generally don't give their dogs the care they need to be happy and healthy. The puppies that come from these mills almost always are in extremely poor physical condition — riddled with parasites, beset with kennel cough, and often malnourished. They also tend to have way more behavioral problems, especially when it comes to housetraining, than dogs who come from other, more reputable sources. And to add insult to injury, these stores often charge more for their puppies than reputable breeders charge for theirs.

But here is an important caveat: A pet store can be a great place to look for an adult dog — if the dog is there as part of a rescue group event. Many organizations that care for rescued dogs like to bring those dogs to enlightened pet stores as part of a meet-and-greet event for the public. A prospective adopter gets to meet a dog in the flesh, apply to adopt the dog, and buy whatever dog care supplies he needs, all in one place at one time. Log on to the Web site of the rescue group you're interested in, where you'll almost certainly find a list of such adoption events.

Proceed with Caution: Adopting from the Internet

Log onto the Web, and on just one puppy-selling Web site alone, you can find well over 600 baby Beagles to choose from. There you are, sitting in your comfortable home, poring over photographs of adorable-looking puppies. Kinda like Internet dating, you think. What's not to like?

Well, actually, you should take some time to pause and reflect. The folks who advertise their Beagle puppies on the Web probably don't know any more about proper breeding practices than those who advertise in the classifieds. Worse, you probably won't be able to see most of these puppies in person.

But that doesn't mean that you should avoid all Web sites advertising Beagles. For example, on the American Kennel Club's Web site you can search a database consisting of thousands of breeders from all over the United States. After you read the educational materials the AKC has conveniently added to the site, log onto www.akc.org/classified/search, type in your search terms as directed, and begin your search. The Beagle breeders who pop up will be individuals who are members in good standing of the National Beagle Club of America, and they'll all be within a half-day's drive from your home.

The Internet can also be a good place to look for an adult Beagle. Many breed rescue groups, including for Beagles, cooperate with the American Society for the Prevention of Cruelty to Animals (ASPCA) to list adoptable dogs on Petfinder (www.petfinder.org). The listings also provide contact information for the rescue groups that are posting, so if you see a Beagle you like, you can get in touch with the group directly. This humongous Web site should be the first stop for anyone who's looking to adopt a homeless animal.

Chapter 4

Choosing Your Beagle Soul Mate

In This Chapter

▶ Exploring options when choosing a Beagle

▶ Knowing what to look for in a Beagle puppy

▶ Evaluating an adult Beagle

▶ Learning about contracts and other important documents

*Y*ou're ready. You've determined that yes, the Beagle is the breed for you. You've figured out where the best place to find *your* dream Beagle is: reputable breeder, animal shelter, or breed rescue group. Now comes the trickiest part: choosing your Beagle.

Picking the Beagle who will be your canine companion is much more than falling for the first endearing face you see. This chapter explains what you need to know to select the Snoopy-dog who's right for you, your family, and your way of living.

Narrowing Your Choices

The beauty of Beagles is that you have so many options to consider. Do you want a boy Beagle or a girl Beagle? Do you want a dog who wins ribbons in dog shows, a dog who can hunt, or a dog who's simply your wonderful best friend? Does raising a cute little puppy appeal to you, or would you rather skip the puppy stuff and welcome home an adult dog? And if having one Beagle is great, is having two Beagles even better? This section doesn't answer any of those questions for you, but it gives you the info you need to answer them for yourself.

Male or female?

Most experts agree that little difference in temperament exists between male and female Beagles. Both are friendly to people and other dogs. Both would follow their noses to the ends of the earth if they were given the chance. Both are capable of being bossy or of being meek. Both are known to engage in that inimitable Beagle-song otherwise known as howling. And both should be altered in some fashion — spaying for females, neutering for males — unless you plan to breed them. (Chapter 11 provides more info on breeding.)

So if male and female Beagles have similar temperaments, should you favor one gender over the other for any reason? The answer to that question depends on your individual situation and personal preferences. Here are some gender differences to consider:

- ✔ If you already have a dog and want to add a Beagle to your household pack, your best bet is to choose a Beagle of the opposite gender. In other words, if your first dog is male, your Beagle should be a female — and vice versa. Opposite-sex dogs tend to get along better with each other than same-sex dogs do, even if the same-sex dogs are neutered or spayed — although there are plenty of exceptions to that principle.

- ✔ The male Beagle is probably less likely to keep his private parts private than his sister is. Males will lick their genitals and will hump inappropriate objects, such as the table leg or your leg, with little or no fanfare. Females are much less likely to engage in such behavior — although girl dogs have been known to hump other dogs and even humans to show that they (the humpers) are in charge.

- ✔ Males and females deal with bathroom issues differently. The adolescent and adult male Beagle lifts his leg and pees on nearby vertical surfaces, and at times, targets a specific surface and subjects that surface to repeated anointings. This behavior, which experts call *marking,* can ruin the surface that bears the brunt of the dog's attention. By contrast, females squat daintily to pee and rarely engage in marking.

Neutering your male Beagle before he reaches adulthood is likely to put an end to marking, or at least diminish it considerably. Neutering may also enable your Beagle guy to be more discreet in dealing with his remaining private parts than is the case with the typical intact male.

- ✔ Adult female Beagles are ready for love approximately twice a year unless they are spayed. These events, or *heat cycles,* signal that your dog is ready for mating. The scent of her discharge will lure male dogs from all over creation — or at least from all over your neighborhood — to your doorstep, ready to service your Beagle girl. To prevent an unplanned pregnancy, you need to confine your Beagle when her heat cycle occurs. Better yet, if you don't plan to breed your Beagle, have her spayed before she reaches adulthood.

Spaying your female Beagle not only prevents unwanted litters of puppies but also virtually eliminates the chance that your dog will get mammary (breast) cancer if done before her first heat cycle.

Field dog, show dog, or pet?

Just because they're the same breed doesn't mean that all Beagles are the same — not by a long shot. The task a Beagle was bred to perform has a very significant impact on that dog's temperament, personality, and suitability for your lifestyle.

The *field dog* is a Beagle who's been bred to hunt rabbits. As such, she's likely to be much more energetic and require much more exercise than the dog who's been bred for the show ring or for life as a pampered pet. She also probably will be much more vocal — a trait that will not endear you to your neighbors. A Beagle bred for hunting won't be happy in your average pet-loving household, and you probably won't be happy with her, either.

The *show dog* is a Beagle who comes exceptionally close to meeting the breed standard, which is the National Beagle Club of America's blueprint for a perfect Beagle. (See Chapter 2 for more info on the breed standard and the ideal Beagle.) For that reason, she's likely to be far more expensive than a Beagle who doesn't epitomize the standard quite as well. Moreover, the breeder may want to retain some ownership of the dog as well in order to show her, or he may require you to sign a contract specifying that you will show her. If the breeder opts to show the dog, she'll probably spend quite a few weekends away from you to compete in shows. If you opt to show the dog, the two of you will be spending more than a few weekends going to dog shows. And even though the show dog can make a lovely pet, just because she's a gorgeous example of a Beagle has absolutely no effect on what sort of pet she'll be.

The *pet* is a wonderful Beagle who, for one reason or another, just isn't suited to the show ring. The reason may be as simple as a breeder expecting a puppy to grow over 15 inches in height — which disqualifies a Beagle from being shown. Other problems or faults such as ears set too high on the head or eyes deemed too small could end a Beagle's show career before it even starts, but these traits would have absolutely no effect on whether that dog would make a marvelous pet for you.

Puppy or adult?

Deciding whether to get a juvenile Snoopy-dog or an adult Beagle isn't necessarily a clear-cut matter. The right decision depends on your personal preferences and also on how much time you can spend taking care of your dog.

Without question, Beagle puppies are extremely cute and cuddly. And a lot can be said for raising a dog from near-infancy. For one thing, you can control what kind of adult a puppy becomes. You can teach that puppy what you want her to know, and you can make sure that she doesn't develop any bad habits. You can start her training at the best possible time — in puppyhood — and you can make sure that her earliest experiences in life are all positive and happy.

However, raising a puppy is a lot of work. You'll have to contend with the whole business of housetraining, for one thing. Despite what I tell you in Chapter 14 to help make the whole process as painless as possible, you nevertheless will have to get up during the night to give your Beagle baby a bathroom break — at least for the first couple of weeks after you bring your dog home. And for at least a few months, you or someone else need to be around during the day to give your puppy potty time at least every couple of hours — and possibly even more often. Puppies also need regular meals and constant vigilance to prevent bathroom accidents and to keep them from destroying your house and otherwise getting into mischief.

Adult Beagles, on the other hand, don't need such close monitoring — at least not when it comes to bathroom matters. They also generally have a pretty good idea as to how they should behave in a human household, so they're less likely to make your house look like a rock star's hotel room than the juvenile Beagle is. However, depending on where your adult Beagle lived before she met you, she may come with some emotional baggage or at least some bad habits that require time and patient remedial training to redo — or undo.

For many people, the puppy-or-adult decision depends on whether someone can be home during the day to care for a youngster. If you're away from home for more than a couple of hours each day, and no one else is around to give a puppy the constant attention she needs, do that puppy a favor: Get an adult dog instead.

Double your pleasure, double your fun? Maybe not

More than few prospective owners consider getting two Beagles at a time. They may think that the two dogs can keep each other company and out of mischief. Or, they may feel unable to choose between two adorable Beagle puppies and decide to get both. But even though two Beagles, such as those in the color section, may mean double the cuteness, they won't necessarily double your pleasure. Here's why:

- ✔ If one puppy is a lot of work, two puppies are a lot *more* work. Trying to keep track of one frisky puppy is tiring enough; monitoring two Beagle mischief-makers may be a short trip to utter exhaustion, if not a complete nervous breakdown.

- ✔ A solitary puppy will bond with her human, but two puppies who enter a household at the same time are more likely to bond with each other than with any human beings in their household. You, the owner, end up getting double the puppy care with much less of a payoff in the form of a cute, cuddly little puppy worshipping the ground you walk on. The two puppies you work your tail off raising are more likely to be interested in each other than in you.

- ✔ Adopting two adult Beagles also means double the work of adopting one — and that's assuming the two dogs get along.

In short, bringing two Beagles into your household at the same time probably isn't a good idea, unless you're a very experienced dog owner. If you absolutely must have two Snoopy-dogs, wait a few months before you acquire dog number two. Then you'll have time to get to know your first dog and give her the one-on-one attention that gets any new dog — puppy or adult — off to the best possible start.

Selecting a Puppy

Finding the puppy of your dreams is a two-part process. The first task is to find a reputable breeder, which I describe in Chapter 3. After you've found a breeder who has puppies available, the second task begins: picking your puppy.

Selecting one puppy isn't easy when you've got a bunch of wiggly little darlings crawling all over the place and breathing their sweet, milky puppy breath on you. How do you decide which puppy is right for you? Heck, how do you know if any of these puppies are right for you?

Start by answering the second question first. A good way to determine whether this litter is one for you to look at is to meet Mama Beagle. A *dam* who's clean, healthy-looking, and friendly is likely to produce puppies who are as healthy and friendly as she is.

Then watch the puppies as they play together. Pay close attention to their movements; make sure that they walk and run without difficulty. A puppy who limps or appears to lack energy may have health problems you probably don't want to take on.

Should you meet Dad?

Maybe. But then again, maybe not.

Meeting the mother of any Beagle litter you're looking at is a good idea, but the same is not necessarily true of meeting the father, or *sire*. If Daddy Beagle's on the breeder's premises because the breeder owns him, chances are that sire and dam may be related rather closely to each other. Breedings of closely related dogs, even if they appear healthy, may result in puppies who have congenital conditions or other less-than-desirable qualities.

On the other hand, if the sire belongs to another breeder and is just staying with your breeder temporarily, go ahead and give him a look. Getting acquainted with Papa Beagle can give you that much more information on what sorts of dogs his puppies will grow up to be.

As the puppies play, give yourself time to distinguish one from the other. Eventually, you'll either find that one particular puppy appeals to you or that you appeal to one particular puppy (as in, she'll come over to say hello).

The puppy who's confident enough to approach you and who behaves in a friendly fashion when she's there will probably keep that good temperament into adulthood. In other words, the puppy who chooses *you* may be your best bet.

Either way, as you cuddle the little darling, check for the following:

- ✓ **Bright, clear eyes:** The puppy should have clear, bright eyes like the youngsters featured in the color section of this book. Discharge from the eye or cloudiness in the eye itself may signal the presence of an infection or other eye problem. The pup also should be able to follow a moving object with her eyes. (If she can't, she may be blind.)

- ✓ **Dry, odor-free ears:** The smell of baking bread is lovely when it comes from a kitchen, but not when it comes from a Beagle's ears. A yeasty odor in the ear area probably means the pup has a yeast infection; other odors also indicate infection is present. Check the pup's hearing, too; just clap your hands to see whether the pup responds to the sound. If she doesn't, she may have a hearing problem.

- ✓ **Clean skin and full coat:** The pup should have no dirt or scabs on her skin or bald spots on her coat. Also check for fleas; if you see little dark specks hop around the coat, the pup is carrying these unwanted critters and probably hasn't gotten the care she should have.

Breeder's choice

If your breeder wants to select a puppy for you instead of allowing you to choose a pup, don't fret. Many breeders prefer to control the puppy selection process. Such breeders believe that they know their puppies better than anyone else and that they're in the best position to match puppies with people. If your breeder is part of this camp, share your preferences with her — for example, whether you want a male or female Beagle pup — but then trust her to make a good choice for you and your family.

✔ **Healthy stools:** I know it sounds gross, but take a peek into the puppies' living area to see what their poop looks like. The stools should be firm and formed, not runny.

✔ **Sound temperament:** Use the time that you spend with the puppy to try to get a feel for her personality — and whether that personality meshes with yours. Is she a little firecracker, or is she content to cuddle quietly? Does she roll over onto to her back for a tummy scratch, or does she fight efforts to put her in that position? The quiet cuddler who submits to belly rubs is likely to be easier to live with and train than the fractious firecracker. On the other hand, the firecracker pup may be better suited for life in a busy, active family than that low-key little cuddler.

Be wary of the shy little darling who won't come to you at all. Beagles shouldn't be timid — and a dog of any breed who's that reticent may turn out to be a dog who bites out of fear.

Selecting an Adult Beagle

Choosing an adult Beagle is similar to selecting a puppy — to a point. You want to look for the same traits in a full-grown Beagle as in a pup: healthy eyes, ears, and skin; sound temperament; good movement; and a full coat. But unlike with a puppy from a reputable breeder, you don't necessarily want to reject an adult Beagle who doesn't look or act quite as healthy as the well-bred puppy.

Most adult Beagles come from animal shelters and rescue groups — and many of these dogs find themselves in these settings because their original owners couldn't or wouldn't take proper care of them. Consequently, these dogs may have a couple of physical problems or behavioral issues. But with the help of shelter or rescue personnel, your veterinarian, and/or a professional dog trainer, you and your adult Beagle can overcome these challenges and live happily ever after.

A family affair

Here's how to max the odds that everyone will live happily ever after with your Beagle — and vice versa:

✔ **Ban surprises.** Giving a Beagle puppy or adult dog as a holiday, birthday, or Valentine's Day surprise gift is not a good idea. The commotion of the holiday practically guarantees that the new dog won't get off to a good start, and the recipient may be unprepared to care for a dog.

✔ **Make a promise.** Instead of giving a Beagle as a gift, create a gift certificate or I.O.U. promising to choose a dog together after a birthday or holiday passes. Meanwhile, present the recipient with a collar and leash — and to give him a really good head start on raising a Beagle, give him this book!

✔ **Bring your partner, spouse, and children with you to the breeder, shelter, or rescue foster-care provider.** Allow everyone to look at the puppies or dogs, to handle them (children should be carefully supervised, however), and to weigh in on which dogs they like — and don't like.

✔ **Include your other pets.** Ask your breeder, shelter professional, or rescue group member whether you can introduce your current pet to your possible future pet before you make a final purchase or adoption decision.

✔ **Make it unanimous.** If one family member doesn't like the puppy or dog the others have chosen, don't overrule that lone veto. Make sure that the Beagle you take home is the puppy or dog that everyone in your family wants.

Don't reject the adult Beagle because of the following:

✔ **Her ears smell yeasty.** Your vet can prescribe antibiotics to knock out the infection causing the yeasty odor, and he can show you how to clean the ears to keep the infection from coming back.

✔ **Her coat and skin aren't perfect.** A trip to the vet to deal with minor skin rashes, combined with an optimum diet (as described in Chapters 6 and 8), can turn a not-so-great-looking Beagle exterior into a picture of perfect hound health.

✔ **She's coughing.** Dogs confined with a lot of other dogs are more vulnerable to *bordetella,* also known as *kennel cough.* This condition is treatable — and after you treat the disease, you can keep it from coming back by having your vet give the dog a shot designed for just that purpose.

✔ **Her temperament's not perfect.** Experiences of abandonment, neglect, and even abuse can cause an otherwise healthy dog to be anxious, hyperactive, or a little shy, but don't rule out such a dog automatically. The stress of being in a noisy shelter can affect a dog's temperament, too. Time spent in a loving home coupled with consistent, patient training can go a long way toward helping a shelter or rescue Beagle's true personality to emerge.

If you're having trouble evaluating a shelter dog's temperament, ask shelter personnel if you can take her to a quiet room or out into a fenced courtyard. A little bit of one-on-one time away from the noise of the shelter kennel may be just what a shelter Beagle needs to show you what a sweetheart she really can be.

Of course, some problems you may encounter with an adult Beagle should result in an automatic thumbs-down, no matter how much you otherwise like the dog. Deal-breaking problems include these:

✔ **A Beagle who growls at you for no apparent reason:** Aggressiveness in a dog is a problem you do not want to have to deal with.

✔ **A dog who cringes in the corner of her crate or kennel:** The very shy dog may turn out to be a fear-biter.

✔ **A dog who bites:** The adult Beagle who literally puts teeth in her interaction with you should not get any additional interaction opportunities — not with you or your family, anyway.

Pushing Papers

After much deliberation, you and other members of your family have chosen a Beagle of your very own. (Or perhaps she chose you!) Either way, now that you've made your choice, you need to seal the deal. At the very least, the breeder, animal shelter, or rescue group will give you a purchase or adoption contract to sign and probably also some written instructions on how to care for your new family member. Here's the scoop on what you'll get and why.

Buyer or adoption contract

Once you agree to buy or adopt a Beagle, you need to formalize the transaction with a written contract. Such documents protect the puppy or adult dog by clarifying the rights and responsibilities of the buyer or adopter, and the breeder, shelter, or rescue group. The document should address the following issues:

✔ **Terms of sale:** The contract should state whether the puppy is a companion animal or a show dog. If the latter is the case, the contract should state whether the breeder retains partial ownership of the puppy (often the case with show dogs). If the breeder is selling the puppy as a pet, the contract should state when the dog needs to be spayed or neutered.

- **Financials:** The contract should state what the breeder is charging for the dog and how that money is to be paid (by cash or check? All at once or in installments?). This provision should also specify the terms of any deposits, such as a deposit for altering a dog or completing basic obedience training.

- **Health guarantees:** At minimum, a contract should let the buyer return a dog for a refund if the animal gets sick shortly after the sale or becomes ill because of a hereditary defect. A better contract permits the exchange of a sick puppy for a healthy one or lets the owner keep the sick dog but be reimbursed by the breeder for reasonable costs.

- **Return provisions:** The best breeders agree to take a puppy back at any time after the sale, even if several years have passed. They understand that sometimes life deals a hand that just doesn't allow a person to keep a pooch, even if that pooch is a much-loved Beagle. Breeders also understand that sometimes people bring their new puppies home and find that puppy care is more than they can handle. For that reason, a fair contract allows a person to return a puppy for any reason within a few days after purchase and get a refund.

Shelter and rescue adoption contracts are quite similar to breeders' contracts, except that they don't contain any provisions for showing the dog. That's because shelter and rescue dogs are all spayed and neutered — if not by the shelter or rescue group, then by the adopter as a condition of the adoption — which means they aren't eligible for dog shows. Adoption contracts may also contain more provisions than breeders' contracts as to how the adopter is expected to care for the Beagle. Adoption contracts commonly:

- **Require that the owner has a fenced yard:** This condition especially applies for Beagles, who are known to follow their noses to the ends of the earth, unless confined properly.

- **Forbid keeping the dog outdoors:** Such provisions result from the Beagle being a very social individual who spends most of her time with her family and in her family's house, not banished to the backyard to live on her own.

- **Prohibit tie-outs:** Shelters and rescue groups understand that tying a dog to a post or pole outdoors not only endangers the animal but can result in aggressive behavior.

AKC papers

A reputable Beagle breeder should provide you with papers to register your puppy with the American Kennel Club. You're not required to register your puppy — but you can't compete with her in AKC sports such agility or obedience unless you do.

If you're buying a show-quality Beagle, you'll apply for a *full registration* for your puppy. This registration certifies that your Beagle is a purebred dog, lets her trip the ring fantastic, and permits her offspring to be registered with the AKC. If your Beagle isn't destined for the show ring, you'll apply for a *limited registration*. A dog with this registration is also a certifiably purebred dog but can't enter dog shows. The offspring are ineligible for AKC registration. However, a Beagle with a limited registration can enter AKC sports.

Either way, the breeder will fill out parts of the form (called the *blue slip*) dealing with your pup's breed, birth date, names of the parents, the breeder's name and address, and the AKC registration number for your puppy's litter. She'll give the forms to you to complete, sign, and send (along with a fee) to the AKC. The AKC then transfers ownership of the puppy to you and sends you a certificate with your puppy's new AKC number.

Make sure that you get your AKC papers before you leave your breeder's premises with your new puppy – or your Beagle can't enter any AKC events.

The breeder also should give you a copy of your puppy's *pedigree,* which is a chart that depicts your Beagle's family tree. The pedigree includes the names of your puppy's sire and dam, their sires and dams, and offspring from the previous three to five generations. If you plan to breed your Beagle, such info is essential; if breeding's not on your agenda, the info is still fun to have.

Health clearances

Your breeder should give you copies of any health clearances given to your puppy's sire and dam, such as approved hips and elbows from the Orthopedic Foundation for Animals (OFA) (or a PennHIP clearance, see Chapter 3) and the Canine Eye Registry Foundation (CERF). Keep these clearances with your puppy's health records.

And speaking of health records, your breeder should give you information as to whether and when your puppy received any immunizations and which diseases she's been immunized against. You also need to know about any treatment for worms or other parasites your pup may have received. A shelter or rescue group should provide similar info about an adult Beagle.

Care instructions

The breeder, shelter, or rescue group should provide you with basic information on how to care for your new Beagle. The info should include a description of when to feed your Beagle and what the dog's been eating up until now.

Try to feed your new Beagle the same food she's been eating at the breeder, shelter, or foster-care provider, at least for a couple of weeks or so. Consistency in feeding helps keep her tummy from getting upset during the exciting and sometimes stressful transition from her previous living environment to her new home. Some breeders will even give you a small sample of the food they've been feeding your puppy; ask your breeder if she can give you a couple of meals worth of your puppy's current chow. If you plan to switch from the dog's current diet to another food regimen, Chapter 8 explains how to do so.

If your Beagle has recently been spayed or neutered, the shelter or rescue group should provide instructions on how to care for the incision and let you know about any other care she needs.

Homeward Bound? Maybe Not

Just because you've signed a contract and paid some money doesn't mean that you'll be able to take your new Beagle home right away. Here are some reasons why you may need to delay your gratification:

- ✔ **The puppy is too young.** Good breeders don't let puppies go to permanent homes until they're 8 weeks old. A puppy needs those first weeks to wean herself, learn to eat solid food, and learn how to interact politely with other dogs.

- ✔ **The shelter needs to check your home.** Many shelters hold off on finalizing adoptions because they want to see the adopter's home first and make sure that it's a good place for a Beagle to live. Normally, such delays are only a matter of days. When your home passes muster, your new dog can come home.

- ✔ **The dog needs to be fixed.** Cash-strapped animal shelters (which most seem to be) often delay spaying or neutering a Beagle until that dog has an adoption pending and the would-be adopter has paid a fee for the procedure. After the surgery is completed and the dog has had a few days to recover, the adoption proceeds and the Beagle goes to her new home.

Part II
Starting Life with Your Beagle

"Okay, before I let the new puppy out, let's remember to be real still so we don't startle him."

In this part . . .

To get your Beagle off to a good start, you need to know what to expect on that first crucial day in your home — and how to deal with the unexpected. Part II helps you get ready for your Beagle's arrival with guidance on prepping your home, getting proper Beagle gear, and managing the pandemonium that will inevitably occur after your Snoopy-dog crosses the threshold into your home and his.

Chapter 5

Preparing for Your Beagle's Arrival

*C*hoosing the Beagle of your dreams involves much more than heading to a reputable breeder, a local animal shelter, or a breed rescue group. Before you start life with your new four-legged friend, you need to prepare yourself and your home for his arrival. This chapter tells you how to accomplish both tasks.

Choosing a Veterinarian

No one can raise a Beagle alone. As hard as you'll work to keep your new family member healthy, he inevitably will get sick. To cure him of his ills (not to mention prevent him from being struck by some nasty disease), you need a veterinarian for your Beagle — and you need one now.

You may be tempted to wait until your Beagle gets sick before you find a vet for him. But your dog deserves better than such a haphazard approach to his health care.

Choose your Beagle's veterinarian with the same care that you would use to select a pediatrician for your child. Start by asking for recommendations from friends who have the same attitude toward owning pets as you do. Other options include going online or opening your printed telephone directory to choose a few animal clinics to visit. Then, after you cross the threshold of the clinic you're considering, ask yourself some questions, such as:

✔ **Am I comfortable?** Probably the most important question to ask yourself is whether you feel at ease with the veterinarian you're considering. You need to be able to communicate with the vet, ask any questions that come to mind, and understand the answers she gives you.

✔ **Do I like the facility?** Just looking at the veterinary clinic or animal hospital where a veterinarian practices can help you decide whether this vet is the right one for you and your pet. Ask for a tour, and check to see whether the clinic is clean, the staff is helpful, and — if the clinic has several vets — you can see the same practitioner at every visit. Seeing the same vet every time you visit means you'll have a practitioner who really knows you and your Beagle.

✔ **Does the staff keep current?** Veterinary medicine evolves at lightning speed, with new treatments, techniques, and discoveries being unveiled almost constantly. Your Beagle's vet should stay on top of these developments. How can you tell whether the vet you're considering is staying ahead of the curve? Look for certificates and diplomas on the walls. They show that the vet is learning how to perform new treatments, such as laser surgery (which is less painful to the dog and shortens recovery time from surgery), or developing discipline-specific specialties, such as dentistry or emergency care. And make sure the clinic itself is certified. Look for a seal that shows membership in the American Animal Hospital Association (AAHA), a voluntary accreditation association for animal hospitals and clinics.

✔ **Is the location satisfactory?** Notice that I use the word "satisfactory," not "convenient." Although you want to find a clinic or animal hospital that's convenient to your home, the best clinic isn't necessarily the closest. A facility that offers great customer service may be worth a little extra travel time.

✔ **Does the clinic have procedures for dealing with after-hours emergencies?** Beagles and other pets have a maddening habit of developing health crises at night, on weekends, or at other times when most clinics are closed. Ask the clinic staff how they cover after-hours emergencies. At minimum, the clinic should have an after-hours telephone number for clients to call and, if the vets can't treat the problem, procedures to refer you to a nearby emergency veterinary clinic.

Shopping for Beagle Basics

Sure, you could wait till you're on your way home with your new Beagle before you stock up on dog gear. However, sprinting in a frenzied fashion up and down the aisles of your local pet super-store and throwing stuff into the shopping cart while trying to manage a Beagle you don't know isn't an effective way to shop for Beagle belongings, much less start a good relationship with your new friend. A better plan is to pick up everything he needs a few days — or even weeks — before you bring him home.

Repeat after me: Crates aren't cruel, crates aren't cruel . . .

I can hear you now. "A crate?" you say. "Don't you mean a cage? There's no way I'm going to cage up my Beagle!"

But if your Beagle could talk, his opinions about crates may sur-prise you. He'd probably tell you that a plastic or metal crate is just what he needs to feel secure when he rests, sleeps, or just wants to beat a retreat. Everyone, even the sociable Snoopy-dog, needs a place to call his own — and in the Beagle's case, a crate fills the bill. Figure 5-1 shows a metal crate; Figure 5-2 shows a plastic crate.

Figure 5-1: A metal crate contains your Beagle but lets him see the world.

Crates help people as much as they help pooches. That's because they're a great place to keep your Beagle out of mischief when you can't watch him. Crates are also an invaluable housetraining aid, because they teach a dog to hold his water (not to mention the other stuff) until you can get him to his outdoor potty. Chapter 14 details exactly how crates can help civilize your Beagle's bathroom behavior.

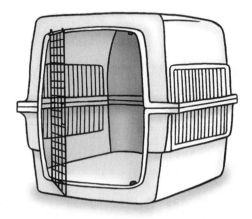

Figure 5-2: A plastic crate encloses your Beagle in a cozy, dark den.

When considering crates, either plastic or metal is fine. Bypass mesh crates until you're sure that your Beagle won't chew through the mesh! Consider size carefully, though. Any crate you choose must be big enough for your dog to stand up, turn around, and stretch out to sleep — but not so large that he can pee at one end and sleep at the other.

The crate that's big enough for an adult Beagle is too big for a puppy. But you don't need to buy a new crate every few weeks as your puppy grows. Instead, consider buying a metal crate with a divider. The divider restricts the area of the crate available to the young puppy so the crate won't be too big for him. As your puppy grows, adjust the divider accordingly until he's fully grown. At that point, you won't need the divider at all, but you will have saved money by only having bought one crate.

Borrowing from baby: Gates and pens

At times, you may want to limit your Beagle's access to some areas of your house without having to confine him to a crate. To that end, *baby gates* and *exercise pens* (ex-pens for short) do a fine job of keeping your dog contained without totally restricting his movements.

Baby gates are available in pet stores and baby supply stores. Gates come in several different styles:

✔ **Pressure-mounted gates:** These gates rely on pressure to ensure that they adhere to the walls. They're easier to install than hardware gates, but they're also easier for a rambunctious Beagle to knock over. Some pressure-mounted gates swing open; check the gate or the label on the gate's packing box for details.

✔ **Hardware gates:** These gates are very sturdy, but they offer another advantage: They generally swing open, allowing you to walk through the gate instead of having to hop over it (see Figure 5-3).

✔ **Wooden accordion-style gates:** Don't buy this type of gate at a thrift store or yard sale. Such gates pose a strangulation hazard to Beagles and young children.

No matter what style you choose, make sure that the gate has a straight top edge (it will be safer for the puppy who wants to stand on his hind legs and easier for you to hop over), and either rigid metal bars or a mesh screen. If you choose a gate with metal bars, make sure that it has a mesh cover so a puppy or dog can't get his head stuck between the bars.

You can also choose to keep your dog contained with an exercise pen.

Ex-pens resemble children's playpens — except ex-pens don't have floors or bottoms. Some are made from the same sort of wire used in wire crates, but others are made from hard plastic. Many ex-pens have eight panels, plus a door, but others such as the one in Figure 5-4 have only six panels. Either way, they generally range from 2 to 4 feet high and are available at pet supply stores.

Figure 5-3: A baby gate keeps your Beagle out of unauthorized areas.

Figure 5-4: An ex-pen can help keep a Beagle out of mischief.

Picking out dishes

Dog dishes come in a wide range of sizes and shapes — but for a Beagle, the options are reasonably narrow, literally. A narrow, deep bowl allows your Snoopy-dog to eat and drink with his ears outside the bowl. As for the dish's material, you have several options:

- ✔ **Stainless steel:** Your best bet probably is a stainless steel dish, because it's easy to clean and can't be demolished by a teething puppy.

- ✔ **Ceramic:** Ceramic is also a good choice, as long as it's not imported. No, I'm not bashing foreign trade here; my concern is that ceramic dishes manufactured outside the United States may contain lead, which can be toxic to Beagles and their people.

- ✔ **Plastic:** Plastic dishes are cheap and easy to clean, but can cause some dogs to lose their nose pigment (the loss is temporary; after you switch to a nonplastic dish, the pigment should return) or to develop little pimples (yup, dogs can get acne) on their chins.

 Invest in three dog dishes: a water dish and one dish for each of the two meals per day that you'll feed your adult Beagle. That way, you won't have to wash a dish after every doggy meal. You can just pop each dish into the dishwasher, run the dishwasher at night, and — voilà! — have clean dishes at the ready the next morning.

Chow time!

Plan on having a week's worth of dog food on hand before you bring your new Beagle home. What to buy? Ask the breeder, animal shelter, or foster-care provider what they've been feeding your dog and buy the same product. You may want to change food later — if so, Chapter 8 will give you some ideas on what changes you may want to make — but for now, at least, stick with what your dog's already eating. The transition to your home will be challenging enough for your new friend; don't ask him to deal with dietary changes, too.

Lay in a couple of 15-ounce cans of pumpkin — just straight pumpkin, not prepared pumpkin pie filling — before you bring your Beagle home. If your new dog's stress results in overly loose or overly hard stool, a dollop of pumpkin mixed in with his food can rebalance his system in a jiffy.

This Beagle's made for walkin': Collars and leashes

Abandon any thoughts you have of getting your Beagle to walk beside you off leash, at least for the immediate future. The Beagle is much more likely to obey his nose than to obey you — and if his nose takes him in a direction away from you, it's bye-bye, little friend. To keep your dog securely tethered to you, you need to buy him a collar and leash.

The collar holds not only the leash, but also the identification tag, rabies inoculation tag, and license tag needed to keep your Beagle legal. Stores offer plenty of collar styles to choose from, and Chapter 15 discusses those options in detail. For now, though, all you need is a soft nylon or thin leather buckle or snap collar. For an adult Beagle, get a collar for 20- to 30-pound dog; for a puppy, size down accordingly.

Chapter 15 also discusses leash options — but for now, opt for a 6-foot leather leash. Nylon leashes are cheaper, but if your Beagle decides to get in touch with his inner sled dog and pull you down the street, the nylon could leave a nasty burn on your palm as the leash crosses your hand. Leather is easier on the hands, and it lasts longer, too.

Think twice — no, make that 20 times — about using a retractable leash. These contraptions may give your dog the illusion of freedom because they allow him to wander up to 15 feet — maybe even farther — away from you. However, many communities ban the use of leashes that extend more than 6 feet, because unsuspecting pedestrians don't always see the leashes and can easily trip over them. In addition, the leash's retractability encourages your Beagle to pull you down the street as though he's running a one-dog chariot race straight out of the movie *Ben-Hur*. Trust me: You don't want to give your Beagle the means to exhibit any more independence than he's already likely to show!

The same is true of harnesses. Unless you use a special no-pull harness (more about that in Chapter 15), you won't have the control
you need to keep your Beagle from pulling. Harnesses are appropriate for a teeny-tiny dog who may injure his windpipe if subjected to a leash and collar. But Beagles are stronger than that!

Grooming gear

Beagles require relatively little grooming equipment, but you need
to have a few basic items on hand for when your dog could use a
canine makeover. Put these items on your shopping list:

✔ **Shampoo:** A mild shampoo formulated just for dogs will give
your Beagle a pleasurable bath whenever he needs one. An
oatmeal or hypoallergenic shampoo is an especially good
choice. Don't bother with flea shampoos; they're much too
harsh for a Beagle's tender skin — and your vet can offer far
better ways to rid your dog of fleas.

Don't use your own shampoo on your Beagle. The stuff that
keeps your tresses gleaming is too harsh for his coat and skin.

✔ **Brush:** Either a soft bristle brush or rubber curry brush will
do the trick for the weekly brushings he'll need.

✔ **Nail clippers:** Doggy nail clippers are the equipment of choice
for regular Beagle pedicures.

✔ **Toothbrush and pet toothpaste:** To keep your Beagle's teeth
clean, pick up a doggy toothbrush (or soft child's toothbrush)
and pet toothpaste. Don't use human toothpaste, which can
upset your dog's tummy.

Everything you need to know about grooming your Beagle is in
Chapter 10.

Clean-up equipment

As a responsible Beagle owner, you need to clean up any poop that
your dog deposits outdoors — and as a person who presumably
wants to keep a reasonably sanitary house, you need to clean up
your dog's indoor bathroom boo-boos.

For outdoor cleanup, all you really need is a goodly supply of plastic grocery-size bags or larger. The scoop on cleaning up your dog's poop appears in Chapter 11.

Indoor cleanups require specialized products. Check out the appropriate aisle in your local pet superstore, where you'll find a boatload of *enzymatic cleaners* that remove not only the stains from your Beagle's bathroom transgressions, but also the odors. Chapter 14 has a thorough explanation of why odor removal is crucial for housetraining to succeed.

Extra comforts of home

Of course you want to pamper your new pooch! Here are some suggestions on stuff to buy to help you do just that:

- ✔ **A crate pad:** You wouldn't want to sleep on a hard metal or plastic surface, and your Beagle probably won't want to, either. A crate-sized foam mattress will give your dog a comfy reason to love his den, which is a big plus while you're trying to housetrain him. Many of these pads are also waterproof, which is another plus during the housetraining process if, for some reason, your Beagle has an accident in his crate.

- ✔ **A few toys:** Most Beagles love toys of some sort, but you may need to experiment for a while until you figure out your own dog's plaything preferences. Start with a few inexpensive, durable items such as balls or rubber bones. Other good toys are pooch puzzlers such as Kongs and Busta Cubes in which you hide tasty treats for your Beagle to ferret out.

   Avoid toys that have parts (including squeakers) that are small enough to swallow; are easily destroyed by canine teeth; come with long strings that can get stuck in the digestive tract (for example, rope toys); and resemble real-life objects that you don't want your dog to chew on (for example, a sock, shoe, or newspaper).

- ✔ **A few treats:** The food- and scent-obsessed Beagle responds well to food rewards for learning basic doggy etiquette. Chapters 8 and 15 give you the lowdown on giving treats for tricks and just plain doing what you ask your Snoopy-dog to do.

Designating Beagle Spaces in Your Home

Getting Beagle gear is only half of what you need to do before you bring your new family member home. The other half is making sure that your home is ready for when the little hound crosses your threshold for the first time.

Before your Beagle comes home, figure out where in your house he's going to be conducting the major activities in his life: sleeping, eating, pooping, peeing, and playing. The sooner you determine where you want him to do his thing — and where you don't — the smoother his transition into your household will be.

Note that in the previous paragraph I said "in your house." That's because I strongly believe that Beagles — and all dogs, for that matter — belong indoors with their families. The more time your dog spends with you, the more bonded to you he will be. He'll be a better companion, too.

The Beagle boudoir

The best place for your Beagle to sleep is in the same room that you sleep — and not just the first few nights, but every night you and he are in the same house. Beagles are pack animals, which means they want to sleep in close proximity to other family members. Your Beagle, as independent as he is, will still count on you to feed him, play with him, train him, exercise him, and take good care of him. He'll want to be with you as much as possible, even if he won't necessarily want to do everything you ask of him.

Sleeping in the same room that you do gives your dog a chance to be with you and your scent for an extended period of time. Repeated nights together help your Beagle build trust and confidence in you, and also help him feel that he really belongs in his new pack.

Many people, especially first-time dog owners, think that inviting a dog into one's bedroom is the height of lunacy. Their objections generally take the form of plaintive questions such as:

✔ **What if he's noisy and won't let me sleep?** No matter where your Beagle sleeps, he'll probably be noisy, at least for the first few nights. He'll whine, he'll bark, and he may even howl.

But can you blame him? He's in a strange place with people he doesn't know. If he's a puppy, he's away from his mom and siblings for the very first time in his young life. Either way, he's scared and needs comforting.

Put him in his crate, bring the crate into your bedroom as close as possible to your bed, and extend your fingers down from your bed toward the crate door so he can sniff them. I guarantee that your Beagle's nocturnal vocalizing will be much less than it would be if you banish the poor little guy to the other end of the house just so you can get some zzz's.

✔ **What if he has an accident?** Any accident anywhere should draw the same response: Just clean it up. But you can limit the likelihood of accidents in your bedroom by taking your new Beagle out to potty just before bedtime, putting him in his crate at night, and, if he's a puppy, taking him outside to pee once or twice during the middle of the night. Chapter 14 explains how to prevent accidents anywhere in the house.

Don't let your Beagle sleep on your bed with you — at least not until you're sure that he's fully housetrained, as described in Chapter 14.

✔ **What if we're, um, doing something?** Please. Who's your Beagle going to tell? Put him in his crate and enjoy yourselves! He'll probably sleep through the whole thing.

The doggy dining area

The kitchen is probably the best place for your Beagle's dining area. You'll undoubtedly fix his meals in the kitchen, so feeding him there means fewer steps for you. Spillage doesn't ruin a bare kitchen floor the way it might ruin a living-room carpet. The kitchen also is the center of most human household action, so your sociable Snoopy-dog won't feel that he's missing anything important just because he's stopping to have a meal. That said, your Beagle should be able to eat all of his meals without being disturbed. In other words, no matter where your little hound eats, don't let anyone — kids, other pets, even adults — bug him. To create just the right atmosphere for your Beagle's dining pleasure, turn to Chapter 8.

The Beagle bathroom

The best place for your Beagle to do his duty is outdoors, but not far away from your house. If you have a backyard, select an area that's a few feet away from the house and take him there each and every time he needs a bathroom break. If you don't have a yard, walk with him on the sidewalk and let him eliminate on the median strip between the sidewalk and street — taking care to clean up immediately afterward. No sidewalk? Find a small park or lot where you can take your friend and clean up after he unloads.

Don't take a Beagle puppy to areas where other dogs eliminate until he's had all of his puppy shots. Until his immunization program is complete, he's vulnerable to contracting diseases, such as distemper, parvovirus, and intestinal parasites, all of which may lay waiting in the droppings of infected dogs. Chapter 11 gives more information on immunizing your Beagle.

The Beagle hangout zone

Giving your Beagle the run of the house while you're not home isn't a good idea, especially when he still holds newcomer status. A better option is to escort your Beagle to his cozy crate if you'll be gone for just a couple of hours. Longer jaunts away from the house require that you set up another place for your dog to stay until you return; possible options include a laundry room or the kitchen. Put his crate in that new place, set up baby gates, or shut the door and leave him a couple of safe toys to play with. By taking these precautions, you'll greatly reduce the likelihood that your Beagle will chew on your upholstery, tear down the wallpaper, or otherwise trash your domicile before you return.

No-Beagles zones

Picking the places you don't want your Beagle to go is really a matter of personal preference. In my household, the dog-free zones include our living room furniture, all human beds, and my husband's art studio. Think of a few areas where you positively, absolutely, never, ever want your Beagle to be, and take steps to restrict his access to them. The following section offers ideas on exactly how to restrict your dog's access to areas and items that may get him into trouble.

Beagle-Proofing Your Home and Yard

Every child needs boundaries in order to thrive and grow to be a healthy, well-balanced adult — and in that respect, Beagles are no different than human kids. Your Beagle needs clear, consistent boundaries not only to stay in your good graces, but also just to stay safe.

Securing the perimeter

Those boundaries start with the outdoors: specifically, with enclosing part or all of your yard so it's virtually escape-proof. Fencing comes in a wide variety of materials and price ranges, but the most important consideration for the fence-building Beagle owner is that whatever you build be impermeable. Ask your local hardware store or fencing professional what materials best keep Beagles on their own turf. And after you or the contractor start to install the fence, make very sure that no openings or crevices exist above or below ground that may allow your Beagle to make his bid for freedom. And check at least weekly after installation is complete: Beagles are masters at fashioning creative escape routes by digging under or chewing holes in fences.

If you choose not to install a fence, don't let your Beagle out in your yard without you holding the other end of a leash. No matter how much your little hound loves you, he'll love the great outdoors more. If he gets the chance to explore the world beyond his backyard without being tethered to you, he will jump at it — and the results could be tragic. Some dog owners install an electronic fence thinking it will protect their Beagle just as well as a traditional fence. The sidebar, "How about electronic fences?", explains why you shouldn't opt for this high-tech solution.

How about electronic fences?

For many Beagle owners, the prospect of installing conventional fencing either offends their visual tastes or wreaks havoc on their household budgets. Either way, electronic fencing appears to provide an attractive, cost-saving alternative. After installing underground wiring around the perimeter of your property, you buckle a special collar around your dog's neck. If he crosses your property line, he receives a mild electrical shock.

Unfortunately, all too many Beagles and other breeds venture beyond their property lines despite getting shocked — but then refuse to come back to their domiciles because they don't want another mini-jolt. And that's not the only potential problem with electronic fencing; another is that other dogs, animals, or people can cross freely into your yard, but your Beagle can't get away from them unless he's willing to risk getting shocked. In other words, electronic fencing can make your dog more vulnerable to being attacked or stolen.

The bottom line: Don't rely on electronic fencing to contain your little hound. The Beagle who gets lost could be your own.

Even though you've provided an outdoor play area for your Beagle, don't leave him outdoors unattended. The great outdoors, even within the confines of your yard, offers too many hazards for your little hound — hazards that range from dangerous plants to kids' toys to uncovered swimming pools. When your Beagle's outside, be there with him — or at least be watching him from a window.

Conducting a sweep

Inside the house, your main task is to make sure that your Beagle can't come into contact with anything that could get him into trouble or, worse, jeopardize his safety. The prudent dog owner takes steps to Beagle-proof his home before the little hound actually sets paw in the house. Here are some tips to do just that:

- ✔ **Get down to his level.** Assess the field from your Beagle's perspective: down low and on all fours. Get down on your hands and knees, and crawl throughout your home's interior so you can get a pup's-eye view of what will attract his attention or land him in trouble.

- ✔ **Stash your stuff.** Shoes, socks, underwear, kids' toys, books, and magazines are all fodder for a curious Beagle's teeth. Keep your Beagle from shredding your stuff by putting it out of view and out of reach. Put clothes in closed closets and drawers, place books and magazines out of reach, and cut off access to any items that you don't want your little hound to find during one of his many search-and-destroy missions.

- ✔ **Batten down the wires.** Dangling electrical cords could entice a curious Beagle who wants to paw or chew on them. Fasten them to the floor and/or wall with duct tape.

- ✔ **Block off staircases.** A tumble down some stairs can break a Beagle's leg or other bones. Close any doors that lead to flights of stairs; if that's not possible, put baby gates at both ends of the staircase. After your Beagle gets used to your home and learns to navigate stairs, you can probably get rid of the gates.

- ✔ **Secure the cabinets.** Install door guards to keep your Beagle out of cabinets that contain household cleansers or other substances that may be dangerous to him. Door guards are available at any toy or baby supply store.

✔ **Lids down!** I'm sorry to have to tell male readers that leaving the toilet seat up is not an option if you share your home with a Beagle. A Beagle puppy who finds his way into an open toilet could drown — and no Beagle benefits from drinking water out of the toilet. Bottom line: Keep the seat down at all times.

✔ **No trashing.** Dogs love to dive into wastebaskets to ferret out undesirable goodies. Make sure your Beagle can't find any. Empty your wastebaskets often, and/or limit his access to them by closing doors or moving the baskets off the floor.

Ladies, not to get gross, but many dogs love the scent of used feminine hygiene products. Wrap used maxi-pads, tampon inserters, and pantiliners securely with toilet paper before stashing them in the trash — and make sure your dog can't get to the basket you've stashed them in.

Planning Mayhem Management

Take a deep breath, look around your home and savor the moment. It may be the last peaceful moment you'll have in your house for quite a while. That's because the first few days of having a Beagle in your home inevitably will be somewhat chaotic. The newcomer won't have a clue as to what's going on, other than that he's in someplace new that bears exploring. Meanwhile, the current residents — human and nonhuman alike — are struggling to figure out what to do to keep the new dog off their turf or get some love time in with the way-too-cute Snoopy-dog. Still, you can limit the chaos by mapping out a first-day mayhem management plan. Here's what to consider:

✔ **Who's the boss?** Figure out who makes the rules, who controls the interactions between your Beagle and the rest of your family, and who does which dog-care jobs. If you're the decision-maker — well, congrats. You're top dog.

✔ **Where will the other critters be?** Plan how your current pets will meet the new critter in the house. Do you want them to be out of the house until your Beagle can settle in? Will the cats be at large or confined to a small room away from the new family member? Check out Chapter 6, which offers tips for managing your new dog's first encounter with the other nonhuman members of your pack.

✔ **How will your kids meet the dog?** Depending on their ages, you may want them to wait until you bring the new dog to them, or let them greet the newcomer immediately. Consider, too, whether you want to let them bring any of their friends over to meet the Beagle — and if so, how many and for how long. Stumped? Hop on over to Chapter 6.

Have a conference with your kids before you bring your Beagle home. Help them understand that your new puppy or dog may be feeling a little scared at first, and that he needs everyone to stay calm and give him some space for a while. Then, make some rules — no screaming, shouting, or squealing; no roughhousing; gentle petting only — and enforce them.

✔ **Does everyone know what will happen when the Beagle comes home?** Make sure everyone in the household — the kids, your roommates, and your partner — knows what you plan to do when you bring the Snoopy-dog home. Will you give him a bathroom break first? How long will you let him explore the house? How will you handle the introductions to the other animal members? When everyone knows what's going to happen, you stand a better chance of keeping mayhem to a minimum. Chapter 6 offers suggestions to help you do just that.

Chapter 6

Welcoming Your Beagle Home

*A*t last the big day has arrived: Today you bring your new Beagle home. The first 24 hours or so with your Beagle can be a dream come true or an absolute nightmare, depending on how you handle some potentially tricky arrival maneuvers. This chapter gives you the scoop on how to not only survive but thrive during your Snoopy-dog's first day and night in your abode.

Picking Up Your Beagle

Bringing home your little darling requires more than just motoring to the breeder, animal shelter, or foster-care provider, stashing the Beagle in the front seat, and boogeying back home. A little preplanning makes the trip a lot less stressful for both your new dog and yourself. Here are some suggestions on what to do before and during the trip home.

What (and whom) to bring

Driving home with a new Beagle puppy or dog can be a real challenge. Your new friend may be a little confused and more than a little carsick. She's very likely to need a bathroom break if you have to travel very far from her old home to her new one. And although you may be tempted to keep your little one in your lap while you drive, reconsider. If you have an accident and the air bag deploys, the impact could kill your dog. By the same token, letting her crawl around the back seat while you drive in the front seat is almost as bad an idea as having her in your lap. If you stop suddenly or have an accident, your new pet could literally fly off the seat and into you, resulting in serious injury to you both.

You can prevent these and other calamities if you bring a few simple items with you when you pick up your Beagle. Here's what to take with you before you take off:

- ✓ **Another person:** Bringing along a second person — preferably over the age of 10 — can make the drive home a lot easier for all concerned. Your new dog can lie on that person's lap, allowing you to concentrate on driving safely. If you'd rather be the designated lap, then let the other person drive, assuming he has a license.

  If you're driving, have the other person sit in the back seat with your Beagle. That way, if the dog gets squirmy or escapes from the designated lap, the dog is less likely to end up on the gear box, the gas pedal, or *your* lap. If the other person is driving, you should sit in the back seat with your Beagle.

- ✓ **Several towels:** Your Beagle may get carsick during the journey home. To limit the damage to your car or your human companion's clothes, bring some towels and have your friend place one across his lap. That way, if your dog tosses her cookies, the cookies can be easily whisked away. And don't bother pulling over if your dog starts to upchuck; she'll be done before you turn off the motor.

- ✓ **Collar and leash:** A drive of more than an hour may be too long for your confused or nervous new dog to hold her water or the other stuff. Having her collar and leash along makes a midjourney bathroom break both easy and safe. Make sure that you put the new collar on the dog before you head for home.

- ✓ **A couple of plastic bags:** Cleaning up your dog's poop is essential to being a good dog owner — and you should get in the habit of doing your dog's dirty work on the trip home. For the poop on how to pick up poop, check out Chapter 11.

- ✓ **A roll of paper towels:** You'll be glad you brought this item along if your little sweetie has a bathroom boo-boo or upchucks in your car.

- ✓ **A crate:** If you can't bring another person with you — or if the only other people who can come are your very young children — bring your Beagle's crate. Place the crate in the back seat and secure it with a seat belt. Stick a crate pad or a few towels inside to create a cozy nest for your four-legged traveler.

A doggy seat belt is a great safety option for your Beagle — but not necessarily on the day you bring her home. These devices can be a little bit daunting to use at first, and may add to any stress you and the dog already are feeling. However, having a canine seat belt is a great idea for future trips. Get the goods on these devices by checking out Chapter 13.

✔ **A chew toy:** Having a durable, medium-sized toy to chew on can distract your Beagle from any apprehension she may feel as she leaves her old home and moves to her new home with you.

Receiving the necessary papers

Hooray! You've made it to the breeder, shelter, or foster home, and you've got your new friend. Before the two of you embark on your journey home, however, you should receive a few additional items:

✔ **A signed contract:** No matter where or from whom you adopt your new Beagle, you should receive a document that transfers ownership of the dog to you. The contract also should specify your obligations and those of the individual or institution from whom you're acquiring the dog.

✔ **Your dog's health record:** The breeder, shelter, or rescue group should provide you with a copy of your Beagle's health record. This document should include when she was born and/or arrived at the shelter or foster home, and the veterinary care she has received, such as immunizations, spaying or neutering, deworming, and/or other procedures.

✔ **Some food:** A breeder or rescue volunteer may also give you a few days' supply of the food she's been feeding your Beagle. If you aren't given any food, at least ask what your new dog's been eating so you can pick up the same product (if you haven't done so already).

✔ **A scent cloth:** To get your Beagle puppy's housetraining off to a good start, consider asking her breeder for one more item: a paper towel that's been scented with a bit of your pup's urine. This pretreated sheet will speed up your pooch's potty-training process. More about scent cloths and housetraining appears in Chapter 14.

From there to here: The trip home

After you have your four-legged friend safely ensconced on a human lap or in her new crate in your car, you're ready to roll. If your trip home takes more than an hour, give your pooch a pit stop midway through the journey — or whenever you notice that your doggy passenger is getting restless.

Just find a grassy place and pull over. Put a leash on your Beagle before you open the car door, and then take her to the spot where you want her to do her business. To help her figure out where that spot is, place the prescented paper towel that you got from her breeder, shelter, or foster-care provider on the spot where you want her to go — and then let her unload on it.

Make sure this spot is away from any other doggy deposits. Until your dog is fully immunized, she's vulnerable to picking up nasty diseases from other canines — and stool is a prime transmission vehicle. Contact with stool can also put your pooch in contact with roundworms and other parasites.

If your Beagle poops or pees, tell her in a soft, cheerful voice what a good girl she is, and take a minute or two to pet her. Use one of the plastic bags you brought to clean up any poop, and drop the bag into a trash can.

If your Beagle puppy pees, wipe her urinary area very gently with a clean paper towel, and then put that towel into a plastic bag. You've just made a brand new scent cloth that will come in handy when the two of you arrive home.

After your little love-fest, take your new Beagle back to the potty spot to give her another chance to do her doo. Maybe she will, maybe she won't — but at least you've given her a chance. Either way, you can then continue on to your home and know that you've already started to not only teach her basic bathroom manners, but also form a lifelong bond.

We're Here! Arriving Home

You've truly arrived: You and your new Beagle buddy are about to cross the threshold into your abode. But before you open the door and are greeted by the other members of your household, consider how you're going to help your Snoopy-dog handle the first few hours of life in your household.

First things first: A potty break

When the two of you arrive at your home, don't go inside right away. Car rides often prompt a dog to open her floodgates almost immediately after she emerges from the vehicle. You can use this tendency to continue your Beagle's introduction to housetraining.

As soon as you get out of the car, leash up your little darling and either carry her or walk her to the potty area you've selected (Chapter 5 gives you the scoop on where that area should be). Place the scent cloth that you created during the trip home on top of the spot where you'd like her to potty. Let her sniff it — and tell her what a good girl she is when she decides to unload atop it.

If you haven't already made a scent cloth for your puppy — perhaps because the trip was very short — make one now. The previous section tells you how.

If she doesn't go, be patient. Give her a few minutes to explore her new bathroom; if she hasn't done the doo already, she probably will shortly after beginning her investigations.

Even if your Beagle does take a whiz or make a deposit, don't bring her inside your house immediately afterward. Many Beagle puppies and even some adult Beagles may need to make multiple deposits or take several whizzes before they're totally empty.

Checking out the new digs

When you're reasonably sure she's done, take your Beagle inside, and let her explore your domicile for a little while off lead. If at all possible, keep the kids and other family members out of her way for a few minutes and avoid fussing over her yourself — just let her do her thing in peace. At the same time, though, watch your little one closely to see if she needs to pee or poop again. Signs of an imminent bathroom event include a sudden stop in her explorations, an equally sudden onset of intense sniffing, and walking in ever-tighter circles.

If you see any such signs, get your dog back out to the potty spot she used before. The scent from her previous anointing or deposit almost certainly will prompt an encore. When that happens, praise her for doing her business where she's supposed to.

Meeting the rest of the pack

After your new Beagle has had a few minutes to explore her new domicile and, if necessary, take another bathroom break, she's ready to meet the other members of her family. Make these introductions carefully so you minimize the stress on everyone. You want these initial meetings to be positive and happy; they'll set the tone for your new friend's future interactions with her housemates.

The human members: No trauma please!

The other adults in your household, if any, should know how to handle themselves around a Beagle or other small dog, but your kids could be another matter. They're undoubtedly thrilled with the arrival of this new family member, and they probably can't wait to cuddle and hug her. However, they may not know their own strength, especially if they're under the age of 6. They may think they're giving your Beagle lots of love, but your Beagle may feel as though she's just met a couple of boa constrictors.

As a parent, it's your job to make sure that neither your children nor your Beagle are traumatized by their initial meeting. If you haven't had a family conference with your kids to explain the ground rules — no yelling, screaming or shouting; no rough handling; no squeezing; gentle petting only — have one now. Explain to your kids that your new dog is probably scared and almost certainly doesn't understand what's happening to her. Make sure that the kids give your Beagle some space while she explores, and allow her to have time to nap and just relax.

Never, ever leave any dog — Beagle or otherwise — alone with a child under the age of 6. Even the gentlest Beagle may nip a small child that pulls her tail or yanks her ears. Kids under 6 often don't understand that a Beagle is a living creature with real feelings, not a stuffed toy that just happens to walk and bark. For the sake of your dog and your kids, stick around to make sure that everybody stays out of harm's way.

As for your neighbors, the best course of action is inaction, at least for the first couple of days after your dog comes home. Even if your wonderful neighbors want to give your puppy a welcome-home party, decline politely. Your Snoopy-dog's got as much as she can handle just meeting you and your family. Let her get used to life within your household before she meets people and other individuals outside your four walls.

The canine members: Don't let the fur fly!

The other dogs in your family may not be totally thrilled to meet the newest doggy family member. For that reason, first meetings are best accomplished in neutral territory, such as a park or someone else's fenced yard. Let the dogs have a chance to sniff each other and check each other out.

Let your dogs sniff and lick each other's bottoms, even if the sight of such activity grosses you out. Such interactions are proper pooch protocol — kind of the canine version of humans shaking hands.

Keep the dogs on leash, but don't tighten up. Loose leashes keep the doggies relaxed.

After you're sure that everybody likes each other — or at least will tolerate each other — walk the entire pack home. Continue to monitor their behavior; use baby gates to separate them if necessary. Meanwhile, make sure that you don't neglect the dogs you already have in order to lavish attention on the newcomer!

The rest of the critter crew

Without a doubt, you're thrilled to be adding a Beagle to your family, but don't expect your resident kitty or other critters to share your enthusiasm. Exercise some caution, though, and chances are you'll achieve mutual tolerance, if not mutual admiration.

Introducing your new Beagle to your cat requires that you show some respect for the kitty having been in your home first. Place your Beagle in her crate, and let Fluffy the feline investigate the newcomer and her environs.

If no fur flies, and the hisses or barks are minimal, hold your Beagle on your lap and let your kitty approach if she chooses — or run in the other direction if she prefers. Either choice is fine as long as nobody's getting hurt.

Continue to monitor both animals closely until you're absolutely sure that they'll co-exist in peace, or that one can safely escape the other. For those times that you can't supervise, keep them separated — either behind closed doors or with baby gates — to keep them from fighting like, well, cats and dogs.

Other animals such as rabbits, guinea pigs, hamsters, birds, and reptiles generally spend most of their time in cages. When your Beagle's around, that's where they need to stay. A dog has a strong instinct to chase and catch prey, which is what these critters will look like to her (especially if the critter is a rabbit). The result, unfortunately, will probably be the critter's demise. Allow your critter floor time only when your Beagle's not around.

Introducing (or re-introducing) the crate

If you're lucky, your new Snoopy-dog has already seen the inside of a crate and will welcome a chance to spend a little alone time there. But that's not always the case. Some dogs — Beagles or otherwise — have no idea that crates even exist. Others have gotten up close and personal with crates, but need some time to appreciate the virtues of having one's own den. These latter dogs often are adults who've spent way too much time inside crates and have, understandably, come to view these structures as puppy prisons rather than as doggy dens. You don't want your Beagle to view her crate in such a negative light, because if she hates her crate, housetraining and traveling with your canine companion could become very complicated.

Such complications don't have to happen. By carefully introducing your Beagle to her home-within-your-home, you can teach her to view her crate as the divine doggy den it's supposed to be. Here's how to help your Beagle consider her crate a great place to chill:

- ✔ **Start with an open-door policy.** Successful crate introduction is a gradual process that forestalls any events that could spook your little hound. One such event is the accidental closure or slamming of the crate door before she's fully acclimated to the crate. Prevent such events by tying the door open and leaving it that way until your dog ventures into her crate under her own steam.

- ✔ **Let her check out the crate.** Let your Beagle walk around and sniff the exterior of the crate. After a couple of minutes of investigation, place a treat or toy just inside the crate door. If she enters the crate to retrieve the goody, praise her extravagantly and let her enjoy the treat or toy. If she's unsure about setting foot in the crate, encourage her to try — but don't force her. Allow your dog to decide when she's ready to enter her crate on her own. When she does, tell her what a very good girl she is.

Playing the name game

If you haven't done so already, now's the time for you to give your Beagle a name. Your Snoopy-dog is a distinct individual and should sport a moniker that reflects her endearing, irrepressible individuality. For adult dogs adopted from shelters or rescue groups, a new name can take on an added significance: The new appellation reflects the dog's new life in a happy household.

But coming up with the right name for your little hound may be more of a challenge than you anticipated. To help you negotiate those challenges and come up with a name that truly fits your magnificent canine companion, consider the following suggestions:

Pick a name that says something about your pooch. For example, a good name for a Beagle might be Elvis, reflecting The King's classic song "You Ain't Nothin' but a Hound Dog."

Choose a name that's easy to learn. Most experts suggest limiting a name to one or two syllables. Such names take less time for a dog to recognize than a longer one does — and will be easier for your kids to use, too.

Pick a name your dog will grow into. Sure, calling your Beagle puppy Baby Snooks sounds cute now, but that name will sound doggone undignified when your puppy reaches adulthood.

Avoid sound-alike names. Names that sound like either the names of other people in your house or common commands will confuse everyone in your home, including your Beagle. For example, the name "Kit" wouldn't work for a dog, because it sounds too much like the word "sit." Similarly, if your husband's name is Manny, don't name your dog Fanny.

Don't choose a name associated with negative behavior. Prime examples here: aggressive names for dogs. In other words, don't name your Beagle "Killer." And even if your Beagle has had an accident or two, avoid calling her "Piddle-puss."

Pick a name you can use in public. Okay, okay — your Beagle has made an unauthorized deposit in the middle of your Berber carpet. Worse, you have tween-agers who think potty humor is the greatest thing going, and they want to immortalize that deposit by christening your Beagle with a name that rhymes with "sit." Tell them no. If they accuse you of being an uptight fuddy-duddy, refer them to the "Avoid sound-alike names" suggestion.

Google for some ideas. The World Wide Web has a gazillion sites that list common dog names. Just type "common dog names" into a search engine and you'll come up with scores of sites that are stuffed to the gills with suggestions.

Follow the leaders. If you can't come up with something suitable on your own, consider what's worked for other people and pooches. For example, PR Newswire reports that the most popular names for dogs in 2005 were Max, Bailey, Buddy, Molly, Maggie, Lucy, Daisy, Bella, Jake, and Rocky.

✔ **Shut the door — but not for long.** When your Beagle consistently chooses to enter the crate to retrieve a treat or toy, take the next step: shutting the door quietly for just a few seconds. While the door is shut, praise her, then open the door and coax her out. Praise her again and give her another treat. Repeat this sequence, gradually increasing the time the door remains closed, until your dog stays calmly in the crate for five minutes or so.

✔ **Leave the room.** When your dog can spend five minutes in her crate without getting hysterical, try leaving the room while she's inside her little den. Lure her into the crate with either a safe chew toy or several treats (not just one). When she's in, shut the door quietly and leave the room for just a minute. When those 60 seconds are up, come back and see how she's faring. If she's content, leave again and come back in a few minutes. Continue checking until she's finished her chewing or eating, or acts restless or distressed. At that point, let her out of the crate and praise her for her remarkable achievement. Keep practicing until she can stay in her crate alone for about 30 minutes.

Surviving the First Night

The first night or two home with your new Beagle can be, well, challenging. Your friend is likely to have difficulty settling down for a good night's sleep in her new home. And if she has difficulty, you're likely to have difficulty as well. But before you get too frustrated with your sleepless sidekick, consider why she may be having trouble sleeping.

Yes, your new dog is beginning a wonderful life in a fabulous new home with you — but she hasn't had time to realize how terrific this new phase of her life is going to be. If she's a puppy, this is her very first night away from the only home she's ever known. Gone are her mama and brothers and sisters, not to mention all the sights and smells she's grown accustomed to. Instead, she's all by her lonesome in a strange new place. And even an adult Beagle may have some issues the first few nights. She may be wondering what's going to happen next after having endured one or more moves to new homes, a shelter, and/or foster care.

Understanding what your Beagle is going through can help you respond with kindness and sympathy to her bedtime issues. Happily, too, that same kindness and sympathy also can help you keep those nighttime cries and whimpers to a minimum. Here are some suggestions.

Keep your Beagle with you . . .

Yes, you'll be tempted to put your noisy Beagle and her crate in the kitchen, basement, or laundry room so her nighttime vocalizing doesn't keep you awake. But having to sleep all alone in a strange place will only worsen her distress. Better to keep your Beagle with you — and if you do it right, you'll not only reduce her need to vocalize but also help her realize that you're her new best friend.

Just pull your Beagle's crate close to your bed — close enough so you can dangle your fingers right outside the door. Such close proximity allows your new family member to see you, smell you, and hear you breathe — all of which helps reassure her that she's not alone and that you're there to take care of her. If your Beagle sleeps in a wire crate, you might want to drape a towel or sheet over three sides to block out light or other distractions.

. . . But keep your bed to yourself

You may think that bringing your canine companion up on your bed to snuggle with you will help calm her even more. And you're probably right. However, by inviting your dog up on your bed, you may open a Pandora's box of other problems For one thing, she may have a bathroom accident on your bed. In addition, she may become confused as to who really is top dog in your pack. So let your little darling stay in her crate. Bringing your Beagle close to you at night doesn't mean that you should surrender your personal boundaries completely! Chapter 5 offers suggestions on where your Beagle should sleep.

Play some (not so) funky music

Soothing music can go a long way toward helping your four-legged friend relax. Think classical or New Age fare: Vivaldi (not Beethoven or Wagner, please!) or Enya or something else along those lines is perfect. You may find yourself falling asleep faster, too.

Use your hands

If your little one is still fussing, consider using your hands to help her settle down. No, this doesn't mean using your hands to open the crate door and scoop your Beagle up and under the covers. Instead, try the following:

✔ **Keep it dangling:** Your hand, that is. Dangle your hand in front of the crate door or slats so your dog can sniff and maybe even lick it. This superclose proximity to your scent and your person can help even the most unhappy new puppy feel better and settle down to sleep.

✔ **Give a pat:** To the crate, not the canine. If your dog still refuses to wrap up her nighttime concert or otherwise won't settle down, give the top of the crate a little pat and tell her "Jessie (or whatever her name is), go to sleep." This maneuver works better if you've chosen a plastic crate rather than a wire crate for your dog, because the plastic crate has a solid surface that makes a sound when patted.

Have your shoes ready

If your Beagle's whining or restlessness awakens you from a sound slumber, she probably needs a bathroom break. Grab your shoes, her collar and leash, and your coat, and take her outside to the designated potty area. As she poops or pees, praise her extravagantly — but then go back to bed. Stand firm if she thinks now's the time to play. Give in to her playtime invitation now and you'll have a hard time convincing her a few nights from now that the two of you need to get some sleep.

Keep your outdoor gear close by the first few nights your Beagle is with you. You'll get her outside more quickly, thus preventing more than a few potty accidents. Few aspects of dog ownership are worse than cleaning up dog doo in the middle of the night!

Be patient

Repeat after me: This won't last forever, this won't last forever . . . I promise you that your Beagle *will* learn to sleep through the night. After a few nights she'll decide that sleeping in a soft warm doggy den next to you beats nighttime concerts anytime! In the meantime, do what you can to help her feel that she can count on you to be there for her and help her through this transition from old to new.

Chapter 7

Beginning a Beautiful Friendship

*T*he next few days can be a lovely time as you and your new Beagle get to know each other. For your Beagle, this is when he begins to learn the lay of the land, including how things work in his new home and who takes care of him (that would be you). For you, these days are when you need to attend to certain details, such as that first veterinary exam, establishing your dog's daily routine, laying the groundwork for training, and — most important of all — falling in love with your Beagle.

Bonding with Your Beagle

The biggest reason to get a Beagle — or, for that matter, any dog — is to build an attachment to him that enhances both your life and his. Why else would you agree to clean up Beagle poop, risk damage to your furniture, and experience the dubious pleasures of hound dog concerts? Simple. You want to have a loyal friend who worships the ground you walk on, and lets you know he worships you every time he looks up at you adoringly with those big, soulful eyes of his.

But this attachment doesn't develop automatically. Bonding with your Beagle results only when you commit yourself to spending time with him and teaching him what he needs to know to be a happy household member. Doing both tasks with a generosity of heart and spirit will sooner or later (hopefully, sooner) result in your falling in love with each other.

Jump-starting the bonding process

Your Beagle is relatively independent, as dogs go. But he's also a social creature. He loves being with people. He has his own ideas about what he wants to do — but chances are whatever he wants to do doesn't call for solitude. He wants a partner in crime, or at least an audience.

And although the Beagle may be an independent, even stubborn individual, he can't get along without you. He needs you. You provide the food, water, and shelter that he requires to survive. You can take advantage of this dependence to bind him to you — and, in the process, you'll find that you're also binding yourself to him. When the love flows both ways, the real joy of Beagle ownership begins.

Need some ideas on how to jump-start the bonding process? Start with these:

- ✔ **Commit some time.** Plan on taking a few days off — or, at the very least, a weekend — to acclimate your Beagle to life in your household and to acclimate yourself to living with your Beagle.

- ✔ **Forget business as usual.** Don't try too hard to keep up your usual routines these first few days. Immerse yourself in Beagle care and Beagle love. There's time enough to get back to everyday life. Enjoy these precious new days with your little hound.

- ✔ **Keep your sense of humor.** Your Beagle is a canine clown. As he gets used to his interesting new home, he will look for ways to entertain himself. His explorations may include diving into wastebaskets, shredding magazines left on coffee tables, running off with a family member's lingerie, and other creative diversions. You can view these sparks of mischief as annoying, and no one would blame you. But a better approach — for the sake of your sanity, not to mention your bond with your Beagle — is to laugh at his antics, even as you take steps to ensure that he has as few opportunities as possible to indulge in those antics.

Minimize the hassles that often accompany life with a hound dog by keeping your home as Beagle-proofed as possible. Keep drawers, doors, and closets closed; place wastebaskets beyond your Beagle's reach; and remove stray items from coffee tables and other furnishings. For more Beagle-proofing tips, see Chapter 6.

✔ **Tether him to you.** Help your Beagle learn to look to you for what he needs by keeping him with you whenever possible. Keep his crate in your bedroom at night, and move his crate to wherever you are during the day so he can be with you at all times. And when he's out of his crate while you're bustling around the house, put his leash on and bring him with you. The next section has tips on how to teach your Beagle to accept his collar and leash.

Investing this time with your Beagle now can jump-start a beautiful friendship between the two of you. Take the time and make the commitment now, and the rewards will be sweet later on. When you're ready to take the bonding process even further, check out Chapter 9 for more fun activities to do with your pooch.

Getting a new leash (and collar) on life

When your Beagle's not on leash, let him run around without his collar. But when he needs to be leashed for any reason, he needs that little nylon or leather ring around his neck.

Ideally, your Beagle will become joyful the minute he sees you pick up his collar and leash because he'll know that means you and he are going for a walk. However, some Beagles — especially puppies — may initially balk at having to be leashed or otherwise restricted. For these freedom-loving Fidos, you'll both have an easier time if you slowly introduce the leash and collar. Here's a game plan:

✔ **Start with the collar.** Buckle or snap the collar around your dog's neck, and then just let him react to it. Let him paw it, run around, and otherwise demonstrate his displeasure. Keep the collar on for a few minutes, then remove it, and try attaching it again a little while later. Eventually, he'll accept it. I promise.

✔ **Let him be a drag.** After your little hound accepts the collar, attach the leash — but don't pick up the other end. Just let him drag the leash around until he gets used to the way it feels.

✔ **Perform a quick pickup.** When your Beagle matter-of-factly accepts the leash and collar, pick up the other end of the leash but don't move. Just hold the leash for a minute or two.

✔ **Take a hike.** Once your dog is cool with you holding the other end of the leash, try walking with him a little bit. While you move, hold a treat within sniffing distance to encourage him, and give him the treat if he cooperates. Pretty soon you'll be ready for Chapter 15 and serious walking lessons.

Visiting the Vet: The First Exam

Within a day or two of arriving home with your new dog, you need to take him for his first visit to the veterinarian you've selected. (If you haven't found a vet yet, please read Chapter 5 for guidelines on finding a qualified doggy doctor.) The visit allows you and your Beagle to get acquainted with a person who will play a key role in keeping your dog healthy. In addition, the exam allows your vet to learn more about your dog's inner workings — knowledge that will be crucial during future visits. Finally, the exam may uncover hidden health problems plaguing your new dog, problems that you can start solving immediately.

Bring any health records you have for your new Beagle, and, if possible, a stool sample. The records enable the vet to determine what immunizations and other medications your dog needs, while the stool sample can reveal the presence of parasites, such as worms. Information on how to collect a stool sample appears in Chapter 11.

In addition to examining your Beagle's health records and analyzing the stool sample, the vet will also weigh him; measure his vital signs; check his skin for lumps, bumps, rashes, parasites, and signs of infection; look inside his ears for signs of parasites and infection; peer into his eyes for signs of abnormalities; check his genitals for correct formation and absence of any discharge; and look at his gums and teeth to make sure they're healthy and properly formed. The vet also will use a stethoscope to listen to your dog's heart and lungs, and will gently feel around the dog's abdomen to make sure everything's as it should be.

After the vet examines your Beagle, she may give him one or more immunizations, depending on your four-legged friend's age and health status. Those shots may include:

- ✔ A single shot to prevent *rabies,* a disease that's deadly to both dogs and people. Almost all state laws require that dogs and other domestic animals be vaccinated against rabies. The first rabies shots are given at around 16 weeks of age; the second shot, a booster, comes about a year later. After that, dogs get rabies shots every one to three years, depending on local laws.

- ✔ A series of combination shots to prevent other serious diseases, such as *parvovirus, distemper, hepatitis, leptospirosis,* and *parainfluenza.* Puppies often receive the first of these shots, often called the *DHLPP,* at the age of 6 weeks, with three subsequent shots dispensed at three-week intervals.

✔ A shot to prevent *bordetella,* also known as *kennel cough,* if you plan to board your Beagle often or take him to places where other dogs gather, such as a dog park, doggy day care, or obedience class. Your vet also may recommend shots to prevent Lyme disease or other illnesses, depending on where you live and your dog's needs.

Ask your vet whether she can give your dog each of these three shots during separate visits. Spacing out these immunizations can help avoid overtaxing your Beagle's immune system.

If your dog's stool sample reveals the presence of parasites, your vet will also give you some medicine to rid him of all such freeloaders. (Chapter 12 has advice on how to get meds into your dog.) These unwelcome minicritters include roundworms (very common in puppies), hookworms, whipworms, coccidia, and tapeworms. Because these little beasties can sap your dog's energy and health, they need to be banished. Your vet also may suggest that you give your dog medications to combat other parasites, such as fleas and heartworms.

Don't buy over-the-counter deworming products. Your vet can prescribe far more effective deworming products that deal specifically with the particular wiggly critters that are bothering your Beagle.

If necessary, your vet will talk to you about arranging to have your puppy or dog spayed or neutered. Your contract with the animal shelter, rescue group, or breeder may require you to have this procedure performed on your four-legged friend, if it hasn't been done already. Most vets opt to do the surgery on puppies when they're about 6 months old, although some veterinarians do so earlier. Spaying or neutering adult dogs can occur just about any time, except when a female is in *heat* (a three-week period during which she has a bloody discharge from her vagina and can mate with a male dog). More about spaying and neutering — pro's and con's — appears in Chapter 12.

Starting Daily Routines

Nothing will give your new Beagle a feeling of comfort and safety faster than a consistent daily routine.

Divining a dining schedule

The number of meals you dispense to your four-legged friend each day depends on his age. Young puppies generally need three meals daily: breakfast, lunch, and dinner. After your little hound passes the 4-month mark, though, you can cut back to two meals per day, morning and evening.

Keep up the twice-daily meal routine throughout your Beagle's life. Morning and evening meals are easier on his tummy — and easier on you. The reason: A hungry Beagle is more likely to be bored, less likely to sleep, and if alone, more likely to vent his frustration by eating things in your house. Chapter 8 offers tips for what to feed and how to feed your dog.

Pacing potty breaks

The number of trips your Beagle needs to his outdoor potty depends on his age. The baby Beagle may need to take a whiz as often as once every hour or so, not to mention one or two bathroom breaks during the night. Take heart: When he hits the magic 4-month mark, he'll be able to hold his water and other stuff a little longer. Going out before and after mealtimes, after naps, and after strenuous play should be enough to keep him (and you) content. And (joy!) nocturnal potty breaks should be a thing of the past.

After 6 months of age, potty breaks should occur first thing in the morning, midday, dinnertime, and just before bedtime — a pattern that should continue throughout the rest of your Beagle's life. Chapters 6 and 14 deal with teaching your Beagle where and when to do his doo-ty.

Playing around

You can pretty much play with your pooch whenever you want, although giving him a predictable schedule can help him adjust faster to life in your household. For what it's worth, I take my own dog to a field every morning to play fetch for about 15 minutes. This daily session helps her work off excess energy and keeps her mellow for the rest of the day.

Your Beagle may not need to run around in a field, but a 10- to 15-minute play session morning and evening can keep him happy and content. Make sure, though, that those play sessions don't occur immediately after meals (vigorous activity could cause indigestion or worse) or just before bedtime (because he'll have a hard time settling down to sleep).

Setting snoozing cycles

Your Snoopy-dog will probably set his own snoozing cycles, but you can help him along a bit. Certainly he should sleep at night when you sleep, and he'll probably want to do some sleeping during the day, especially during puppyhood. If you want to set nap times for when you're busy and can't watch him, place him in his crate, turn on some soft music, and watch him head to Dreamland.

Glamming it up

Unlike other breeds, the Beagle doesn't need a whole lot of grooming. A weekly brushing, pedicure, and ear cleaning and a monthly bath should pretty much do the trick. The lowdown on how to beautify your Beagle appears in Chapter 10.

Socializing Your Beagle

A crucial component of helping your Beagle settle in — not to mention becoming and staying emotionally healthy throughout his life — is the process of *socializing* him. This process means that you do everything you can to enrich your dog's social life. That means not keeping him confined to the four walls of your home, but rather getting him out and about safely.

By exposing your Beagle to new people and places, you help him learn to deal with the unexpected with poise and confidence. The well-socialized Beagle can handle most new situations without getting bent out of shape. Visiting other people's houses, dealing with crowds, and welcoming visitors to his own home don't faze him in the least. By contrast, the unsocialized Beagle is more likely to be fearful or even aggressive, simply because he doesn't know how to cope with new experiences.

Exploring the home front and beyond

If your new Beagle is a puppy, the breeder should have started socializing him before you brought him home. However, you need to continue the process. Here are some activities you can do with your dog, whether he's a puppy or adult, to help him become the social butterfly he's meant to be:

✔ **Encourage exploration.** Encourage your pooch to explore his home environment — under your supervision, of course.

✔ **Show him your stuff.** Show him umbrellas, vacuum cleaners, blow dryers, and other potential fear-inducing objects. Start from a distance and work your way closer. Check out the "Taming the monsters: Vacuum cleaners and blow-dryers" section later in this chapter for more pointers on dealing with these appliances.

✔ **Introduce novelty.** Introduce him to stairways, doorways, and other novel structures; this chapter tells you how.

✔ **Have some company.** After you've had your Beagle home for a few days, invite friendly people and their pets (make sure the critters are vaccinated!) over to meet your new family member.

✔ **Go gadding about.** Take your Beagle out and about. Bring him to a school yard to watch the kids play at recess; take him to a public area to see the goings-on. I brought my puppy to a supermarket parking lot and sat on a bench with her. When passersby stopped to pet her, I gave them a treat to give her. To this day, my now-grown dog is crazy about people and works a room like a politician.

If your Beagle puppy hasn't had all his shots, carry him to new places and hold him in your arms. Don't let him walk on surfaces where other dogs may have been; such dogs may not have been fully immunized and could transmit communicable diseases to your puppy. Make sure, too, that any animals that visit you and your puppy at home are fully immunized.

✔ **Go mobile.** Take your Snoopy-dog for short, frequent car rides to many places — not just to the vet! The "Learning to love car rides" section in this chapter provides advice on helping your Beagle avoid getting automotive issues, or over-come those he may already have.

Easing a fearful adult dog into the big, bad world

Not every Beagle has the good fortune to be socialized during puppyhood — and if you have a grown-up fraidy-dog, you need to help him catch up. Introduce him to the people, places, and experiences that he should have encountered while he was a little guy. Some tips for socializing an adult Beagle include:

✔ **Set up a routine.** Feed, potty, play with, and exercise your hound at the same time every day, if at all possible. By doing so, you'll give your Beagle feelings of predictability and structure, both of which will boost his confidence.

✔ **Let him set the pace.** The undersocialized adult Beagle may be more hesitant than a puppy to check out new people or places. If your dog's hesitation results in clear stress — tail between the legs, trying to hide — stop what you're doing immediately. But don't give up. Try again another day.

✔ **Divert him.** If your Beagle shows signs of stress over something you can't immediately control, try some diversionary tactics. For example, if he's stressing over loud construction noises in the next block, play with him or try some basic training to help him forget that he's scared.

✔ **Squelch the sweet-talk.** When your Beagle cowers, trembles, or otherwise exhibits scaredy-dog behavior, you'll probably want to cuddle him and sweetly tell him something like, "It's okaaaaay huh-neee — Mommy's here." Don't give in to that temptation. By doing so, you're rewarding him for doing what you don't want him to do.

Fighting the Fear Factor

The typical Beagle is an intrepid little pooch; not much fazes him. Still, even the most laid-back dog may find that he's got issues that he didn't know about until he's confronted with something big, noisy, or just plain new. But your Beagle should have nothing to worry about as long as you're by his side. You can help him maintain his confidence by showing him how to deal with the unexpected with poise and aplomb.

Taming the monsters: Vacuum cleaners and blow-dryers

Cleaning dust from your house is a necessity — and when your Beagle arrives, you'll need to clean up Beagle hair, too (unfortunately, Beagles do shed). For these and other domestic tasks, you undoubtedly make good use of a vacuum cleaner. Your little hound (or, for that matter, any dog), may not appreciate the vacuum cleaner's virtues. In fact, its loud noise and giant sucking sound may positively spook him. He may run and hide, bark fearfully and frantically, or show other signs of stress.

For many of us, another noisy appliance is almost as necessary as a vacuum cleaner. The blow-dryer helps many of us tame our tresses into highly styled coiffures that give us at least the illusion that we are beautiful. However, your Beagle may object to the noise emitted from this contraption. His objections may be similar to those he registers when confronted with the vacuum cleaner.

In either case, you can take one of two approaches to help your Beagle cope with these noisy monsters:

- **Help your dog face his fear.** I outline specific steps for teaching your Beagle to face new or scary situations in the "Tried and true de-spooking" sidebar that appears in this chapter. (Make just one adjustment: Instead of speaking to him, use a tasty treat to persuade him to deal with the situation.) The upside to this approach is that, if successful, your Beagle will gain confidence and be better able to cope with the unexpected. The downside is that you may need considerable time to implement this approach — and, if you're like me, you just want to get the vacuuming done or your hair styled without having to play therapist to your beloved Beagle.

- **Accept his issues.** Put your dog in his crate when you wield either the blow-dryer or the vacuum cleaner. The advantage here is the simplicity and ease of this approach, plus the fact that your Beagle will quickly learn to associate his crate with being safe. The downside is that your dog will probably always be afraid of these two appliances — but heck, we all have our little foibles. There's no reason why your Beagle shouldn't have a few issues, as long as those issues don't interfere with your well-being or his.

Learning to love car rides

Some Beagles love car rides. Others, however, are less than thrilled with automotive travel and demonstrate their displeasure by trembling, howling, or even vomiting while they go mobile. You could, of course, allow your Beagle to be a perpetual stay-at-home dog. But his life and yours will go a lot easier if he learns to love, or at least tolerate, being in the car. To help change your car-hating Beagle's mind, try some of these tips:

- **Desensitize him.** Get your dog used to being in the car very gradually. Start by just sitting with him in the car for a minute or two, then work up to several minutes. When he's able to tolerate sitting still in the car, try moving the car up and down your driveway — once. Gradually work into driving up and down your block, around the block, and through your neighborhood until he's able to tolerate being in the car.

✔ **Make it positive.** If you don't want your Beagle to freak out at being in the car, make sure that car trips take him to a pleas-ant destination most of the time: a park, a puppy friend's house, or someplace else that's fun. If your dog's only car trips are to your vet, overcoming his aversion toward the car will be even more challenging.

✔ **Talk to your vet.** Most canine carsickness results from anxi-ety, not motion sickness, and your vet may be able to pre-scribe a mild sedative or other anti-anxiety medication for your car-phobic friend.

✔ **Go for flower power.** Some owners of car-hating dogs have found that flower essences can help ease their pooches' fears. Some of these essences are formulated and combined specifi-cally to help the scaredy-dog deal with life with more equanim-ity. An especially popular formula is Bach Flower Essences' Rescue Remedy, which is a combination of more than a half-dozen floral essences. More information is available at www.bachflower.com.

Check out Chapter 13 for tips on keeping your Beagle safe in the car, including using a doggy seat belt.

Dealing with stairways and doorways

Doorways and stairways are no big deal to you; you probably nego-tiate each without even thinking about it. But for your Beagle or any other small dog, doors and stairs may be quite another matter. Your puppy probably has never encountered a set of steps before and may never have had the opportunity to deal with a doorway. He needs your assistance to help him cope with both.

To help a stair-shy Beagle deal with stairs, the one-step-at-a-time principle is worth following:

1. **Sit at the bottom of the staircase and put your little guy on the bottom step next to you.**

2. **Put a treat or interesting toy on the floor and let him hop down to reach it.**

3. **When he's comfortable negotiating one step, move up one so he needs to clamber down two.**

4. **Keep adding steps until he's going down the stairs with ease.**

Tried and true de-spooking

Sometimes during walks a dog gets the willies totally unexpectedly and decides to deal with that fear in ways that aren't convenient for you. My own dogs have gotten spooked over seeing paper skeletons dangling from trees at Halloween (gotta love those creative decorations); a sailboat parked on a suburban street; and a garbage can that's rolled onto its side and is partially blocking the sidewalk — among other items. Their responses to these objects of fear have included running and pulling me out into the street and into the path of an oncoming car. They've also plunked themselves down in the middle of the sidewalk and become trembling — but otherwise immovable — objects. Either way, their methods of dealing with the unexpected haven't been conducive to safe, much less pleasant, excursions.

However, you can capitalize on your Beagle's trust in you to help him face his fear and literally get past whatever spooks him. Here's what to do:

✔ **Get between your dog and the object.** If your Snoopy-dog suddenly stops or changes direction, check to see what's bothering him, and then position yourself between him and whatever's causing him to spook.

✔ **Start moving slowly.** Keeping yourself between your dog and the object, turn and face him. Then, take one or two steps backward (which will be forward for him).

✔ **Coax him along.** In a high, happy tone of voice, coax your little guy to come along with you. Tell him what a brave boy he is. Make sure you keep yourself between your dog and the object.

✔ **Check it out.** If your dog responds to your entreaties, see if you can get him to be even braver. Suggest that the two of you check out the feared object. In an excited voice, tell him, "Hey Bowser, let's check this out! Look at that garbage can! Isn't it funny looking?" If you're close enough, pat the object and otherwise investigate it. Chances are, your Beagle will do the same.

✔ **Move on.** If your Beagle continues to balk, don't push the investigation; just keep walking slowly, remaining between him and the object, and commend him for his courage. If he does investigate, praise him lavishly, and then resume your walk. Either way, you're likely to see that your pooch has recovered his composure quite nicely, thank you.

Your Beagle doesn't have to learn to negotiate the entire staircase in a single session or even a single day. Break your Stairs 101 course into several sessions if your dog gets tired or distracted.

Until your dog has mastered the art of going down the staircase, keep him away from stairs. For extra protection, install a baby gate at the top of the stairs (see Chapter 5 for info on baby gates). An unexpected tumble down a flight of stairs can seriously injure your dog, not to mention undo all of your efforts to teach him how to negotiate the stairs.

If your dog does take a tumble, examine him carefully. The pup who picks himself up and goes on about his business is probably OK, but keep a close eye on him for a day or two. However, if your dog limps, cries when touched, or otherwise shows any sign of discomfort, call your vet immediately.

Reverse the process to teach your dog to go up the stairs — although, generally, going down stairs is more of a challenge for most small dogs than going up.

Doorways are simply a matter of taking care. Go ahead of your Beagle when going through doorways, and take care that a door doesn't slam in your little guy's face.

Part III
Caring for Your Beagle

"Let me guess — the vet's analysis of the Beagle's fleas showed them to be of the 100 percent fresh ground Colombian decaf variety."

In this part . . .

Raising your Beagle to be the best Snoopy-dog she can be means giving her the best of care: feeding her good, nutritious food; ensuring that she gets plenty of exercise; grooming her coat, teeth, feet, ears, and other body parts; keeping her as healthy as possible; dealing with any and all health issues that inevitably will arise; and planning for her care when you travel. Part III gives you the lowdown on all these aspects of basic Beagle care — and more.

Chapter 8

Feeding Your Beagle

*B*ack when you were a kid, you probably got sick of hearing your mother tell you to eat your peas, drink your juice, or that you'd have no dessert until you finished everything on your plate. Your health teacher probably irritated you just as much when she lectured you about needing to drink four glasses of milk every day, and then proclaimed that you are what you eat.

But you know something? They were right — and not just when they applied their adages to you and your peers. Good nutrition is just as important to the Beagle body as it is to the human bod.

That said, good nutrition doesn't always mean holding your nose and eating those veggies. And eating right certainly doesn't preclude eating for fun. This chapter not only gives you the lowdown on what to feed your Beagle, but also tells you what you need to know to make eating a pleasure for your little hound — and a great training tool for you to use.

What a Dog Wants . . . What a Dog Needs

Many a food-loving Beagle would probably love to give you her idea of what a dog wants and needs to eat happily. Of course, her idea of happy dining (dumpster diving, anyone?) may bear little resemblance to her nutritional needs. That's one reason why your Beagle needs you. You're the parent in this relationship, and your knowledge of canine nutrition enables you to devise a food regimen that's not only good for her, but also good to eat.

What about carbs?

Traditionally, experts have included carbohydrates on the list of must-have canine nutrients — but these days, that opinion isn't unanimous. Most carbs come from grains, such as wheat and corn, which not only are tougher for dogs to digest than other food sources, but also may cause allergic reactions in some dogs. Consequently, some veterinarians and breeders now advocate keeping grains out of a dog's diet. Such dogs ingest relatively few carbohydrates, but that absence of carbs doesn't deprive them of robust health.

"Um," you're saying. "I don't know beans about canine nutrition." Not to worry. Here's a primer on the nutrients that every Beagle needs to stay in tip-top condition:

- **Proteins,** which enable your dog's body to change food into energy, come mainly from meats, vegetables, and grains. However, all protein sources are not created equal. Most dogs, for example, can digest a protein that comes from meat more easily than a protein that comes from grain.

- **Fats,** which play a huge role in keeping a dog's hair and skin healthy, are found not only in foods but also in special dietary supplements. Fats also help promote healthy digestion and keep your Beagle's body temperature stable.

- **Vitamins and minerals,** which help the dog's body maximize all those other nutrients, are already present in many foods. Vitamins and minerals also keep your dog's immune system and coat healthy and prevent many health and behavioral problems.

Choosing Your Beagle's Chow

In just a few short years, the food choices available to the discriminating Beagle and her person have expanded exponentially. Just pick up a copy of a high-end dog magazine, such as *The Bark* (a great read for any dog-lover, by the way), and you'll see a cornucopia of food options to buy from a store or online, not to mention a bunch of ideas for making your dog's food yourself. Such an abundance of options can make you crazy, unless you have some basic info on your Beagle's possible dining choices. Without further ado, here's the scoop.

Store-bought and savory

The vast majority of Beagle people and other dog owners prefer to have someone else create their dogs' meals. Who can blame them? Most people are so busy these days that they don't have time to cook their own dinners, much less their dogs'. Not to worry, though. Pet food manufacturers have created two basic types of chow for you to buy for your beloved Beagle.

Consuming kibble

If you're looking for the ultimate in convenience and value, dry food is the way to go: Just pour, serve, and count your change. Often called *kibble,* dry food consists of baked pellets that are bite-sized or smaller. They're derived from grains, meats, and sometimes vegetables, with supplements such as vitamins added. In addition to its ease of preparation, dry food generally is nutritionally complete, which means you don't have to feed your Beagle anything else to keep her healthy. A Beagle whose daily fare consists of nothing but kibble also produces poop that's easy to scoop, and she's likely to have cleaner teeth than a dog that consumes softer fare. Need more advantages? How about the fact that kibble doesn't need refrigeration and costs less than any other type of dog food.

Alas, however, no food is perfect — and for many dogs, kibble carries a big disadvantage: It's relatively bland. Many dogs like to have some variety in their diets — and to such dogs, kibble may seem boringly, depressingly the same. More than one dog in my acquaintance has gone on a partial hunger strike after being subjected to too much kibble for too long a time. And face it, the most economical, nutrient-packed food is a total waste of money if your dog refuses to eat it.

Canning it

If your Beagle turns up her nose at kibble, try giving her canned dog food. I'll bet that as soon as you pour it into her dish and serve it, she'll practically fall into the dish. Dogs everywhere generally prefer canned food to dry, because of canned food's enticing aroma and better taste. It's also just as easy to fix as dry food: Just pour and serve.

But for all that ease of preparation and great taste, canned food does have some disadvantages. For one thing, it generally costs more than dry food does. Moreover, because canned food contains quite a bit of water, it delivers less nutrition than the equivalent quantity of kibble does. Other disadvantages: It's got more calories, and thus is more likely to pack pounds onto your pooch; it's too soft to scrape tartar from your dog's teeth; it's much more perishable than dry food; and it results in bigger, moister, harder-to-clean-up poop compared to the poop a kibble-eating Beagle produces.

No one says that you have to choose between kibble and canned when it comes to feeding your Snoopy-dog. If you want to give your Beagle the good nutrition that comes from dry food but also the great flavor of canned fare, give her both. For example, try giving her a meal that's 90 percent dry food and 10 percent canned.

Deciphering dog food labels

You can be overwhelmed by the variety of dog foods at your local grocery or pet store. Some foods are vastly superior to others. But the uninformed consumer may struggle to distinguish between a truly good product and one that's simply drowning in commercial hype. That's where knowing how to read a dog food label comes in mighty handy.

Look at the list of ingredients. Are meats listed first? That means that the food contains more meat than anything else — and that's a sign of good quality. Foods of lesser quality usually list grains first.

Check, too, to see what form the meat takes. If the label says "beef" or "chicken" or "aardvark" or some other meat, you've got a high-quality food. If the label lists a meat byproduct without specifying what that byproduct is, you may be subjecting your Beagle to eating such unsavory products as chicken beaks — not exactly a great form of nutrition.

Look, too, for additives and preservatives, such as ethoxyquin, BHA, and BHT. The short story here: The fewer the better.

Homemade and delicious

Are you a control freak? If so, instead of buying your Beagle's food off the shelf, you may want to fix her food yourself. Being your dog's personal chef gives you complete control over what goes into your dog's tummy. Such control can go a long way toward helping you deal with any food allergies your Beagle may have or the rare problem of a Beagle who's a picky eater. Even better, you could save yourself some money.

Still, the do-it-yourself option has a downside. For one thing, fixing your dog's meals can be inconvenient and time-consuming. The inconvenience multiplies if you travel, whether your little hound accompanies you or stays in a kennel.

But the biggest disadvantage to DIY-feeding is that preparing a nutritionally balanced regimen for your dog is far from simple. To keep your Beagle at her very best, you need to make sure that her food contains the proper proportions of all the nutrients that she requires.

If you decide that the advantages of cooking your Beagle's food outweigh the disadvantages, be sure to consult your veterinarian. He can help you devise a meal plan for your Beagle that keeps her not only healthy but happy. Consider, too, consulting a book such as *Dog Health and Nutrition For Dummies*, by M. Christine Zink (Wiley).

To BARF or not to BARF? Feeding a raw food diet

No, I'm not suggesting that you give your Beagle food that makes her hurl — or makes you hurl, for that matter. The acronym BARF refers to *Biologically Appropriate Raw Food*. Theoretically, you can concoct such a diet yourself, but I don't recommend doing so unless you enjoy spending way too much time involved in a way too messy (not to mention potentially unsanitary) enterprise. Instead, consider buying USDA-approved raw foods made specifically for pets. No matter how you go raw, however, this feeding method has advocates and detractors, and both are equally passionate.

Those who favor going raw contend that a doggy menu based entirely on uncooked meats, vegetables, and bones not only most closely approximates what wild animals eat, but also allows dogs to live longer, healthier lives. BARF proponents also believe that dogs that are fed raw food have

- ✔ Cleaner teeth
- ✔ Glossier coats
- ✔ An end to food allergies
- ✔ Infection-free ears (Full disclosure here: My own dog has enjoyed a near-total absence of ear infections since I put her on BARF two years ago.)

Many breeders, dog show enthusiasts, and owners of performance dogs wholeheartedly endorse the BARF diet, as do many veterinarians who practice alternative veterinary medicine.

However, more traditional vets, along with pet food manufacturers, beg to differ. Their concerns include:

- ✔ Raw bones can cause internal injuries or choking.
- ✔ Raw foods increase the odds of contracting salmonella or other bacterial poisoning — either by the dog or by the person handling the food.
- ✔ A diet of raw food causes some dogs to develop chronic diarrhea or vomiting.

One formerly formidable argument against the BARF diet — that it's time-consuming and inconvenient to prepare — has pretty well evaporated. Several companies now prepare and sell raw food for dogs and cats. Some of their offerings include exotic items, such as quail, rabbit, and ostrich — which benefit dogs who suffer from allergies — to more conventional proteins, such as beef and chicken. Among these companies are Aunt Jeni's Natural Pet Food (www.auntjeni. com), Bravo (www.bravorawdiet.com), and Oma's Pride (www. omaspride.com). You won't find their products in most stores, but by checking their Web sites you can find distributors near you from whom you can purchase the products. Failing that, you may be able to get the products you want shipped directly to your door.

If you choose to feed your dog a BARF diet, know that the costs can vary widely, depending on how much your Beagle eats, what you feed her, and which manufacturer you patronize.

A raw diet isn't for every dog or for every owner. If the idea of handling raw food makes your stomach queasy, then bag the idea of BARF-ing without feeling any guilt. If your dog has a compromised immune system or a lot of chronic illnesses, a BARF diet probably isn't a good choice.

Before you decide to do the BARF diet with your Beagle, consult some expert sources. A great book to start with is *The Holistic Dog Book: Canine Care for the 21st Century* by Denise Flaim (Howell Book House).

But is your chow of choice good for her?

After you choose your Beagle's chow, check to see whether your choice agrees with her tummy and the rest of her body. How can you tell whether her food is good for her? Here are some ideas:

✔ **How does her poop look?** Food that's good for your dog is easy for her to digest — and the clearest indication of digestibility is small, compact stools. If your Beagle's poop is big, bulky, soft, and/or stinky, she may be having trouble digesting the food you're giving her. Try switching to another brand — but do so gradually (see "Making the switch" later in this chapter).

✔ **Is she getting flaky?** If your Beagle's coat is littered with flakes, her food may be lacking vital fats. Consider switching to a food that has a higher fat content, or ask your veterinarian whether your Beagle needs a fatty acid supplement.

✔ **Do her toots clear the room?** If your Beagle's gaseous emissions are frequent and/or make you want to keel over, her daily fare may have too many carbohydrates. A higher protein/lower carb regimen may reduce the flatulence and restore a fresh smell to your home.

✔ **Is she porking out?** A dog food that's loaded with calories and fats will probably cause your little hound to lose her girlish figure. A switch to a low-calorie food — or smaller portions of what she's currently eating — can help her regain her svelte shape.

A new take on table scraps

Almost every dog care book exhorts the reader to refrain from feeding table scraps to her dog. But anyone who's been subjected to the guilt trip that a dog can inflict (courtesy of those big, soulful eyes) knows that such restraint is almost impossible to sustain. Consequently, I offer a new take on table scraps: an approach that bows to reality.

The short version of this approach is that it's okay to feed your dog table scraps, within the bounds of good taste, your Beagle's health, and simple common sense. The long version includes these tips for healthful, guilt-free sharing of your food with your Snoopy-dog:

✔ **Don't be literal.** Don't dispense table scraps directly from the table unless you enjoy having your Beagle stare at you and your plate while you eat. (And even if you don't mind, other members of your family — not to mention dinner guests — may take exception to the sight of Beagle begging.) Instead, wait until you and your family or friends have finished eating, and then place some carefully chosen leftovers into your dog's dish.

✔ **Go bland.** Limit those leftovers to foods that don't contain a lot of spices or fats, both of which could cause your little hound to have a major digestive upset. Opt instead for veggies, fat-free meat, fish, or white-meat portions of chicken or turkey. And don't feed cooked bones or gristle. Ingesting either can cause intestinal obstructions or pancreatitis, both of which can make your dog really sick.

✔ **Waste not, want not.** Neither you nor your Beagle should consider the contents of the garbage can or any other waste receptacle a food source for her. Food from these locations quickly becomes laden with disease-causing germs and bacteria. In other words, after the scraps leave the literal table, they should be off the figurative table — permanently.

Making the switch

If you plan to switch your dog from one food to another, consider doing so gradually — especially if you know she's got a sensitive stomach. Start by serving her three-quarters of her current food mixed with one-quarter of the new food for a couple of days. Assuming she tolerates the new food, move to a half-and-half mixture for another few days, then one-quarter old to three-quarters new. After that, she should be fine with the new chow.

On the other hand, many dogs do well having diets that rotate among two to four different types of food. If your dog is one, you don't need to be gradual about the switches.

Getting the Skinny about Your Hound's Pounds

No discussion of the art and science of Beagle feeding is complete without at least touching on how to help the Snoopy-dog who eats too much or too little food. Keeping your Beagle svelte but not skinny should be the balance you aim for in her feeding program.

Slimming the portly pooch

One of the many advantages to having a Beagle is that you can tell almost immediately whether she's packing on too many pounds. Although other breeds such as Keeshonden or Collies can hide their jelly bellies under mounds of fur, the Beagle has no such cover. That means that just a quick glance or a touch can tell you what you need to know.

Start by looking at your Beagle from above. Can you see an indentation at her waistline? If so, she's probably not overweight. If not, try running your hands along her sides. A dog who's at the proper weight has ribs that you can feel easily. Too much fat, and you'll need to exert a little pressure to find her ribs.

If you've concluded that your little hound is a little too heavy, here's what to do:

> ✔ **Ask your vet for help.** Your Beagle's veterinarian can help you help your dog in two ways. First, he can see whether your Beagle's extra inches result from a health problem such as those described in Chapter 12. Second, if he can rule out a health problem, he can help you develop a diet and exercise program that will help your dog slim down safely.

✔ **Reduce portions.** It's simple: Dogs who weigh too much need to eat less. Your vet can tell you how far to cut back your Beagle's rations. Your goal here is to help her take off weight, but not to starve her!

✔ **Limit treats.** Reducing your Beagle's mealtime portions will be useless unless you also reduce the number of treats you give her. Don't let your little hound have a snack attack!

✔ **Give more meals.** Make those reduced rations go further by dividing them up into three or more meals. That way, you'll help your dog's tummy stay fuller for a longer period of time. And don't think that *free feeding,* or leaving large amounts of food out for your dog to dine on as she feels like it, is an acceptable alternative to feeding your Beagle three times a day. See the "Free feeding forbidden" sidebar for drawbacks on this practice.

✔ **Add some fruits and veggies.** A low-cal way to fill your dog's tummy is to add some fruits and vegetables to her regular fare. Good stuff to try includes apples, carrots, frozen green beans, frozen Brussels sprouts, and frozen broccoli. Be careful not to feed too many of these items, though, or you'll find that your dog will need to poop more often.

Cut any fruits and vegetables into very small pieces or, better yet, run them through the blender so your Beagle can eat and digest them more easily.

✔ **Get her moving.** Exercise is as important for your Beagle as it is for you. Your dog's small size makes it easy for you to give her extra exercise opportunities without tiring her out or taking too much of your own time. A couple of extra walks or longer-distance strolls can burn up extra calories; so can swimming. More info on great exercises and activities for Beagles is in Chapter 9.

Picky, picky, picky

Some dogs just aren't that into food, or so it seems. These dogs may simply not like the atmosphere in which they're eating; for these environmentally conscious individuals, the next section, "Attending to Ambiance," can help. However, other apparently picky eaters may object not to how they're eating but what they're eating. To help your fussy Fidette learn to enjoy her food, try these suggestions:

✔ **Add something special.** A diet that's all kibble all the time may be nutritious, but for some dogs it's also way too bland. Back in my less-enlightened dog-owning days, my dog went on a hunger strike after enduring an exclusively kibble diet for way too long. Adding canned dog food or nutritious table scraps — or even just pouring some warm water on the kibble to create a rich gravy — can lure your bored Beagle gourmand back to her dish.

✔ **Make a change.** Another way to combat gastronomic boredom is to change the food your Beagle's been eating. Look for something that's a little more flavorful than what you've been giving her, and gradually switch her from one food to another over several days.

✔ **Add some variety.** Some experts advise Beagle owners and other dog owners to refrain from varying their dogs' menus. They contend that consistency keeps a dog healthy. However, consistency may also result in a dog who's less than thrilled at mealtime. In my many years as an enthusiastic dog owner, and almost as many as a student of all things canine, I've concluded that many dogs enjoy variety in their meals, just like we do. Consequently, I rotate three or four different meats in my dog's fare. You can do the same — and give your sweetie something to look forward to at mealtime.

The suggestions here apply only to those Beagles whose pickiness is habitual and long-standing. If your usually ravenous Beagle suddenly loses interest in food for more than a meal or so, she could be seriously ill. Call your veterinarian as soon as possible.

Attending to Ambience

Do you like to eat your dinner at the table with music playing in the background, or on a TV tray while you watch the evening news? Do you like to have quiet while you eat, or does music improve the atmosphere? Is Sunday not quite right unless you have breakfast in bed? The answers to these questions add up to your special dining preferences and underscore the fact that good eating isn't just a matter of what you eat, but how you eat it.

The same principle holds true for your Beagle. Just like you, she may have definite dining preferences. If you make an effort to determine those preferences, your dog is likely to eat better, feel better, and behave better.

For example, some dogs prefer to eat alone, while others like to have the rest of their family around them. Some prefer to eat in one place, while others have such a strong need to be where the family is that you need to bring the dog's dish to wherever the action is. In any case, catering to these preferences won't spoil your Beagle. Instead, your thoughtfulness will help her eat more regularly (and thus, eliminate more regularly) and cut down on digestive troubles that unnecessary stress can trigger.

Free feeding forbidden

The idea of leaving food out for your Snoopy-dog 24/7 may seem like a great idea — or, at the very least, a practice that would be really convenient for you. And if your dog is like most Beagles, she'd probably like nothing better than to have food at the ready instead of having to wait for you to feed her. But this is one case where the convenience for you and desirability for your Beagle of leaving food out all the time — a practice that experts call *free feeding* — don't offset the downsides of this practice. Here's why:

✔ **Free feeding = housetraining hassles.** As Chapter 14 explains, a basic principle of teaching your Beagle basic bathroom manners is understanding that what goes into your dog eventually comes out. If you know when your Beagle's been scarfing down food at one end of her body, you have a better chance of forecasting when that food will reappear at the other end. Such predictability helps you anticipate when your housetrainee needs a bathroom break, and you can get her outside before she has an accident. By contrast, free feeding makes it impossible for you to figure out when and how much your dog has eaten, which makes forecasting her need for pit stops equally problematic.

✔ **Free feeding = weaker bond.** If your Beagle sees food in her dish all the time, she's likely to forget who's providing that food: you. Banning free feeding and turning daily meals into a twice-daily ritual reminds your dog that you are the source of all good things in her life. That understanding makes her likely to want to please you, which will strengthen your relationship with her.

✔ **Free feeding = lost clue.** Still not convinced? Here's another, potentially serious downside to free feeding: the loss of a vital indicator of your dog's health status. The symptoms of many canine illnesses — including serious ailments, such as cancer — include a lack of appetite. If you feed your Beagle twice a day, you'll see any changes in food intake immediately, and get her the help she needs right away. By contrast, keeping your Beagle's bowl filled all the time may mask this vital sign of health and wellness, unless you're keeping track of how often you're filling the dish.

But while every dog, Beagle or otherwise, is unique, certain eating principles apply to every member of the canine race. Those principles include

✔ **Letting her eat in peace:** When your dog is scarfing down her rations, don't interrupt her — and don't let anyone else do so, either. That includes not only human family members, but also animal family members, such as cats and other dogs.

✔ **Forestalling food fights:** If your Beagle is one of several animals in your family menagerie, feed each nonhuman member separately — either in different locations at the same time or at the same location but at different times. Such forethought will prevent the battles over food that almost always result when you attempt to feed all pets at the same time in the same place.

✔ **Not rushing her meal:** Good food is an even bigger pleasure for dogs than it is for people — for dogs, breakfast and dinner are among the high points of their day. So don't be in a rush to pick up her dish; give your Beagle sufficient time — at least 15 minutes — to savor her daily fare. By doing so, you'll reduce her chances of getting an upset stomach.

✔ **Doing the dishes:** Washing your dog's dishes not only constitutes good hygiene, but also enhances your dog's meal. In fact, many dogs refuse to eat food from a dirty dish. Can you blame them? Do for your Beagle what you would do for yourself: Give her clean dishes to dine from.

Treating Your Beagle Right

Should treats be part of your Beagle's diet? Absolutely. As you see throughout Part IV, treats make a terrific tool for teaching your Beagle how to be a well-mannered Snoopy-dog. The prospect of scoring a tasty morsel can spur almost any dog — including the occasionally stubborn Beagle — into figuring out what you want her to do and then doing it.

But dispensing treats isn't a risk-free proposition. Unless you're careful, the treats that are great for your Beagle's brain may end up being not-so-good for the rest of her body. In other words, too many treats can make for a Beagle with too many pounds. At the same time, though, a low-cal treat will get you and your Beagle nowhere if she decides she doesn't like what you're offering.

Selecting scrumptious snacks

A good treat is a goody that your Beagle absolutely adores — so much so that she will do anything, just anything, to earn one of those tasty (and often smelly) morsels. At the same time, though, the treat shouldn't be so fattening that your Beagle will pork out. Here are some suggestions for treats that many dogs adore:

✔ **Fish-based treats,** such as those available from high-end dog product Web sites, such as SitStay.com (www.sitstay.com).

✔ **Fruits and veggies,** such as tiny pieces of carrot, apple, and frozen vegetables.

✔ **Meaty treats** that you cook to reduce the fat content. Small hot dog pieces microwaved to a crisp smell like bacon — a heavenly smell to a Beagle. Those goodies will contain a lot less fat if you wrap them in a paper towel before you feed them to your dog. The paper towel will absorb much of the fat.

✔ **Semi-moist dog foods,** such as those that come in a tube, can make wonderful treats. They smell delicious to your Beagle, and that great smell can be a wonderful incentive for her to learn what you're trying to teach her. These foods are full of calories, though, so feed in moderation — and scale back your Beagle's regular fare.

✔ **Commercial dog biscuits and treats** are OK — if you feed them in moderation and if they don't contain artificial colors or dyes. Those colors may catch your eye, but they do nothing good for your dog's health and well-being.

Keeping calories under control

Treats can work wonders to boost your Beagle's mental prowess — but all the calories in those little morsels also can cause her to pack on the pounds.

To make sure that your Beagle has the incentive to learn without losing her sleek physique, start by downsizing her mealtimes. If you're feeding commercial treats, check the manufacturer's label to see how many ounces a certain number of treats is equivalent to — and downsize your dog's meals accordingly. For homemade treats, try cutting meals by 10 to 20 percent during the initial training phases, when you're dispensing a lot of goodies to teach good behavior.

After your Beagle's learned a new trick, command, or other maneuver, start cutting back on the number of treats you give her for obeying your command. Instead of rewarding her every time she complies, start rewarding her every other time, then every third time, and so on. Eventually, she should be satisfied with some lavish praise and petting as a reward for a job well done.

Avoiding Dangerous Dining

Alas, your Beagle doesn't necessarily have a clear sense of what's good and what's not so good for her to eat. She needs you, her knowledgeable human, to keep her away from those foods that could make her seriously ill, not to mention very uncomfortable. Here's a sampling of food items that you need to keep your Beagle away from if you want to keep her healthy:

✔ **Cooked bones:** The big rib from that roast may smell wonderful to your Beagle, but the effect on her digestive tract could be decidedly unwonderful. Cooked bones splinter easily, which could result in small pieces of bone getting stuck anywhere in the digestive tract.

✔ **Onions and garlic:** We humans like these flavorful root veggies to flavor our foods, but they can be poisonous to our canine companions if used in raw form. Make sure that your Beagle doesn't get any! Garlic powder is okay, though.

✔ **Grapes:** Another food that your Beagle needs to avoid; too many grapes are toxic to all breeds of dogs.

✔ **Chocolate:** I once lived with a dog who would have done anything to get a taste of mint chocolate liqueur, and most canines adore the scent of chocolate. But here, too, the siren smell of a food meant for humans is toxic to members of the canine race. Don't let your Beagle anywhere near your Godivas — or any other brand.

Your Beagle's Drinking Habits

Water is vital to all living things, including Beagles. And just like people, Snoopy-dogs need more water after they've been running around than after a nap, and more during the hot days (notice I didn't say "dog days") of summer than the frigid days of winter. Moreover, individual dogs' cravings for water vary; for example, dogs who eat nothing but dry food will probably pay more visits to their water bowls than those who eat canned or other types of food.

Adult Beagles should have access to fresh water all day. Keep your little hound's water dish full, but don't just top it off when the water level gets low. Instead, empty the dish and give her some fresh water. Another time to change the water is when you see food residue or other stuff floating in it. And even if the dish contains nothing but water, you should wash the bowl every day.

Beagle puppies, as well as adults who haven't quite mastered the art of proper potty deportment should get plenty of water, but they shouldn't have unlimited access. Chapter 14 includes guidelines for giving water to the dog who's still learning her basic bathroom manners.

And do make sure that your Beagle drinks only the water in her dish. Pond water, water in the toilet, and swimming pool water contain substances that could upset her tummy.

Chapter 9

Getting Physical: Exercising Your Beagle

. . . .

. . . .

For most of my life, I was an intermittent exerciser. Workouts weren't part of my thinking, much less my schedule. Every time I read an article by some buff expert extolling the benefits of exercising for at least 30 minutes three times a week, I'd mutter to myself, "Yeah, and who's got the time? Not me."

Then I went on a cruise to the Caribbean, and to rid myself of the guilt that I felt after I ate way too much delicious food, I headed to the ship's gym to put in some time on the treadmill and exercise machines. To my considerable surprise, I enjoyed myself — and to my supreme relief, my clothes still fit me at the end of the cruise. Those results sold me, and when I returned to dry land, I joined a nearby gym. Today, my clothes still fit me, I've toned up, and I deal with stress a heck of a lot better than I did before I joined the gym.

The same benefits that we get from exercise our dogs also get, if we take the time to make sure they get their daily workouts. This chapter explains how exercise not only benefits your Beagle, but also you. In addition, I list a bunch of sports that can keep your Beagle trim and toned well into his golden years, not to mention mentally sharp and much better behaved than might otherwise be the case.

Keep Him Moving, Keep Yourself Happy

Dog trainers constantly tell their human clients that a tired dog is a happy dog — and for good reason. The pooch who has had the chance to flex his muscles and use his brainpower is generally too pooped to get into mischief such as unwinding toilet paper, pilfering laundry, and engaging in other activities that don't please his people. Put another way, a dog who stays out of mischief results in a happy dog owner — and that generally leads full circle to a happy dog.

Plus, getting and staying in shape feels just as good to your Beagle as it does to you. Regular exercise not only prevents the boredom that gets him into hot water with you — it also does wonderful things for his body and overall health. The Beagle who stays in shape has a healthier heart and lungs, less fat on his body, greater mobility, and fewer aches and pains than his couch-potato counterpart. Those health advantages will become increasingly important to your Beagle as he ages.

Finally, exercise gives your Beagle a chance to be with the individual who matters (or should matter) more to him than anyone else: you. That's because Snoopy-dogs are social creatures, and they're not likely to exert themselves to any great extent unless their people are there to do it with them. They need their people not only to show them the moves that will keep them in shape, but also just to keep them company.

And isn't your Beagle's company the reason that you added him to your life in the first place? He's a delightful little guy, and having the chance to do stuff with him gives you opportunities to enjoy him for the unique individual that he is. Helping your Beagle stay in shape keeps your relationship with him in shape, too. Doing so need not take a whole lot of time: A couple of brisk 15- to 20-minute walks per day may be all he needs. Of course, your Beagle may be such wonderful company that you may need and want a whole lot more time with him than that!

Trying Everyday Exercises

You don't have to join a doggy gym or invest in fancy equipment to give your Beagle a good workout. The stuff you do every day can, with a little tweaking, become part of great exercise routine for any dog. Here are some ideas.

Walk on the wild side

In all likelihood, you'll be walking your Beagle anyway, simply to take him to his outdoor potty. But why not go beyond the thrice-daily bathroom break, and go for a stroll with your little guy?

And if you're a couch potato by nature, take heart. A leisurely stroll for you can be a brisk walk for a Beagle, whose little legs have to move at a quick pace to keep up with your relatively long-limbed strides. A 20-minute walk around a couple of blocks gets your Beagle buddy moving and gives the two of you some quality time together. And a daily stroll is especially good for a senior dog, because walking provides gentle exercise that's kind to an older pooch's joints, muscles, and ligaments.

Chapter 15 explains how to teach your dog to walk politely when he's on a leash. When you and he are out and about, though, keep the following safety precautions in mind:

✔ **Keep it cool.** Black-topped pavement heated to furnace-level temperatures by the summer sun is very unkind to a Beagle's tender paw pads. Avoid walking on such surfaces during the summer so your dog's feet don't burn.

✔ **Avoid extremes.** If the weather's too hot or too cold for you to take a long hike, the same is true for your Beagle. Keep the walks short during summer heat waves and winter deep-freezes.

✔ **Heed your dog.** If your Beagle limps, lags, or otherwise can't keep up with you, stop to rest, or at least slow your pace.

If your normally energetic Beagle suddenly can't keep up with you during walks, have your veterinarian check him out. A sudden loss of energy may signal the onset of a serious illness.

✔ **Use the leash.** The Beagle's reputation for wandering off in whatever direction his nose takes him means that you must — absolutely must — keep him on the leash unless you're in an area that's enclosed by a secure fence.

Jog your memory (or at least your feet)

For the relatively fit Beagle, a jog with his favorite person can prove even more beneficial than a walk. The aerobic benefits multiply, and the Beagle expends considerably more calories than he does when walking. Jogging also tires out your little hound faster than a walk does, which could prove helpful if he must spend time on his own later. (A Beagle who's had a good jog will be too tired to get into any mischief!) Jogging also delivers many benefits to *your* body — but that's a subject for another book.

The same guidelines for walking apply to jogging with two additions.

- ✔ If your dog shows any signs of discomfort (such as limping), don't jog him at all.

- ✔ Try not to jog on concrete — for the sake of his knees and yours. Instead, opt for a softer surface such as a jogging trail, bike trail shoulder, or even grass if it's not slippery.

Get in the swim

Doggy-style swimming is one of the best exercises your Beagle can engage in. A dip in a pond or pool gives your dog's joints, ligaments, and muscles a terrific workout without causing the strain that weight-bearing exercises such as walking and jogging may entail — a benefit that's especially helpful for dogs who are overweight, arthritic, or recovering from surgery or injury.

Your local pond or nearby creek can serve as a puppy pool. You can also find an honest-to-goodness heated pool (but probably not your local public pool) for your Beagle to execute his water ballet moves in: Just log onto any Internet search engine and type *dog hydrotherapy* and *United States*. You'll come up with plenty of results. (Some places require referral from a veterinarian.)

But no matter where you take your Beagle to swim, make sure that the experience is positive for him. Swimming is great for any dog, including a Beagle — but some dogs take longer than others to appreciate this activity. If your Snoopy-dog is a skittish swimmer, give him time to get used to the pool or pond. Have him wear a doggy life jacket to help him stay afloat, and throw floatable treats such as oyster crackers into the pool to give him a reason to start paddling. In a pond or creek, go in ahead of him, and use a treat or toy to coax him to come to you and into the water.

Great Sports for You and Your Beagle

Wanna go beyond everyday athletics with your Beagle? This section's for you. Here are descriptions of all kinds of doggy sports and other activities that you and your little hound might enjoy participating in together.

Goin' to the show

The oldest and best known of the organized dog sports is the dog show, which is known more formally as *conformation*. That formal term makes a great deal of sense, because dog shows measure how well each dog conforms to the standard of his breed — that blueprint for a perfect Beagle or other dog breed that I describe in Chapter 2.

Does your dog have what it takes to excel in the show ring? Maybe yes, maybe no. If you're a dog-show novice, take your Beagle to a reputable breeder and have her evaluate him. She can examine your little hound and tell you how he stacks up against the Beagle breed standard. Attend a few local dog shows, too, and get a feeling for how they work. (Flip to the color section to see Beagles participating in a dog show.)

If you've already spayed or neutered your Beagle, forget about showing him. The American Kennel Club, which sponsors many dog shows, does not permit the exhibition of a dog who has been snipped.

If your Beagle does have the stuff — and if you haven't neutered him yet (or spayed your female) — you can read up on the dog-show world. Two books to start with are *Dog Showing for Beginners* by Lynn Hall (Howell Book House) and *The Absolute Beginner's Guide to Showing Your Dog* by Cheryl S. Smith (Three Rivers Press). The resources section at the end of this book lists magazines that can help you pilot your Beagle's show-dog career, or just decide whether you want to start it in the first place.

Stay the (agility) course

Does your Beagle like to race around the house, jump atop the couch, or burrow underneath it? Can he turn corners on a dime while barely slowing down? Then your dog may be a fine candidate for the increasingly popular, exciting canine sport of *agility*.

In agility, a human handler directs her dog through an obstacle course that consists of tunnels (under-the-couch burrowers should find these a cinch to navigate), teeter-totters, hurdles, weave poles, A-frames, and balance beams. Almost any breed can learn this sport, but you may find it tough to teach your dog yourself. Not to worry, though. Plenty of professional dog trainers hold classes in beginning agility. (To get an idea of an obstacle your Beagle may encounter on an agility course, check out the photo in the color section.) And if you plan on competing your dog, plan on getting yourself in shape, too. At the competition level, agility is strenuous exercise for both dog and handler.

You can also supplement your class work with reading. If you think you may want to enter your Beagle in agility competitions, check out *All About Agility* by Jacqueline O'Neil (Howell Book House). If, however, you think you just want your Beagle to do agility for kicks, browse through *Having Fun with Agility* by Margaret H. Bonham (Howell Book House). You can get even more info about agility from the American Kennel Club (www.akc.org); the North American Dog Agility Council (www.nadac.com); and the United States Dog Agility Association (www.usdaa.com).

Fetch that flyball

If your Beagle wants to get in touch with his inner Retriever, you and he may want to take up *flyball,* a sport that's as exciting and fast-paced as agility.

Flyball is a relay race that requires each dog on a team to run to a box-shaped ball launcher. The dog presses his paw on a lever that activates a spring inside the box and releases the ball. After the dog catches the ball, he races over hurdles back to the starting point. The next dog in line starts the cycle all over again. The fastest team wins the competition.

The North American Flyball Association sponsors flyball competitions, and its Web site is www.flyball.org. Here you can find general information about the sport. If you're looking for more specific info, such as where to find a flyball class, log onto the Flyball Home Page at www.flyballdogs.com. There you can find a comprehensive, searchable database of teams from all over the United States — including, in all likelihood, a team that trains in your area. Many of these teams offer classes for prospective flyball pooches and their people.

Opt for obedience

Obedience is exactly what it sounds like: an activity that tests a dog's ability to obey commands amid numerous distractions (for example, a bunch of other dogs and people nearby).

In obedience trials, a judge scores a dog for each command the dog performs. If a dog earns at least 150 out of a possible 200 points in a single match, he earns a *leg* toward an obedience title. Three legs brings an obedience title. Earn more legs, and the dog earns still more titles, up to the ultimate accolades: Obedience Trial Champion and National Obedience Champion (earned by one dog each year at the AKC National Obedience Invitational).

Not surprisingly, Beagles don't dominate most lists of top obedience dogs. The independent, easily distracted Snoopy-dog may have more trouble than other breeds when he tries to execute commands precisely or perform mistake-free maneuvers. But so what? Winning isn't everything. No matter where your Beagle places, obedience can certainly help build the bond between the two of you, and can keep your dog sharp as a tack. Info about the world of competitive obedience is available from the American Kennel Club at www.akc.org/events/obedience.

Rally-ho!

Some people — and probably, their Beagles, too — consider the world of competitive obedience to be incredibly dull. They find the precisely scripted exercises to be too difficult and too yawn-inducing to be any fun. At the same time, though, they find agility too strenuous, particularly if the dog is older or the person doesn't have the energy to run all over the agility course alongside the dog. They'd love to find a sport that's more interesting than obedience but less active than agility.

That sport has arrived, and it's called *rally obedience.* In this sport, a dog and handler complete a course of 10 to 20 stations that's been designed by the rally judge. At each station, a sign tells the team what the dog needs to do there. For example, your Beagle may perform a Sit or walk a figure 8 around the sign. The judge scores the team on how well it performs the maneuvers.

Rally obedience is a great activity for a Beagle and his person. Although the Beagle's independence and distractibility can make this sport more of a challenge for him than for other breeds, he can still do well. In fact, three Beagles accumulated national ranking points during 2005, the most recent year that such information was available when this book was written.

Two organizations — the American Kennel Club and the Association of Pet Dog Trainers — sponsor rally obedience competitions and titles. Information about the AKC Rally program is available at the AKC Web site at www.akc.org/events/rally. To find out more about the Association of Pet Dog Trainers's Rally Obedience program, log onto www.apdt.com/po/rally.

Dance with me: Canine freestyle

Are you musically inclined? Do you like to trip the light fantastic? Is dancing your idea of heaven? Well, surprisingly, you can dance with a four-footed partner — your Beagle — in the relatively new sport of *canine freestyle*. In canine freestyle, you and your Beagle perform maneuvers that are set to music. Your dog might circle around you, spin, or perform a flip in response to your signals and in time to the music.

After you and your dog take some classes in canine freestyle and determine whether this sport is for the two of you, check out the info offered by two groups that promote this rhythmic pursuit. The World Canine Freestyle Organization (WCFO) was founded by Patie Ventre, a dog lover who once was a competitive ballroom dancer. The WCFO Web site is www.worldcaninefreestyle.org. The other group is the Canine Freestyle Federation Inc. This group's Web site includes a list of nationwide organizations that hold canine freestyle classes. Find out more by logging onto www.canine-freestyle.org.

Join the hunt: Field trials

The Beagle's original reason for being was to hunt rabbits and other small animals — and today's dog still has the stuff needed to do just that. And although you may not need your little hound to help you hunt your own food, you can still give him a chance to tap into his deepest instincts by introducing him to *field trials*.

The American Kennel Club has devised field trials for almost every type of hunting dog or hound dog. For example, Golden Retrievers, Labrador Retrievers, and other retriever breeds can participate in events that test their ability to bring water fowl back to their handlers under various conditions. Other breeds, such as the Dachshund, the Basset Hound, as well as all Spaniels and Pointers, have similar opportunities to get back in touch with their roots.

Field trials for Beagles measure the dogs' abilities to track and trail rabbits and other small game. These events have many forms:

- **Brace:** Determines the hunting ability of a pair of Beagles
- **Small pack:** Measures the talent of a group of as many as nine Beagles
- **Large pack:** Rates the performance of between 30 and 60 dogs
- **Gun dog brace:** Ascertains how a pair of dogs reacts to the sound of gunfire

Who can resist an adorable Beagle puppy? If you adopt one from a breeder, you can bring him home when he's 8 weeks old. See Chapter 4.

Beagles are inquisitive little dogs. Their looks, intelligence, and playfulness make them one of the most popular dog breeds. See Chapter 1.

Not only do Beagles bark, they howl. You can minimize these canine concerts by keeping her entertained with toys or activities. See Chapter 16.

Beagles have one of the best senses of smell of any dog breed. They instinctively track a scent, no matter what. See Chapter 2.

Just like you, Beagles need time to rest, especially as they grow older. See Chapter 12.

Kids and Beagles can be a perfect match. Beagles are just the right size to romp with youngsters without worrying about whether one may hurt the other one. See Chapter 6.

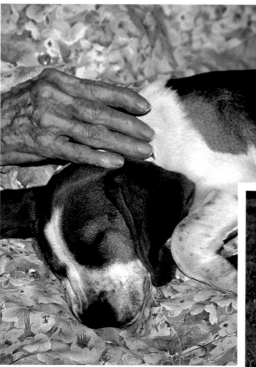

Beagles are happiest w
getting lots of love and
people. That makes the
visit people in hospitals
homes. See Chapter 2.

A Beagle works at getting treats out of
a plastic ball. If your Beagle suffers from
separation anxiety, keep him occupied
with one of these toys when you leave.
See Chapter 16.

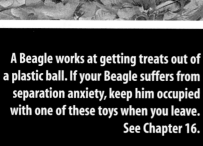

Training to compete in agility trials gives your Beagle a good
workout and allows the two of you to bond. See Chapter 9.

Beagles were bred in the 1500s to hunt rabbits. Today their keen sense of smell is used to detect termites and mold in houses. See Chapter 19.

Dog shows measure how well a Beagle conforms to the standard of his breed. See Chapter 9

Isabelle Francais

After a full day of activities with you and your family, your Snoopy-dog will be worn out. A tired Beagle is a happy Beagle! See Chapter 7

Beagles like to explore every nook and cranny they find. You'll want to Beagle-proof your house and yard before you bring your little hound home. See Chapter 5.

www.jeanmfogle.com

If you and your Snoopy-dog spend a lot of time outdoors, make sure to check her for fleas and ticks. See Chapter 10.

www.jeanmfogle.com

You need a lot of time and patience to train a Beagle to behave and perform tricks, but the results are worth the effort. See Chapter 15.

www.jeanmfogle.com

Beagle pups need three meals a day to help them grow up healthy. As dogs get older, they just need breakfast and dinner. See Chapter 7.

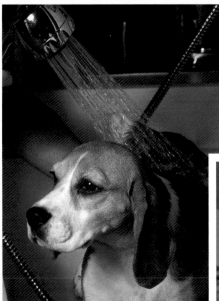

Because Beagles have short coats, they only need a bath about once a month — unless they find something dirty or smelly to roll around in. See Chapter 10.

Isabelle Francais

Your Beagle needs annual checkups with her veterinarian to keep her in tip-top shape. See Chapter 11.

Choosing a Beagle takes time and thought. You have to decide whether you want a pup or an adult, a male or a female, one dog or two. See Chapter 4.

Field trials for Beagles are classified by height and gender. Thirteen-inch Beagles run only with other 13-inch Beagles; the same is true with 15-inchers. Dogs also are separated by sex — no co-ed field trials for Snoopy-dogs! Female dogs in heat may not participate (just think of how distracted all those male dogs would be!). Spayed or neutered dogs may not participate, either, because field trials, like conformation (see the "Goin' to the Show" section in this chapter), aim to showcase the best breeding stock.

The event starts with the flushing out of a rabbit. When a rabbit is sighted, the cry "Tallyho!" is sounded. The dogs are expected to pick up the scent of the rabbit and bark, at which point they're let off leash to track the bunny. Judges assess each participant's tracking ability, determination, and intensity. Certain mistakes, such as going the wrong way and quitting altogether, result in a dog's elimination from its pack until a winner eventually emerges.

More info on Beagle field trials is available from the American Kennel Club at www.akc.org/events/field_trials/beagles. Another place to find out more is at the American Rabbit Hound Association, which you can find on the World Wide Web at www.arha.com.

Get on the right track

Although Beagles were built to hunt rabbits and hares, their incredibly sensitive noses allow them to find just about anything. To harness this ability without involving those sweet little bunnies, Beagle owners may find competing in *tracking* events to be a worthwhile pursuit. Unlike field trials, tracking events are open to all breeds. The objective is to measure a dog's ability to recognize and follow a human scent until the person is found.

The American Kennel Club offers three tracking titles:

- ✔ **Tracking Dog (TD):** For following a track of up to 440 to 500 yards with several turns
- ✔ **Tracking Dog Excellent (TDX):** For following an older track of up to 1,000 yards with more turns
- ✔ **Variable Surface Tracking (VST):** For tracking a scent for up to 800 yards over at least three different surfaces

A dog who earns all three titles is awarded the title of Champion Tracker (CT). More information about tracking is available from the American Kennel Club at www.akc.org/events/tracking.

Adjusting for Age

Exercise is as good for senior Beagles as it is for their younger counterparts, but that doesn't mean that they should conduct their workouts the same way that youthful hounds do. Older dogs are more likely to have special health issues that can limit their endurance or their ability to engage in certain activities. And even senior Snoopy-dogs who don't have specific health issues need to adjust their physical activities to fit the limitations that aging may impose. Here are some ways to do just that:

- ✔ **Go softer.** If you and your Beagle have always jogged on side-walks or streets, move to softer terrain that will be easier on his hips and joints. Grass is good as long as it's not wet (and slippery); so are roadside or trailside shoulders.

- ✔ **Limber up.** A warm-up (such as a slow walk before beginning to jog) will help keep your senior dog from getting injured or overworking his muscles and joints.

- ✔ **Have water at the ready.** Your Beagle needs water to prevent dehydration. Bring some along with you.

- ✔ **Work out regularly.** Regular exercise is the key to minimizing your senior fitness fanatic's pain and strain. Plan to work out with him at least three to four times every week.

- ✔ **Adjust for the weather.** An older dog feels warmth or cold more keenly than a young one does, so don't exercise your senior when the weather is either very hot or very cold.

- ✔ **Watch your Beagle.** Let your dog tell you when he's had enough exercise for now. If he's lagging behind, slowing his pace, and panting heavily, it's time for him to quit.

Lots more information on living with and loving an older Beagle appears in Chapter 12.

Chapter 10

Sprucing Up Your Beagle

. . . .

. . . .

*M*any people choose to share their lives with Beagles because the Snoopy-dog is a relatively low-maintenance canine, at least when it comes to grooming. Those who don't want to pay for a Poodle's monthly trip to a groomer or sit down each day to remove the mats from a Golden Retriever's coat undoubtedly appreciate the Beagle's no-fuss, no-muss coiffure.

But just because the Beagle has a wash-and-wear hairdo doesn't mean that she doesn't need regular grooming. Not only does she need grooming to stay clean and healthy, she also needs grooming to have one-on-one time with you. In addition, regular grooming provides a great opportunity to examine your little hound for lumps, bumps, cuts, and other signs that she's not in tip-top condition.

This chapter gives you the basic info you need to keep your Beagle well groomed from the end of her nose to the tip of her tail — and everywhere in between.

Giving Her the Brush-off

A thorough brushing once or twice a week is crucial to keep your Beagle's coat and skin healthy. The brushing action gently stimulates the skin and distributes the skin's natural oils throughout the coat. Brushing also helps to control your Beagle's shedding — or, at least, to reduce the amount of hair that would otherwise get into your carpets, furniture, or clothes.

You only need one tool to brush your pup: a brush! The best ones have soft bristles; alternatively, you can use a curry comb.

Easy brushing goes like this:

1. **Start by getting yourself and your Beagle into comfortable positions.**

   A safe way to brush your dog is to have her lie down — Chapter 15 explains how to teach her to lie down on command — and roll over onto her side, as shown in Figure 10-1.

   Unless you have a professional grooming station with the means to secure your dog safely, don't place her on a raised surface such as a table. She could be at risk for injury if she decides to end the brushing session prematurely and jump down.

2. **After she's lying down and relaxed, gently stroke her entire body in the direction of the hair growth with the soft-bristle brush or curry comb.**

3. **After you're done with the first side, gently roll her over and do the other side.**

Piece of cake!

It's hard to imagine that any Snoopy-dog could hate being brushed, but if yours is one of those rare individuals, help is at hand. If yours is a hard-to-brush hound, try employing one or both of the following tactics:

- **Turn on the TV.** No, I'm not kidding. Put on your favorite trashy television show (meaning one that doesn't require much of your attention) and invite your Beagle to snuggle up with you. When she does, pet her gently and help her relax. Then, when you see that she's headed toward Dreamland, get out the brush and try a few gentle strokes. If she objects, stop the session immediately but try again later. If she doesn't object, tell her in a soothing voice what a good girl she is and continue brushing.

- **Bribe her.** Any time you and your Beagle are having a love-fest (also known as a petting party), give her a treat. Then, as she's nibbling the treat, wield the brush for a stroke or two. If she doesn't object, give her another treat and praise her for being a good girl. Gradually build up the number of brush strokes you give her. Pretty soon, she'll adore being brushed.

Figure 10-1: Placing your Beagle on her side can make brushing easier.

Establishing a No-Critter Zone

They're teeny-tiny, almost microscopically small — but they can make your Beagle's life (and yours!) miserable. I'm talking about the fleas and ticks that hitchhike their way to happiness on the body of your hound and countless other canines.

Fighting those fleas

Just one flea can drive your dog to distraction. A single bite will cause your four-legged friend to get itchy. Worse, if she's allergic to the fleas, she may scratch so much that she'll lose part of her coat, cause her skin to bleed, and open the door to all kinds of tough-to-treat infections. Even if she's not allergic, without relief from fleas your dog may become anemic, because the flea's dinner of choice is canine blood. However, the flea is an equal opportunity parasite; it has no problem jumping from your Beagle to you. When it does, you'll be scratching, too.

And of course, the flea is not a solitary critter. If you find one flea bite on your dog, you can be sure that a multitude of fleas has been feasting on her.

Hunting for fleas

How do you know if your Beagle has fleas? If she begins scratching almost constantly, take a look at her tummy. Many black specks on the skin of her stomach and/or groin may signal the presence of flea dirt — the blood the flea expels after it's dined on your dog.

Moisten any suspected flea dirt with water. If the specks turn red, your Beagle's got fleas.

You may even see a tiny little critter or two scampering on your dog's skin. Still not sure? Take a flea comb and run it through your Beagle's coat. If she's got fleas, you'll see them crawling around the teeth of the comb. (A flea comb is a small comb with very fine teeth that are very close together. Its single purpose is to help you deal with fleas on your dog.)

Zapping the little buggers

Fortunately, you can give your Beagle permanent relief from fleas. In recent years, pharmaceutical companies have unveiled a variety of products that successfully eradicate these useless parasites. Some stop the flea's eggs from developing, thus causing the population to die off because it can't reproduce. Others kill the adult fleas that make the mistake of biting the treated dog.

Even better are the many flea-control products that are masters of multitasking. For example, the chewable pill that stops flea eggs from developing also kills parasites such as heartworm (which can be fatal if untreated), hookworm, roundworm, and whipworm. A topical product that zaps adult fleas does the same to ticks. Both are available only with a veterinarian's prescription — which leads me to strongly suggest that you consult your veterinarian before starting any flea control program. For one thing, your vet can steer you away from outdated — and frankly, not terribly effective — remedies, such as flea collars, shampoos, and dips.

Banishing those ticks

Ticks are a real danger to canine and human health. They transmit serious diseases such as Lyme disease and Rocky Mountain spotted fever. Antibiotics can zap these diseases, but experts agree that prevention is the better strategy to dealing with these maladies.

Prevention starts with checking your dog often to see if she has any ticks on her body and removing them properly. Depending on the type of tick and how much it's feasted on your Beagle, it will look like a bump that's anywhere from the size of a pinhead to a pencil eraser and be dark brown to brownish-grey in color.

You'll need a pair of rubber gloves, tweezers, a needle, rubbing alcohol, cotton balls, a bowl, doggy shampoo, and water.

To remove a tick, have your dog sit or lie down. Then:

1. **Put on the gloves and grab the tweezers.**

2. **Grab the tick's body with the tweezers, and pull it straight off the dog.**

   Don't twist or jerk while you pull. That way, you're more likely to get the whole tick, not just the headless body.

3. **Check to make sure you got the head as well as the body.**

   If the tick's head appears to have been left behind, remove it from the dog's skin with a needle that's been dipped in rubbing alcohol.

4. **Put the tick in a bowl of alcohol to kill it.**

5. **Clean the area from which you pulled the tick with a cotton ball that has a tiny amount of shampoo on it. Rinse with water and dry. Then use another cotton ball to place a dab of rubbing alcohol on the site.**

6. **Watch for signs of tick-borne disease.**

   Those signs include appetite loss, weight loss, fever, lethargy, and stiffness. Such symptoms probably will appear four to ten days after you've removed the tick, although they may take longer to show up. No matter when your Beagle shows such signs of trouble, though, take her to your veterinarian.

Lather Up! Bathing Your Beagle

Every Beagle needs to be bathed periodically — but unlike you, your Snoopy-dog doesn't need a daily sudsing, or even a weekly one. A monthly bath should keep her clean and sweet smelling, but if she happens to get really dirty between regularly scheduled baths, an extra turn in the tub is fine.

From dirty dog to washed dog

Luckily for you, a Beagle is relatively small and easy to bathe. But before you put your Beagle in the tub, gather the gear you need:

- ✔ Shampoo made just for dogs
- ✔ A hand-held shower attachment or bowl for rinsing
- ✔ Cotton balls to protect the ears from water
- ✔ A rubber bathmat to keep her from her from slipping in the tub
- ✔ A couple of big, fluffy towels

Don't forget about yourself! If you're bathing your dog in a bathtub, place a couple of towels on the floor to cushion your knees. And wear something impervious to water: a waterproof apron or even a swimsuit. (Yes, you will get wet. Maybe very wet.)

After you gather these goods, do two more things:

- ✔ **Protect her ears.** For dogs, water in the ear is very uncomfortable. To keep water out of the ears, place a cotton ball in each.
- ✔ **Dilute the shampoo.** Add three or four units of water to every unit of shampoo you plan to use. That way, the shampoo will lather and rinse more easily.

Now you're ready to get bubbly! Follow these steps to safely bathe your Beagle:

1. **Lay the bathmat in the tub to keep your Beagle's feet steady.**

2. **Carefully lift her into the tub.**

   Keep a steady hand. If your Beagle hasn't yet learned to appreciate the joys of bath time, keep a hand on her while she's in the tub so she can't hop out easily. And in the unlikely event that she does make a break from the tub, keep the bathroom door closed so she doesn't go racing all over your home before you've finished.

3. **With a hand-held shower attachment or a small bowl, pour warm (never hot!) water over your dog, making sure the water goes all the way down to the skin.**

   Start at the top of the head and neck, and then wet the length of the backbone. After that, water her sides, chest, legs, and tail.

4. **Apply enough diluted shampoo to create lather all over the dog's body.**

   Don't OD on the suds. Billowy clouds or multiple floating bubbles mean you've laid the lather on way too thick.

5. **When your Beagle's in a full-body lather, use the shower attachment or bowl to rinse her off.**

   Perform the rinse in the same order you performed the initial wet-down: front to back, top to bottom.

   Make sure you get every last bit of soap off your Beagle; an incomplete rinse will leave her skin flaky, dry, and itchy. Keep pouring on the water for five minutes or until the rinse water runs clear — whichever comes last.

6. **Block the tub and let her shake.**

   With your Beagle still in the tub, hold a bath towel up in front of you so it's between you and your dog. At this point, she'll shake the excess water off her coat — but thanks to the towel, that excess water won't get on you.

7. **Gently lift your Beagle out of the tub and wrap her in a dry towel to speed up the drying process.**

   Don't rub, though; instead, blot the excess water from the coat and skin.

8. **Let your dog indulge in an after-bath running frenzy — after which you can towel her some more.**

   Beagles have short hair and small bodies, so you don't need to bother with a hair dryer.

And . . . that's a wrap! You're done (except for cleaning up the mess in the bathroom, of course)!

Defusing the Beagle stink bomb

Sometimes your little hound may, well, stink. She may smell bad because she's rolled around in something disgusting, such as a dead animal. That's normal doggy behavior — but if your dog engages in such behavior, her next stop should be the bathtub.

At other times, an ear infection or gum disease may be causing her icky odor. Both conditions can be cleared up with medication, regular cleaning, and possibly, a change in diet. Your vet can help you relieve both conditions.

If, however, your normally sweet-smelling Snoopy-dog suddenly sports a foul odor that you can't attribute to any single cause, take her to your vet. A sudden change in odor may signal the onset of a serious condition.

Bottom line: Don't assume your Beagle's BO is normal doggy odor. Chances are it's not.

Tending to Eyes and Ears

A Beagle's eyes and ears need special care, but you need not be a visual or audio specialist to provide the basics.

Cleaning the windows to the soul

Keeping your Beagle's eyes clean is a snap and really only needs to be done whenever you see any little eye crumbs at the inner corners. Just like with you, these crumbs are most likely to appear after she's had a nap — and after a nap may be the best time to remove them.

The only equipment you need is a bit of cotton or small cloth. To tidy up your little friend's eyes:

1. **Have your dog sit in front of you.**

2. **Gently wipe the inner corners of her eyes with the cotton or cloth.**

If you see any goopy, colored discharge from the eye, a red or inflamed eye, cloudiness of the eye, sensitivity to light, or if your dog frequently paws at her eye, take her to a veterinarian as soon as possible. She may have a serious vision problem, and prompt treatment is essential.

Wiping out the ears

A Beagle's ears need more attention than the eyes do. That's because the little hound's long, floppy ears provide a perfect breeding ground for fungi and bacterial infections. The *ear flap* (that's the floppy part) covers the rest of the ear and restricts air flow in and out of it. The result: a perpetually moist ear and lots of potential for ear trouble.

Weekly cleaning can keep the ears dry and help them stay infection free. To do the job right, you need some cotton balls and an ear cleaner made especially for dogs.

Ear cleaners are available from your veterinarian, but you can also make your own by combining two parts water with one part white vinegar in a squirt bottle.

After you've secured your Beagle's ear gear, follow these steps:

1. **Have your dog either sit or lie down.**

2. **Squirt a little bit of cleaner into the ear.**

   If your dog doesn't like to have cleaner squirted directly into her ear, saturate the cotton ball with ear cleaner. Then, place the cotton ball in the dog's ear (but not too far into the canal). Squeeze the cotton ball so the cleaner flows from the cotton ball into the ear canal.

3. **Fold the flap over the ear and massage the base of the ear for about one minute. Let your Beagle shake her head.**

4. **Use your cotton ball to clean the visible parts of the ear, as shown in Figure 10-2.**

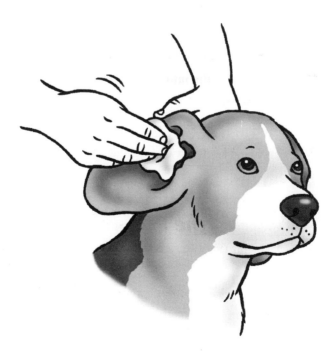

Figure 10-2: Regular cleaning keeps your Beagle's ears healthy.

If your Beagle shakes her head a lot, runs her ears along the ground often, paws at her ears, or has a dark, goopy discharge, she probably has an ear infection. The same is true if your dog's ears smell like baking bread. Take her to the vet. Ear infections are not a trivial matter. They're very painful to your Snoopy-dog — and if left untreated can result in permanent hearing loss.

Brushing Those Pearlies

When your Beagle yawns, do you want to give her a breath mint? If so, your dog isn't alone. According to the American Veterinary Dental College, more than 80 percent of all dogs and cats show signs of dental disease by the age of 3 — and bad breath is a sure sign that dental disease is present (see Chapter 12). This condition not only makes your Beagle not so nice to be near, but also could lead to tooth loss and even bacterial infections in other parts of the body.

However, all those problems are preventable. All you have to do is brush your Beagle's teeth once daily, or at least three or four times a week. Brushing removes the food particles and other crud that coats the teeth with plaque and creates a breeding ground for dental disease.

Before you tackle your Beagle's teeth, you need to have these items on hand:

✔ A soft toothbrush that's designed for either pets or children

✔ Toothpaste created especially for dogs

Don't use human toothpaste; it can upset your Beagle's stomach. Besides, doggy toothpaste — which comes in flavors like chicken and beef — will taste much better to your Beagle.

Here's how to do the job:

1. **Put enough toothpaste on the toothbrush to cover half to two-thirds of the brush. Have your dog sit in front of you.**

2. **Lift your dog's lips and gently brush the outer surfaces of her teeth. Figure 10-3 shows how to pull back the lip.**

   Brush vertically, from one side of the mouth to the other; one pass ought to do it. (Your dog probably won't tolerate any more brushing than that!) Don't worry about the inner surfaces; your Beagle's tongue keeps those areas clean.

   And unlike when we brush our teeth, your Beagle won't need to rinse or have a towel nearby for dainty mouth wipes.

If your four-legged friend has never used a toothbrush before, get a finger brush from your local pet supply store, or just wrap some gauze around your finger. Rub her gums gently with the gauze or finger brush until she's used to having you work with her mouth. Then, gradually introduce her to the toothbrush.

3. Bribe your Beagle with a short walk or play with her for a few minutes after each session with the toothbrush.

A Beagle who can expect something nice to happen right after a brushing is much more likely to put up with the procedure than one who's got nothing to look forward to.

4. Brush at the same time every day.

Having a schedule helps you to remember to brush daily. An added bonus: If your Beagle expects her brushing at a particular time, she may be more amenable to the procedure.

Alas, some dogs simply don't tolerate having their teeth brushed. If your dog is one of them, try giving her special plaque-reducing foods and plaque-fighting treats.

Figure 10-3: Brush your dog's teeth daily to keep her healthy all over.

Trimming the Tootsies

If you saw a Beagle clunking down the street wearing the latest pair of Manolo Blahnik high heels, you'd probably think she looked pretty silly, right? And you'd probably shudder over the strain the poor dog would be putting on her feet and legs.

Well, if you let your Beagle's toenails grow too long, your Snoopy-dog suffers the same way she would if she had her own pair of Manolos — and she doesn't look nearly as good. Overgrown toenails throw your Beagle off balance and can cause her to suffer any number of painful injuries. Regular nail trimmings, however, can prevent such mishaps and keep your Beagle on her right (and left) feet.

The nails should be short enough to be off the ground when she's standing still, and her dew claws (the nails that are found higher up on the leg near the ankle) should be trimmed short enough to prevent them from curving back into the skin of the leg.

You only need a few things to give your dog a pedicure:

✔ A pair of nail clippers designed just for dogs

✔ Styptic powder (available in pharmacies) or baking flour in case you cut the quick

✔ Lots of yummy treats (at least 20 of them!)

Here's how to trim her toenails and help your Beagle put her best foot forward:

1. Have your dog either sit or lie down.

She should be relaxed, and you should be able to reach her paws.

TV time can be a good time to give your dog a nail trim. That's because many dogs relax when they watch the tube with their people.

2. Look for the *quick,* the blood vessel inside the toenail that runs almost to the end of the nail.

Light nails make the quick easy to see; it's the pink area inside the nail. With dark nails, you can't see the quick, so you have to guess where it is.

3. **Pick up one of your Beagle's paws, and gently squeeze it to extend the nails a bit. Place the clippers around the very end of one nail, as Figure 10-4 shows. Squeeze the clippers quickly to trim off the nail tip.**

4. **Continue trimming a little at a time until you see the black dot in the center of the trimmed nail.**

   The black dot is where the quick starts.

5. **Stay calm and apply some styptic powder or baking flour to the nail if you cut the quick.**

   If you accidentally trim the nail too short and hit the quick, the nail will bleed — a lot. Don't panic. The bleeding will stop very quickly after you apply styptic powder or flour.

6. **Give your Beagle a treat each time you finish trimming a nail.**

   Keep rewarding her, one nail at a time. Many dogs decide that pedicures are tolerable if they get a few treats during the process.

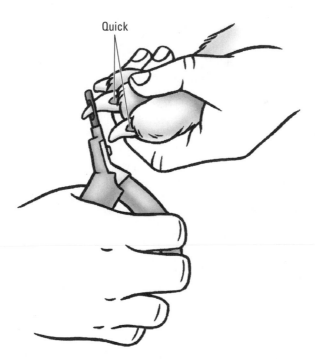

Quick

Figure 10-4: Be careful to avoid cutting the quick when you trim the nail.

Addressing Your Beagle's Bottom Line

No question about it: A Beagle's bottom is cute. One look at that wiggly tush (the wiggles come from that perpetually wagging tail) and you'll be hooked — if the Snoopy-dog's big soulful eyes haven't won your heart already.

But at times, the Beagle's bottom may turn into a real pain in the you-know-what for her. You may see her rub her derrière along the ground after she poops, or perhaps her rear end is sporting a very strong and totally unpleasant odor. Either of these conditions may indicate a common but painful problem: full *anal sacs.*

Every Beagle has two of these little sacs, one on each side of her *anus* (also known as the *rectum,* the opening through which the dog poops). Normally when a dog poops, the sacs release a little bit of incredibly strong-smelling fluid that helps the dog mark territory and leave her calling card. In other words, the fluid identifies the deposit that your Beagle leaves after a bowel movement as *her* deposit.

Sometimes, though, the glands around the anus produce more fluid than the sacs are capable of holding, or the small openings in the sacs become clogged with fluid. That's when your Beagle may start dragging her butt along the ground — a behavior that experts call *scooting* — and you notice a very strong-smelling odor emanating from her tush.

The way to stop the scooting, eliminate the odor, and relieve your Beagle's discomfort is to release — or, in veterinarian-speak, *express* — the excess fluid from the anal sacs. Any veterinarian and most professional groomers are happy to do this literally stinky and certainly unappealing job for you for a nominal charge. But if you want to do the job yourself, you can.

You will definitely want to have some latex gloves and plenty of tissues for this procedure. After the worst is over, you'll also need some petroleum jelly.

Here's what to do:

1. **Take your Beagle to an area such as the bathroom or anyplace else where the floor can be cleaned easily.**

2. **Put on some latex gloves.**

3. **Lift your dog's tail with one hand, and with the other pick up some tissues.**

4. **With the tissued hand, feel around the anus for the anal sacs, which are located at approximately the four o'clock and eight o'clock positions with respect to the anus (see Figure 10-5).**

   If they're full, you'll feel two little bumps at those positions.

5. **Cover the anus with tissues (trust me, you do not want to skip this step!).**

6. **With your fingers on the anal sacs (remember four o'clock and eight o'clock), gently press inward.**

   If your fingers are placed correctly, you'll feel the sacs begin to empty, and you'll see fluid on the tissues that cover the anus. If nothing happens, try repositioning your fingers until you feel the sacs begin to empty.

7. **Continue until no more fluid emerges onto the tissues.**

8. **Apply a little bit of petroleum jelly to the anus and surrounding area to soothe them.**

Figure 10-5: Be gentle when you express your Beagle's anal sacs.

Winterizing Your Beagle

Keeping your Beagle happy and healthy and comfortable in all seasons isn't hard to do. The Snoopy-dog is a hardy soul, and a few adjustments are all that's needed to keep her in tip-top condition all year round, especially during the winter.

The winter-time Beagle may experience the same cold-weather phenomena as the winter-time human: dry, flaky skin. But while human beings can slather on moisturizers and lotions to combat the dryness, your Beagle's dry skin may need treatment from within. Make sure your dog gets plenty of water, and talk with your veterinarian about adding fatty acid supplements to her diet.

We humans have lots of shoes and boots with which to cover our feet during the winter, but dogs generally have the dubious pleasure of walking barefoot over snow and ice. Be considerate of your Beagle. If she's running outside in the snow, make sure you remove any snow or ice that's accumulated between her toes after she gets inside. Leaving those little ice balls intact can spread your Beagle's toes in a most uncomfortable fashion.

During the winter, your considerate neighbors may sprinkle rock salt on their sidewalks to make them less slippery. But while that salt helps keep you upright, it causes your Beagle's sensitive paw pads to dry out and burn. When you and your pooch walk outside during snow season, try to avoid walking her over salted surfaces. If you can't avoid those surfaces, thoroughly rinse your Beagle's feet with warm water when you come back inside.

Bundling up Beagle

Does your Beagle need a sweater to keep her toasty warm during the winter? Probably not, but that doesn't mean she wouldn't appreciate a little help staying warm during those cold winter walks. Pet stores and upscale pet clothing catalogs abound with sweaters and coats to protect Beagles and other canine snow-bunnies (how's that for a contradiction in terms?) from the ravages of Old Man Winter.

How do you know which size is right for your Beagle? First, stretch a tape measure from the base of her neck to the base of her tail. This is her *top line* measurement. Then, measure her chest by wrapping the tape measure around her trunk at the widest point, just behind her front legs. Those two measurements can help you determine your Beagle's clothing size. Generally, Beagles wear a medium — but as with so many other issues, your mileage may vary.

Chapter 11

Managing Your Beagle's Day-to-Day Health

*M*aintaining your Beagle's health means much more than schlepping him to the vet for periodic shots and when he feels sick. You, not your vet, are your dog's primary health-care provider, and you can do a lot right from your own home to keep your little hound in tip-top condition.

That said, you certainly need not (and should not) go it alone when taking care of your Beagle. Your veterinarian is ready to be your partner in your ongoing effort to maintain your dog's health. This chapter outlines what you need to know and do — both on your own and with your vet's help — to keep your Beagle healthy and happy.

Working with Your Vet

Your friendly veterinarian plays an important role in keeping you on track in your efforts to keep your Beagle healthy. He's got the professional training to be the perfect partner for you, the loving owner. His knowledge of overall canine health, coupled with your knowledge of your own, very individual Snoopy-dog, give your dog the best possible odds for living a healthy, happy life.

The wellness exam

Just as you need regular checkups from your doctor, so too does your dog. Most experts suggest bringing your Beagle in for a wellness exam once a year until he turns 8 or 9 years old. At that point, you can consider him to be a senior citizen, and he should see his vet for wellness exams twice a year instead of just once.

But just what is a *wellness exam?* Simple: It's a checkup that a doctor or veterinarian gives the patient when that patient is believed to be free of illness. The exam provides a baseline against which to measure future changes in health status.

During a complete wellness exam, your vet will

- ✔ Measure your dog's vital signs, such as weight, temperature, pulse, and respiration
- ✔ Look into your dog's ears and eyes to see if there's any redness, discharge, odor, or any other signs of ear and eye disease
- ✔ Run his hands over your Beagle's bod to determine if he's got any lumps, bumps, or tender areas
- ✔ Check the heart, lungs, joints, feet, and "private areas"
- ✔ Peer at your Beagle's teeth and gums to see if any redness, puffiness, or plaque is present
- ✔ Check his skin to see if it's flaky, has a rash, or shows anything else that's out of the ordinary

Depending on how your vet clinic does things, your vet also may

- ✔ Ask you to bring in a stool and/or urine sample so he can check for intestinal parasites, nutritional problems, and/or urinary tract infections.
- ✔ Give your dog some shots or other immunizations. But then again, he may not. The next section explains why.

To immunize or not to immunize?

Not so long ago, there was only one answer to the above question: Yes, you should immunize your dog, and you should do it every year. And there's no question that immunizations have done our dogs a world of good. They've saved many Beagles and other dogs from contracting dreaded diseases such as rabies, distemper, parvovirus, and hepatitis. They can also prevent less serious but nevertheless unpleasant conditions such as bordetella, which is also known as kennel cough. Chapter 7 describes the shots your Beagle probably will get the first time he visits your vet.

In recent years, however, many experts have begun to question whether yearly immunizations are necessary or even beneficial. These experts believe that immunizations can protect dogs from disease for much longer than a year. After all, do we get shots every year? Not by a long shot (and yes, that pun was fully intended).

Collecting free samples

If your vet needs a stool or urine sample, he can get them himself, but he'll charge you a fee to do so. Better for you, your Beagle, and your wallet to bring the samples yourself. And you can do it, without making a mess. Here's how.

To collect a stool sample:

1. **Grab a plastic bag (such as a grocery bag or the bag your daily newspaper comes in) and take your Snoopy-dog out for a walk.**

2. **When he takes a dump, turn the bag inside out and pull it over your arm.**

3. **Use the hand covered by the bag to pick up the poop. Then, with your other hand, pull the bag inside out.**

   The poop will now be inside the bag.

4. **Knot the open end, and take the poop to your vet as soon as possible.**

To collect a urine sample:

1. **Get a plastic bag and a clean plastic container such as the kind that margarine comes in.**

2. **Pull the bag over your arm, and hold the container with your bag-covered hand.**

3. **Take your little hound out for a walk and watch to see when he's about to pee.**

4. **As soon as he squats, slip the container under his tush to collect the urine that will stream out immediately thereafter. You don't need much; a teaspoon at most.**

   If some of the urine splashes on your arm, no big deal — you've got it covered!

5. **Seal the container, and take the sample to your veterinarian as soon as you can.**

Conventional or alternative medicine?

Not so long ago, veterinarians in the United States pretty much all took the same approach to treating their patients: They viewed disease as an enemy to be vanquished. The usual battle plan embodied two approaches: stopping the disease before it started or conquering the disease once it occurred. The result has been — and continues to be — a vast array of preventive treatments for dreaded diseases such as parvovirus, rabies, and distemper, and an equally large variety of medicines, surgical techniques, and similar remedies to rid the body of disease that's already taken hold. This approach is known as *conventional veterinary medicine* or *Western veterinary medicine.*

But in recent years, another approach to animal health care has gained ground. This approach, known as *alternative veterinary medicine, complementary veterinary medicine,* or *Eastern veterinary medicine,* focuses on maximizing the body's own defenses against illness. This approach to medicine uses therapies and treatments, such as acupuncture and chiropractic, that may be unfamiliar to conventional practitioners. And because this approach emphasizes treating the whole animal, not just the disease, it's sometimes known as *holistic veterinary medicine.*

So which approach is better for your Beagle?

The answer is both. The best veterinary medicine combines each of these approaches. For example, a Beagle with allergies may need the immunizations developed under the conventional approach, but may also benefit from a change in diet, which often is advocated by alternative veterinary medical practitioners. A good veterinarian will use both approaches in her practice — or, if she can't, refer you to someone who can offer the other approach if hers isn't working.

You can find out more about both approaches by checking out some Web sites such as that of the American Veterinary Medical Association (www.avma.org) and the American Holistic Veterinary Medical Association (www.ahvma.org). The latter site also contains a searchable database that enables you to find a veterinarian who specializes in holistic medicine in your state — either as the primary practitioner whom you consult or someone who works with you and your regular vet to maintain your Beagle's health.

In addition, many vets and knowledgeable owners have become concerned that yearly immunizations actually may endanger some dogs. Among the possible problems they cite:

- ✔ **Tumors:** The possibility is remote, but nevertheless real, that the dog could develop a tumor at the immunization site.

- ✔ **Negative effects on the immune system:** Frequent shots may catapult a dog's immune system into warp drive, which could trigger the onset of chronic, potentially serious autoimmune diseases, such as lupus.

For those reasons, some veterinarians suggest yearly tests for anti-bodies to specific diseases to determine whether immunizations to prevent those diseases are necessary. Others, however, believe that these tests, which are called *titers,* aren't yet accurate enough to be relied upon. Many vets compromise between the old and new theories and recommend giving shots every three years instead of annually. In fact, the American Animal Hospital Association (AAHA) recommends that after 1 year of age, dogs receive their core (essential) vaccinations — against rabies, parvovirus, and distemper — every three years. For dogs who spend a lot of time with other dogs, an annual bordetella shot is recommended.

Should your Beagle have babies?

If you're concerned that your female Beagle will worry about her biological clock if she doesn't have puppies . . . or that your male Beagle will feel like less of a guy if he doesn't have a sex life . . . think again. Your Snoopy-dog's life can be happy and fulfilling even if that life does not include sex or babies — I mean, puppies.

Or maybe you thought that by breeding your female Beagle you could show your kids the miracle of birth? Yes, maybe you could. But you'll have an awful lot of hard work to do after that birth occurs: taking care of several puppies 'round the clock, and then finding good homes for them. If you're like most parents, you barely have time to help your kids with their homework. Do you really think you're going to be able to take care of a litter of puppies? I thought not.

Show dogs get to skip surgery

There's really only one reason to refrain from spaying or neutering your Beagle, and that's if you plan to enter her or him into confor-mation dog shows. The American Kennel Club (AKC), which is the primary U.S. honcho for such shows, does not allow spayed or neutered dogs of any breed to compete. The reason behind that prohibition is based on history: Dog shows were developed in the late 19th century to showcase breeding stock to potential buyers. That thinking still applies to some extent today.

If you think you'd like to show your Beagle, though, get an expert's opinion before you begin to venture down that road. The reputable breeder from whom you bought your Beagle can tell you whether she thinks your dog has what it takes to become a breed cham-pion. And get a book that tells you what you need to know to get started in breeding. A good book to begin with is *Breeding Dogs For Dummies* by Richard G. Beauchamp (Wiley).

Chances are, if the contract from your breeder contains a mandatory spay or neuter provision, she doesn't think your little hound is dog show material. Most breeders evaluate their puppies at a very young age. They identify show prospects at that time and structure the purchase contracts for those puppies accordingly.

Ready, aim, specialize!

If you had a heart condition and needed a triple bypass, your regular family physician almost certainly would not be the person to perform the procedure. Instead, he'd probably refer you to a doctor who specializes in performing surgery on hearts: a cardiac surgeon. Similarly, if you became pregnant, your regular doctor probably would send you to a physician who specializes in prenatal care and the delivery of babies: a obstetrician/gynecologist.

The same is becoming true of veterinary medicine. If your Beagle develops a serious eye problem, your regular vet can refer you to an eye specialist: a veterinary ophthalmologist. If he develops a mysterious rash that doesn't respond to treatment, your vet would probably refer you to a veterinary dermatologist. The world of human medicine has become populated with highly skilled specialists — and so, too, has veterinary medicine.

A national professional organization for vets who work in the United States, the American Veterinary Medical Association, maintains a listing of 20 specialty organizations. Some of those groups, such as the American College of Zoological Medicine, probably don't include vets who would treat your Snoopy-dog. But specialized veterinarians who would treat your canine companion are likely to be a member of the group that represents their field, such as the American Veterinary Dental College, the American College of Veterinary Dermatology, and the American College of Veterinary Ophthalmology. You can find the most current list by logging onto the World Wide Web at www.avma.org/education/abvs/vetspecialists.asp.

Members of each specialty group are veterinarians who have completed post-graduate work in their subjects. They have to pass challenging exams that test their knowledge in their specialties. If they pass, their specialty organization certifies them as being qualified to specialize in their particular field of veterinary medicine. When you hear that a veterinarian is *board-certified,* you know that the specialist brings a ton of knowledge to the work he does with his animal patients.

Some of these specialists work together to create a large referral center. For example, about two miles away from my home is the Southpaws Veterinary Referral Center. This facility houses specialists in emergency care, holistic internal medicine, neurology, oncology, radiology, surgery, and orthopedics. Other specialists work from schools of veterinary medicine attached to large universities. To find a referral center in your area, type "veterinary referral center" into an Internet search engine, such as Google or Yahoo.

The good news about spaying, neutering

If your Beagle isn't a show prospect, there's really no sense in holding off on *spaying* (the canine equivalent of a hysterectomy, in which the dog's uterus and ovaries are removed) or *neutering* (the removal of a dog's testicles). In fact, by "fixing" your Fido or Fidette, you may well prolong your dog's life. A neutered male can't acquire testicular cancer, which is a fairly common scourge among doggy guys. A spayed female won't ever suffer from *pyometra*, a potentially serious uterine infection. And if you have her spayed before her first heat cycle, she's much less likely to develop breast cancer, which is one of the most common diseases suffered by intact female dogs.

Not convinced? Consider this: The neutered or spayed Beagle probably will behave much better than he or she would otherwise. The male Beagle will have much less of a need to mark his territory with a shot of dog pee across the bow or onto your furniture. He won't get nearly as upset as he otherwise would if he were to catch the scent of a female dog in heat and is much less likely to take off for parts unknown in search of that female. That greatly lessens his chances of getting lost or struck by a car. As for your female, she — and you — won't ever have to deal with the mess and inconvenience of coming into *heat:* a twice-a-year, one- or two-week episode that involves keeping her off the rugs and keeping her in doggy diapers to spare your furnishings from the bloody discharge that occurs.

Some veterinarians spay or neuter puppies as early as 7 weeks of age, but many others suggest waiting until the dog is 6 months old or so, when a pup may be better able to tolerate being anesthetized. In any case, you need not wait until your female Beagle comes into heat for the first time, which is usually around 6 to 9 months of age. The surgery will probably involve an overnight stay, and your Snoopy-dog will be sore for a few days as the incision heals — but that's all. And neither a boy Beagle nor a girl Beagle will miss having a sex life. Promise!

Can 1 See Your 1D?

No, no, no — I'm not discussing how to keep underage Snoopy-dogs from bellying up to the local bar and scoring illegal drinks. Beagles need several kinds of identification for other reasons: to enable them to get back home if they become lost (which is way too easy for a wandering Beagle to do), and to comply with state and local ordinances. Read on to see which forms of ID do which — and see which one you might consider not bothering with.

Playing tag (s)

Every Beagle needs to have at least two tags hanging from his collar: a tag that certifies he's been inoculated against rabies and a tag that tells people who he is. Depending on where you live, he may also need a third tag: a dog license.

Rabies tag

Your veterinarian will give you a *rabies tag* after he has inoculated your Beagle against the dreaded and always fatal disease of rabies. The tag certifies that your dog has been immunized against the disease (see Figure 11-1). Your dog needs to have this tag on his collar at all times, especially if the two of you are traveling outside your home state. That way, if your dog is injured or becomes ill while you travel, the veterinarian who takes care of him will know that he is protected against rabies and that she doesn't need to give him another rabies shot as a precautionary measure.

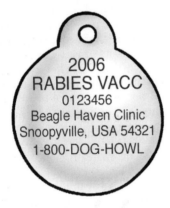

Figure 11-1: A rabies tag indicates that your Beagle is current on his rabies immunization.

Identification tag

An *identification tag* is the quickest way that a person can determine who your dog is and where he lives (see Figure 11-2). You can create these little gizmos on the spot at any local pet superstore, and the cost will be minimal. If, however, you go for fancier fare, you can order a larger, more attractive tag from an upscale pet retailer. For example, Planet Dog (www.planetdog.com) offers a round, silver-plated disk with your dog's name and address on one side and the company logo on the other.

Make sure your dog's tag includes at least his name, address, and a phone number where you can be reached.

Dog license

Many municipalities and towns require that your dog acquire still another tag: a dog license. Having a license entitles your dog to use canine facilities, such as a dog park — although you'll see plenty of people bring their dogs to such facilities without anyone checking to see if the animal has a license. Still, if your beloved but unlicensed Beagle gets loose, you may have to pay a fine to your community for having an unlicensed animal. You make the call.

Tattoo you

Until the use of microchips (discussed in the next section) became widespread as a form of identification, tattoos were the backup ID of choice for dogs. After a number is tattooed on the inside of a dog's hind leg, the number is entered into a national registry, such as the National Dog Registry (www.nationaldogregistry.com) or AKC Companion Animal Recovery (www.akccar.org). A person who finds a dog can call a veterinarian, the police, or animal control, any of whom know to look for a tattoo and contact the registry. Voilà! Your dog is then on his way home.

Figure 11-2: An identification tag gives the who and where information for your little hound.

A chip in the old (or not-so-old) Beagle

In recent years, microchips have become more popular than tattoos (refer to the previous section) as a form of permanent identification for dogs. A veterinarian can easily insert one of these chips under the skin between your Beagle's shoulder blades; the chip is just a little bit larger in diameter than a pencil lead.

At the same time your Beagle gets his microchip, you get a form that registers him with the registry that's administering the microchip, such as the AKC Companion Animal Recovery Program. Just as with the tattoo, animal pros know how to scan your dog (using a special scanning device) to see if a microchip is present. The scanning device activates a unique identification code. The person who performs the scan then calls the appropriate registry, where a recovery specialist has all of the information needed to get your Beagle safely back to you. The registry also will give you a tag that contains your Beagle's microchip number and the registry's telephone number.

However, microchipping is all for naught unless you complete the registration form and send it to the company that administers the chip. And if you move, contact the registry and tell them your new address. Make sure, too, that you register with a large microchip company, such as Home Again or AVID, both of which manufacture chips that are more easily scanned.

Have your vet insert your Beagle's microchip when she or he is being spayed or neutered. That way, you don't have to make a separate trip to the vet to have the job done.

Do not rely solely on an identification tag to help your lost Beagle find his way home. A dog can lose his collar all too easily; my own dog has done so twice — so far. A permanent form of identification such as a tattoo or microchip can reunite you with your lost dog even if he loses his collar.

Maintaining Good Health at Home

Your veterinarian is the best person to know how to treat your Beagle when he gets sick or injured. But you are the best person to know when all's right with your canine companion, and to keep him that way between visits to the vet.

Knowing what's normal

You can't know if anything's wrong with your Beagle unless you know how he looks and acts when everything's fine. That's why it's important to spend time grooming and otherwise caring for your little hound and observing how he behaves when he's free from illness.

Make it a point to note how much your Beagle usually eats during one sitting. That way, you'll know immediately when your dog's appetite is off. A lack of interest in food that lasts for more than a couple of meals can be a sign of serious trouble and warrants a call to your veterinarian.

Another behavioral clue to note is how much water your Beagle drinks when all is well. See how often, generally speaking, you need to fill his water bowl — once a day, twice a day, whatever. If you observe a sudden increase in his water intake for no obvious reason (such as being hot, thirsty from exercise, or thirsty from enjoying a chew toy), your vet needs to have a look at him.

Take note, too, of how often your Beagle does his business, and what that business looks like. Such knowledge will help you spot signs of difficulty quickly. For example, if your Beagle suddenly starts peeing more often than normal, he may have a urinary tract infection — an uncomfortable condition that requires treatment by a vet. And if your dog's stool changes in consistency or color, he could have any one of a number of intestinal ailments; some of those ailments are serious, while others may be less so. Either way, by observing those changes sooner rather than later, you can get him to the vet and start treating his problem that much quicker.

Finally, try to get a sense of what your dog's normal activity level is — whether he's a hyperactive little dynamo, a laid-back kind of a fella, or somewhere in between. Any prolonged changes in that activity level could signal the onset of a medical problem that needs your vet's attention.

Checking vital signs

Your Beagle's temperature, pulse, and respiration (TPR) are crucial measurements of his health status. If your little hound's temperature is above or below normal, if his heart rate is way faster than usual, or if his breathing is quicker than it should be, he clearly needs to see the vet pronto. But for you to know whether those vital signs are normal, you need to know what normal is and how to measure your own dog's TPR.

Table 11-1 tells you what a Beagle's normal TPR should be.

Table 11-1	Normal Vital Signs
Vital Sign	*Normal Range*
Temperature	100.5° Fahrenheit to 102.0° Fahrenheit
Pulse	60 to 140 beats per minute at rest
Respiration	10 to 30 breaths per minute at rest

Here's what you need to know to measure your Beagle's TPR.

Taking the temperature

To measure your dog's temp, gather together three items:

- A clean, digital rectal thermometer (get one just for him, but you can use any thermometer for humans from your local pharmacy)
- Some petroleum jelly
- Another person

After you've got your gear:

1. **Have the other person hold your Beagle still.**

2. **Smear some petroleum jelly on the thermometer bulb (the end with the metal tip).**

3. **Slowly and gently slide the thermometer about 1 inch into the dog's rectum.**

4. **Wait for two minutes — and gently pet your dog or engage him in another activity that will help him stay calm and still.**

5. **Remove the thermometer slowly, and read it.**

Measuring the pulse

All you need to take your pooch's pulse is yourself, him —preferably after a nap or otherwise in a relaxed state — and a timer that counts seconds. Then:

1. **Have your Beagle lie down on his side.**

   Use a treat to lure him into a Down position (see Chapter 15); then move the treat in a two o'clock or ten o'clock direction — depending on which side he prefers to lie on — to lure him into the proper position.

2. **Sit behind your Beagle and place your hand atop his hind leg.**

3. **Move your hand forward until your fingers are curled around the front of the leg.**

4. **Slide your hand upward until your hand touches the wall of your dog's abdomen (see Figure 11-3). Your hand should be resting on his inner hind leg.**

   Here, you feel a pulse beating beneath your fingers.

5. **Count the beats for 15 seconds.**

6. **Multiply that number by four, and you'll have your dog's heart rate per minute; compare that number to the normal pulse rate listed earlier in Table 11-1.**

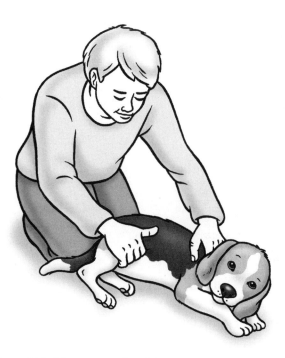

Figure 11-3: Measure your Beagle's pulse by placing your hand atop his inner hind leg.

Measuring respiration

To determine how many breaths your Beagle takes per minute, grab a timer that counts seconds, and then:

1. **Have him lie down on his side.**

   Get him into a Down position (see Chapter 15) by using a treat; then move the treat in a two o'clock or ten o'clock direction — depending on which side he prefers to lie on.

2. **With your hand resting lightly on his rib cage, count how often your hand rises in 15 seconds.**

3. **Multiply that number by four; compare that number to the normal respiration rate listed earlier in Table 11-1.**

Stocking a first-aid kit

You can be ready to deal with any illness or injury to your Beagle by stocking up on first-aid gear and medications. A portion of a bathroom medicine cabinet, a tackle box, or a toolbox are all good places to stash the following items:

- Adhesive bandages (for small wounds)
- Antibiotic ointment
- Benadryl (25 mg)
- Buffered baby aspirin
- Cotton swabs or balls
- Eyedropper
- Flexible plastic digital rectal thermometer
- Gauze sponges
- Hand wipes
- Hydrogen peroxide (to clean wounds)
- Latex gloves
- Muzzle and leash
- Nonadhesive bandages
- 1-inch adhesive tape
- Petroleum jelly (to soothe irritated areas)
- Small pair of scissors
- Soft padded gauze bandage on a roll

✔ Styptic powder or pencil

✔ Tweezers

✔ Phone number for your veterinarian and/or nearest emergency veterinary clinic

✔ Phone number for ASPCA Poison Control Center: 888-426-4435

✔ A good first-aid book, such as *First Aid for Dogs: An Owner's Guide to a Happy Healthy Pet* by Stefanie Schwartz (Howell Book House)

Giving meds

Dispensing pills or liquid medication to a dog is no fun — mainly because the dog often makes the job very difficult. Some pooches fool their owners by holding the pill in their mouths and spitting it out later (my own dog is a master at this maneuver). Others struggle so much that you may be exhausted from the wrestling match that ensues when you try to dispense the meds.

However, the job doesn't have to be difficult. With a little confidence and patience on your part, you can get a drug, whether in pill or liquid form, into your dog with ease.

The pill drill

In most cases, you can bury a pill inside some soft food such as peanut butter, cream cheese, or moist dog food. Alas, though, some dogs don't fall for this ploy: They eat the good stuff and leave the pill in the dish. If your Beagle proves to be one of these crafty canines, you'll need to dispense the pill manually. Here's how:

1. **Place your dog in a sitting position (Chapter 15 tells you how).**

2. **Tilt his head back about 45 degrees.**

3. **Gently run your fingers along his upper lips until your fingers are about halfway back along the lip line. Place a slight bit of pressure on both sides of the lips to open the mouth.**

4. **Quickly place the pill as far back on the tongue as possible.**

5. **Close the mouth and hold it.**

6. **Keeping his head tilted upward, gently rub his throat until you feel him swallow the tablet.**

Liquid potions

Administering liquid medicines is a bit trickier than dispensing pills, because they can't be readily mixed in with food. But you can still do the job. Just find a clean eyedropper and proceed as follows:

1. **Have your dog sit down (Chapter 15 can help).**

2. **Tilt his head upward and open his mouth by gently running your fingers along his lips until your fingers are halfway back along the lip line. Then exert a small amount of pressure on both side of the lips to open the mouth.**

3. **Fill the dropper with the proper amount of liquid, and inject the liquid as far into the mouth as you can.**

4. **Close the mouth, hold it shut, and stroke the throat until you feel him swallow the liquid.**

Chapter 12

Dealing with Health Issues

In This Chapter

▶ Treating common puppy and adult health problems

▶ Helping the senior Beagle

▶ Knowing what's an emergency — and what's not

▶ Bidding a fond farewell

*O*f course you're going give your Beagle the best of care. But no matter how diligent you are in your efforts to keep him healthy, eventually your dog will get sick. Some illnesses are serious; others are not. This chapter helps you determine which of your little hound's health problems are emergencies, which ones are less so — and how to deal with each, in partnership with your vet.

Treating Puppy Problems

Beagle puppies are almost always in the best of health, but occasionally a problem befalls one of these little gals. Beyond the usual cases of worms and such, a Beagle under the age of 1 year may encounter one of the following conditions.

Cherry eye

This condition results when the tissue that holds the tear-producing gland in the dog's third eyelid weakens, causing the gland to pop out of place and become visible at the inner corner of the eye. The gland looks like a cherry: round and bright red. The condition isn't painful — at least not initially — but without treatment, the tear gland can become irritated or infected, or even cease to function. For that reason, you should put in a call to your vet as soon as possible if your Beagle develops this condition.

Treatment consists of surgery that tacks the gland back into its proper position.

Chondrodysplasia

Chondrodysplasia is a big name for a relatively rare disease that keeps a Beagle very small. The condition prevents the bones and vertebrae from growing properly, resulting in deformed vertebrae and legs, and joint pain. Some people call the affected dogs "dwarf Beagles."

The disease usually shows up when the puppy is 3 to 4 weeks old. Affected puppies don't develop as quickly as their littermates, have trouble moving, and appear to be in pain. By the time the pup reaches 6 months of age, the growth plates of the bones have matured and the puppy becomes more comfortable. However, she may limp when she walks, her legs may be deformed, and her back and neck appear abnormal. An X-ray taken when the puppy is no more than 2 months old can illuminate the bone abnormalities that are the hallmarks of this disease.

Chondrodysplasia has no cure, but medications can relieve the pain that comes with the arthritis that results from this condition.

Puppy pyoderma

Sometimes a Beagle puppy develops what looks like mild acne on the hairless area of her abdomen. This condition is called *puppy pyoderma,* and it usually results from the presence of *Staphylococcus* bacteria.

Puppy pyoderma is not a serious condition. Your vet can prescribe special shampoos to treat the belly zits and speed their exit. In severe cases, he may also prescribe an antibiotic.

Handling Adult Health Challenges

Generally, the period between 1 and 8 or 9 years of age finds your Beagle in her prime. She's not as vulnerable as she was when she was a puppy, and she doesn't have to cope with the frailties of old age. Still, some maladies can befall the young and middle-aged adult Beagle. Here's a sampling of the most common.

Allergies

If your Beagle constantly scratches herself or if you just can't seem to get rid of her ear infections, she may suffer from an underlying problem: allergies. Just like people, Beagles and other dogs can develop allergic reactions to a wide variety of sources. These allergy-triggering sources can include grass, pollen, carpeting, or even certain foods.

Treatment for allergies depends on the severity of the problem and the cause. Minor problems may be controllable with simple antihistamines and dietary adjustments, such as adding fatty acid supplements. More severe problems require diagnostic testing. Depending on the results of the tests — which, in the case of food allergies, can take up to four months to perform — your vet may recommend a complete change in diet or even allergy shots.

Allergies can't be cured, but in many cases they can be controlled — with time and patience. The result, however, will be a much more comfortable Beagle.

Dental problems

The vast majority of dogs over the age of 3, including more than a few Beagles, have some sort of dental problem: bad breath, inflamed gums, and yellowing teeth. A veterinarian can take a look at your dog's teeth and confirm a diagnosis of dental disease.

Treatment of dental disease starts with a full cleaning that is performed while the dog is under anesthesia. The cleaning includes not only removing the tartar (the brown and yellow stuff) from the teeth, but also extracting any teeth that have become loose. The vet may also prescribe antibiotics to fight off any infections that the dog's dental disease may have caused.

You can prevent dental disease from occurring in the first place — simply by brushing your Beagle's teeth every day. See Chapter 10.

Hypothyroidism

Most of the time, the Beagle body does just what it's supposed to do, but occasionally the inner workings go awry. For example, if your middle-aged Beagle starts putting on weight for no apparent reason, becomes lethargic, and starts losing hair on both sides of her body, she could suffer from *hypothyroidism*. This condition occurs when the dog's thyroid gland produces insufficient levels of thyroid hormone. The skin may become scaly-looking and rough to the touch, and become infected frequently. Chronic ear infections and skin allergies also could signal the onset of this condition.

A blood test can confirm the veterinarian's diagnosis. Daily doses of synthetic thyroid hormone can control the condition and allow your Beagle to live a completely normal life.

Idiopathic epilepsy

Epilepsy is fairly common among many dog breeds, including Beagles, but very often the cause is unknown. Such epilepsy is called *idiopathic epilepsy,* and it's believed to be genetic in origin.

The first epileptic seizure usually occurs between 6 months and 4 years of age. A seizure usually starts when the dog falls on her side (unless she's already lying down). The head and neck arch, and the mouth opens wide. The limbs extend fully and begin to move in a jerky manner. The dog may lose control of her bowels or bladder, and she may froth at the mouth. The seizure probably will last about two minutes, although it can continue for longer. Afterward, the dog sleeps for about 20 minutes. When she awakens, she may walk aimlessly and be extremely hungry or thirsty.

If your Beagle has a seizure, your best immediate course of action is no action at all. Just leave her alone, unless she is near a flight of stairs — if that's the case, move her to a safe place. And keep kids and strangers away; even the nicest dog may bite during a seizure because she's scared, confused, or just completely out of it.

Your vet needs to see your Beagle if she has more than one seizure or if the seizure is accompanied by other symptoms, such as vomiting or diarrhea. Your vet will perform an extensive examination and lab tests to determine if the seizure has an obvious cause, such as a brain tumor. If nothing turns up, epilepsy is likely and the vet can prescribe medication such as phenobarbital or potassium bromide, both of which can control seizures.

Intervertebral disc disease

If your normally active Beagle suddenly stops, yelps with pain, and refuses to put weight on a paw, she may have developed a condition that's quite common to this breed: *intervertebral disc disease.*

The disease results when a *disc* — the gelatinous cushion (like a jelly doughnut) between two vertebrae — ruptures. When the rupture occurs, the vertebrae no longer have a cushion, and the ruptured disc material may protrude and press onto the spinal cord. Depending on where the rupture occurs and its severity, the dog could experience paralysis in some or all of her legs. If you notice your dog exhibiting symptoms of this disease, your dog needs to see her vet as soon as possible.

At minimum, a *myelogram* — an X-ray of the spine after a dye has been injected into the spinal fluid — is needed to determine whether a dog has disc disease. However, the myelogram may not reveal a disc rupture. In such cases, the veterinarian will order a CT scan or magnetic resonance imaging (MRI) to confirm the diagnosis.

The treatment for disc disease depends on how severe the problem is. For relatively mild cases, a month of strict confinement to a crate (the dog can't leave the crate except to eliminate) plus administration of an anti-inflammatory medication may help. For more severe cases — or if the problem recurs — surgery to relieve the pressure on the spinal cord and remove the disc is the treatment of choice, followed by several weeks of crate rest.

Easing Your Beagle's Golden Years

The Beagle enters her senior years at around 8 to 10 years of age. Why the range? Because every Beagle is an individual. The care she's been given, her genes, and her luck all play a role in determining not only her lifespan but also when she enters the twilight of that lifespan. Rather than assume that your little hound is a golden oldie at an arbitrary point in time, see if she's showing signs of impending seniorhood. Those signs include:

✔ **Slowing down:** Aging dogs aren't all that different from aging people — both species move more slowly than when they were younger. As your Snoopy-dog enters her golden years, she'll probably take more time lying down for a nap, getting up from that nap, and getting up and down the stairs than she did when she was a youngster. She also probably won't want to chase a ball or retrieve a Frisbee for as long as she used to.

✔ **Getting grayer:** Gray or white hair, especially around the eyes and muzzle, is a strong indicator of seniorhood.

✔ **Having accidents:** Many aging Beagles appear to forget proper potty protocol. The causes can range from simply having an aging bladder to developing a condition called *cognitive dysfunction syndrome* (CDS), which I discuss in a later section of this chapter.

✔ **Being "out of it":** The senior Beagle who seems to get lost in her own backyard or ignore you when you call her may simply be showing her age. At this point in time, many dogs lose some of their hearing or vision, which can cause them to act disoriented.

✔ **Freaking out more often:** Loud noises, such as fireworks and thunderstorms, may not have upset your Beagle during her youth, but that could change once she hits seniorhood.

Although all these developments may herald the onset of canine old age, they could also signal the presence of serious illness. Don't attribute any of these changes to mere seniorhood; have your vet check your Beagle over.

Checkups are, in fact, a great way to help your Beagle's seniorhood be truly golden. Start by stepping up her wellness exams. Most vets want to see your aging Beagle twice a year rather than once a year once she's truly an oldie-but-goodie. The reason: Frequent checkups give your vet that much more opportunity to uncover any possible problems.

In between visits, keep a careful eye on your senior Snoopy-dog for any changes in her physical demeanor or behavior. Some of those changes can mean the onset of diseases or conditions that are common to senior Beagles. Here are a few.

Arthritis

Arthritis is most commonly found among older dogs, although it can strike a dog of any age. When the cartilage that covers the bones becomes worn, the bones that form the joints rub up against each other. The joints become inflamed, and painful arthritis results.

The arthritic Beagle has more trouble getting around than the more agile Snoopy-dog does and may have trouble lying down for a nap or getting up from one. Negotiating stairs and taking walks may become challenging.

To confirm a diagnosis, your dog's vet needs to examine the affected limb(s) and the rest of the body. He may also take X-rays of the affected joints. Fortunately, remedies for arthritis abound. They include:

- ✔ **Nonsteroidal anti-inflammatory drugs (NSAIDs):** These range from common aspirin to state-of-the-art meds such as Rimadyl and Deramaxx.

- ✔ **Nutritional supplements:** Glucosamine and chrondroitin sulfate are examples. They come in tablets, liquid, or injectable form.

- ✔ **Acupuncture:** The traditional Chinese healing method employs specially placed needles to bring the body into proper balance.

- ✔ **Dietary adjustments:** Reducing the amount of food your dog eats helps pare poundage from an overweight Beagle and thus reduces strain on the joints.

- ✔ **Surgery:** Your vet may suggest this in certain cases.

Giving your arthritic Beagle moderate exercise can do a great deal to alleviate arthritis pain. One or two daily walks, regular swims, or other gentle, regular exercise can help a stiff, sore Beagle stay a little more limber and reduce her discomfort. Most importantly, keep your dog slim enough so you can feel her ribs. A sleek physique lessens strain on the joints.

Cancer

Cancer is one of the most common diseases to strike dogs of any age. According to the Animal Cancer Institute at the University of Colorado, one in five dogs will develop cancer during her lifetime. Those odds rise considerably when a dog ages. The Veterinary Cancer Center at the University of Colorado reports that 45 percent of all dogs over the age of 10 die from cancer.

The signs of canine cancer are similar to those of human cancer. They include:

- Abnormal swellings that persist or continue to grow
- Appetite loss
- Bleeding or discharge from any body opening
- Difficulty breathing, urinating, or defecating
- Difficulty eating or swallowing
- Hesitation to exercise or loss of stamina
- Offensive, unexplained odor
- Persistent lameness or stiffness
- Sores that don't heal
- Unexplained weight loss

In addition, seizures, unresolved vomiting, and a change in demeanor can signal the onset of cancer, particularly if one or more symptoms in the list above also are present.

Canine cancer can take many forms. Among the most common are lymphoma (cancer of the lymphatic system), skin cancers, and bone cancer. A cancer diagnosis is not necessarily a death sentence for a dog. Treatment can include surgery, chemotherapy (the good news here: Dogs generally tolerate chemo much better than people do), radiation, and a change in diet. In addition, many scientists are working aggressively to improve treatments for cancer in dogs.

What about health insurance?

In theory, pet health insurance sounds like a great idea. Just like with human beings, health insurance for pets allows you to prepay some of the future veterinary costs that your Beagle is likely to incur. However, theory and practice aren't always identical. Before you sign up for any health insurance plan for your little hound, look carefully at the deductibles and reimbursement rates, and crunch some numbers. Check, too, for strange conditions or exceptions. For example, at least one major health insurer covers the cost of spaying or neutering but not the cost of the anesthesia required for either procedure (no, I'm not kidding).

Your objective here is to make sure that you don't end up paying more for your Beagle's health care than you would if you hadn't signed up for insurance at all.

Cognitive dysfunction syndrome

One of the many ways that humans and dogs are similar is that both can acquire a disease in which proteins form plaque deposits on the brain. These deposits cause a wide range of behavioral changes, including apathy, anxiety, confusion, disorientation, and a changed sleep cycle. In human beings, the condition is known as Alzheimer's disease; in dogs, the disease is called *cognitive dysfunction syndrome* (CDS).

To diagnose CDS, a veterinarian may perform blood tests, urinalysis, testing of thyroid and adrenocortical hormone levels, and CT scans or magnetic resonance imaging (MRI) scans.

Two treatments can help delay the effects of CDS.

- **Anipryl:** The U.S. Food and Drug Administration (FDA) has approved this drug specifically to help reduce the symptoms of CDS.

- **Prescription Diet Canine b/d:** Hills Pet Foods, which manufactures the product, says this food is designed to combat the effects of aging on the canine brain, even when those effects are as extreme as CDS symptoms can be.

Diabetes

Many breeds, including Beagles, can acquire *diabetes*, which results when the pancreas produces insufficient insulin, a hormone that enables the body to process sugar in the blood. Older dogs and overweight dogs are especially vulnerable. Symptoms include:

✔ Increased thirst and urination

✔ Weight loss despite an increased appetite

✔ Cloudiness of the eye

Blood tests and analysis of a urine sample confirm the diagnosis. Treatment is the same as for humans: injections of the insulin the body can't produce by itself. The condition can't be cured, but a lifelong program of medication, nutritional management (to reduce or maintain weight), and regular exercise can enable the diabetic Beagle to live a long, healthy life.

Even if your Beagle is disease free, you need to adjust your routines to your little hound's age. If the stairs are getting to be too much for her, pick her up and carry her. If her eyesight is failing, reconsider whether you want to rearrange your furniture. If her hearing is on the wane, start teaching her how to respond to hand signals as well as audio cues (Chapter 14 shows you how). If her metabolism is slowing down and she's starting to look a little pudgy, adjust her food regimen accordingly.

My Beagle Is Sick! What Should I Do?

No matter how careful you are with your Snoopy-dog, the time will come when she's clearly not feeling well. But even though your Beagle may exhibit symptoms of illness that frighten you, not all of those symptoms signal the presence of a life-threatening or even serious condition. In this section, I identify signs of illness that require an immediate trip to your vet or emergency clinic, signs that require a phone call, and signs that may not signify illness at all.

Call the doggy ambulance

There's no such thing as an ambulance for dogs (at least not that I know of), but the following symptoms should prompt you to get your Beagle to your veterinarian or emergency clinic immediately.

Breathing problems

If your Beagle seems to be having trouble breathing, she needs to see her vet right away. She could be suffering from life-threatening heart or lung problems, pneumonia, heartworms, anemia (perhaps caused by an undetected internal injury), or obstructions in the respiratory tract. Even excess weight can force your four-legged friend to literally gasp for breath. A runny nose qualifies, too. If your Beagle has a cloudy or bloody nasal discharge, she needs a vet's attention immediately.

Changed gum color

If your Beagle's normally pink gums turn white, blue, yellow, or red, get her to a vet pronto. The various colors may indicate anemia, shock, breathing problems, liver or gall bladder disease, blood poisoning, severe infection, or heat stroke. Unexplained bruising of the gums is an emergency, too.

Hyperthermia

Hyperthermia is the condition that results when a dog is overheated — and an overheated dog is a dog whose life is in danger. She's likely to be panting to an extreme, have a dark red tongue and gums, and be extremely lethargic. She also may be confused, experience shallow or rapid breathing, vomit blood, and collapse.

Have someone else phone your vet while you cool down your dog. Immerse her body in a tub of tepid to cool (but not icy) water, spray her with water from a hose that's not been out in the sun, or apply cold wet compresses to her face, neck, feet, and armpits. After the soaking, get her to a vet so she can be treated for any problem resulting from the excessive heat.

 Never, ever leave your Beagle in a parked car when the outdoor temperature is 70 degrees or more, not even in the shade with some windows rolled partway down. The interior temperature can exceed 100 degrees in a matter of minutes and kill your little hound.

Hypothermia

If your Beagle has cold legs or rigid muscles, shivers deeply, and acts lethargic, she may be experiencing *hypothermia,* the opposite of hyperthermia. Wrap your dog in blankets, put her in your car, and hot-foot it to your vet's.

 Your Beagle's coat is too short to protect her against extremely cold temps for very long. If you're going to be out on a frigid day for more than a few minutes, put on her doggy coat or sweater.

Obvious trauma

If your Beagle experiences any clearly traumatic event, such as a fall or being hit by a car, she needs to see a vet right away, even if she seems to be OK. She could have a life-threatening internal injury.

Persistent vomiting

A Beagle who vomits frequently over several hours — particularly if the vomitus contains blood or foreign material — may have a major malady. The many possible causes include ingesting a foreign object, poisoning, pancreatitis, kidney disease, cancer, or inflammatory bowel syndrome. Some of these causes are life-threatening, while others aren't. But only a vet can tell you why your dog can't keep anything down, and to do that, he needs to see her. For that reason, persistent vomiting qualifies as a symptom that requires a vet's immediate attention.

If you think your dog's problem is caused by poisoning, have someone call the ASPCA Animal Poison Control Center. The specialists there can determine what antidote your Beagle needs, and the caller can forward that info to you and your vet. A phone consult to the center costs $55; you can pay with plastic. The phone number is 888-426-4435. More info is available at www.aspca.org/apcc.

Significant bleeding

If your Beagle bleeds from anywhere so extensively that the bleeding continues even after a pressure bandage has been applied for 15 to 20 minutes, she needs to see a vet right away. Bleeding that spurts or pulses outward for any length of time also requires a vet's immediate attention.

If you accidentally cut the quick of your dog's nail while trimming, don't panic and don't call your vet. Just check out Chapter 10.

Staggering

Is your Beagle walking as though she's had several beers too many? If so, she may have ingested antifreeze — a potentially fatal dietary indiscretion — or have a metabolic problem. Get her to a vet pronto.

Sudden collapse

A Beagle whose legs suddenly buckle underneath her needs to see a vet pronto, even if she remains conscious. She could be suffering from heart problems or the worsening of an illness.

Sudden eye change

An eye that suddenly becomes red, changes color, or shows a change in the size of the pupil needs prompt veterinary attention. Possible causes are *glaucoma,* which leads to blindness if not treated promptly, or another eye condition called *anterior uveitis.*

Give your vet a heads-up

The symptoms listed here may signal problems that are potentially serious but not immediately life-threatening. Your best response to these problems is to call your veterinarian as soon as possible. If you first notice any of these symptoms after hours, though, it's okay to wait until morning to make the call.

Appetite changes

If your Beagle bypasses her meal more than a couple of times, she could have a serious medical problem. The same is true if your dog suddenly starts eating much more food than usual. Increased food intake is a common symptom of diabetes, a condition that often befalls older dogs.

Bad breath

Hoochy poochie breath is no laughing matter, despite all the joking references to "dog breath" that we hear. Your foul-mouthed Beagle may have dental disease — discussed earlier in this chapter — or other problem such as diabetes, kidney disease, sinus problems, or a problem with her immune system. All require a vet's attention.

Behavioral changes

A sudden or extreme change in your Beagle's behavior or personality can indicate that something physical is amiss. A disoriented older dog may have cognitive dysfunction syndrome or may be losing her eyesight or hearing. Lethargy and depression can signal the presence of many dangerous conditions.

If your dog's personality has changed significantly, check on your own for any physical signs of illness — but also call your vet. Share with him what you've discovered to put your Beagle on the road to recovery that much faster.

Body odor

A Beagle with BO is not necessarily normal. Unless your dog has rolled in something gross, her stinkiness could result from *seborrhea* (which also causes hair loss, flaking, and greasy skin), an infected wound, or cancer. In any case, she needs a vet's attention.

Constipation

A dog who goes for more than two days without taking a dump may simply be constipated, or may have an intestinal blockage caused by a foreign object or a tumor. Call your vet.

Diarrhea

All dogs get the runs sometime, often more than once. Such instances usually result from a dietary goof or a tummy bug. A 12-hour fast, followed by a bland diet of hamburger and rice, usually gives the digestive tract time to recover. But if your Beagle's diarrhea lasts for more than a day, put in a call to your vet. Call sooner if she exhibits any other symptoms listed in this chapter.

Hair loss

Doggy baldness is not normal. If your dog is losing so much hair that she's got bald spots, she could be suffering from one of several conditions. Call your vet.

Lameness

The Beagle who favors one leg over the others needs to see her vet as soon as possible. This condition isn't a dire emergency, but it could reflect serious problems that range from arthritis to bone cancer. A dog who favors one leg, then the other, may have arthritis or a heart valve infection. Either way, she needs to see her vet.

Lumps and bumps

If you find a lump under your Snoopy-dog's skin, call your vet as soon as possible during business hours, and make an appointment for him to see your four-legged friend. But don't panic: The lump may not be cancerous. Warts, fatty tumors, and cysts also can make your dog feel lumpy. Your vet can tell you what's going on.

Sores that don't heal

A cut or sore that doesn't heal may signal a serious condition such as cancer, or a less serious (but frustrating) condition called *acral lick granuloma*. Either way, the dog needs to see her veterinarian, who can run the proper tests and determine the cause of the problem.

Stinky ears

A stinky-eared Beagle is probably a pretty unhappy Beagle. Her problem probably results from a painful ear infection. If such infections occur frequently, they may reflect an underlying problem such as allergies or hypothyroidism. Successful treatment requires a vet to address not only the infection itself but also determine the cause.

Unexplained weight gain or loss

A Beagle who's porking out or getting skinny for no clear reason could be more than a little sick. If you notice a change in your Beagle's bod either way, but can't figure out why, make that call.

Unusual fatigue

If your Beagle seems to suddenly lose energy and fails to regain it, your vet needs to know. Such lethargy could be a symptom of anemia, kidney disease, liver disease, hypothyroidism, obesity, arthritis, or cancer.

Weird-looking poop

Poop that changes from its usual color or otherwise looks odd could signal one of many problems, and requires a vet's attention. Unusual-looking poop includes:

- ✔ **Black or dark brown poop:** This indicates bleeding that could result from a tumor, an ulcer, kidney or liver problems, or inflammatory bowel disease. Other possibilities are parasites, a bleeding tooth, bleeding in the mouth, dental disease, or even swallowing the blood that results from an overlicked paw.

- ✔ **Grayish, greasy-looking poop:** Poop that looks like this may indicate that your Beagle can't digest the fats in his food. Other possible causes of gray poop may be urinary stones, a tumor, or an inflammation of the pancreas.

Not to worry . . .

The following conditions appear worrisome but actually don't require a vet's attention.

Butt-dragging

Nothing is seriously wrong if your Beagle starts dragging her bottom across the ground. The likely cause is anal sacs that need to be *expressed,* or emptied. You can do this thankless task yourself by following the steps in Chapter 10, or you can ask your vet to do the job.

Cloudy discharge from the penis

If your Beagle boy discharges a bit of cloudy stuff from his penis, watch his bathroom behavior. If he has no problems peeing, there's no need to call the vet.

Noisy breathing

Sometimes a dog starts to breathe in a way that resembles a human asthma attack. Vets call such breathing *reverse sneezing,* and it's nothing to worry about. The condition generally abates within a few minutes — but if it doesn't, call your vet.

Saying Goodbye to Your Beagle

Living with a Beagle — or, for that matter, any dog — has to be one of life's greatest joys. But for all those joys, dog ownership brings one sorrow that is almost certainly inevitable: We almost always live longer than our dogs do. That means the time will come when you will need to face your Beagle's impending death and say good-bye to her.

In all likelihood, that time will come when your Beagle is 10 to 14 years old. In some unfortunate instances, it could occur sooner; if you and your Snoopy-dog are very lucky, it will occur later. No matter when the end comes, however, you need to be prepared for it — not only for your sake but also for your dog's.

Fortunately, we can limit the suffering of our canine companions and allow them to die with dignity, thanks to euthanasia. But with this ability comes the responsibility to use this power wisely — to know when the time is right to euthanize. How can you tell when the time has come? Answering these questions can give you clues:

- ✔ **How's my Beagle doing?** If your dog is still interested in the world around her, eating with gusto, and enjoying your company, she may be able to stick around a little longer. On the other hand, if she's apathetic, in constant pain, and losing her appetite, now may be the right time to let her go.

- ✔ **How am I doing?** Your state of mind should count for something in this decision. If your Beagle has a terminal illness but still seems healthy, you may not want to euthanize her yet. On the other hand, if you're providing nursing care for your terminally ill dog — and if that care is becoming more than you can handle physically, emotionally, and financially — it may be time to consider euthanasia.

- ✔ **What will happen?** Find out from your vet how your dog's condition will progress. If your dog will suffer or lose her dignity, or if you and your family will face undue hardship, now may be the time to let her go.

When you've decided that the time has come to let your dog go, you can follow these suggestions to make the process a little easier:

- ✔ **Make arrangements with your veterinarian beforehand, if at all possible.** Most clinics will allow you to pay for the procedure in advance and will allow you to choose how you want your dog's body to be disposed.

✔ **Try to book your appointment at the end of the day.** This allows your vet to spend some time with you and not have to rush off to see another patient.

✔ **Arrange to be off work at the time of the procedure, if you can.** At this time, it's hard to even put up a pretense of working, much less actually get something done.

The procedure is brief and painless for your Beagle. Your vet or a technician probably will prepare an intravenous catheter (IV) and place it in one of your dog's veins. The vet then pumps a sedative through the IV to cause your dog to go to sleep, and then administers the euthanasia solution. Some vets do the procedure in one step.

Many owners choose to stay with their pets during the euthanasia procedure. If you can maintain sufficient composure to comfort your Beagle, you won't regret having stayed with her as she goes to a better place. On the other hand, if you can't bear the thought of watching your Beagle die, don't feel you have to stay — your reaction could add to your dog's stress. Either way, you are in the best position to decide what's best for both of you.

Afterward, you're likely to feel devastated — but, if your Beagle had a prolonged illness, you may also feel relief. Either feeling is okay. What's important is that you've given your Beagle the gift of a dignified death — the final gift in life that was filled with love.

For more information on euthanizing a beloved canine companion — making the decision, experiencing the actual process, and coping with the aftermath — consult my own book, *Senior Dogs For Dummies* (Wiley), which contains an extensive discussion on coping with the end of a beloved dog's life.

Chapter 13

Traveling (or Not) with Your Beagle

*I*nto almost every person's life comes some travel — but if you have a Beagle, travel leads to questions: What shall I do with my dog? Should I take him with me — and if so, how? Should I leave him home — and if so, with whom? Should I take him somewhere else — and if so, where?

This chapter answers those questions — or, more accurately, helps you find answers that are best for you, your Beagle, and the circumstances in which you find yourself traveling.

Taking Your Beagle with You

Does the thought of leaving your Snoopy-dog behind when you go away on vacation induce more than just a pang of sadness? Does the idea of traveling with your little hound elicit feelings of excitement? Perhaps, then, you should give in to your feelings and take your Beagle with you when you head out of town.

Notice, though, that I say *perhaps*. Not every trip you take is one that your Beagle should take as well. It's crucial to consider whether the trip will be as much fun for your Beagle as it will be for you.

For example, if your planned sojourn involves tooling around all day while your dog cools his heels in a hotel room (even at a pet-friendly hotel), you may want to reconsider. Even if you contain your Beagle in a crate, and even if he doesn't bark from sheer lone-liness, he most certainly won't be as happy as he would be if he were either in his own home or at a place where he can play and have a good time.

On the other hand, if you're going someplace where you can hang around with your Beagle most of the time and can keep him safely crated during the few occasions when he can't be with you, bring-ing your little hound along may be a good idea.

Your Beagle's welfare *must* be your first consideration when you're trying to decide whether to bring him with you when you travel. I guarantee that if he's not happy on your trip, you won't be happy either.

Riding in cars (and trucks) with Beagles

Your Beagle's most frequent form of transportation is likely to be in a car — after all, that's probably how you get around most often. But just as you need to take certain precautions to keep yourself safe while motoring down the highway, so must you protect your little hound while he's along for the ride.

The most important step you can take to keep your dog safe in the car is to secure him in the back seat with either a doggy seat belt or in a crate that's buckled into the back seat. A Beagle who's allowed free rein of the back seat could be in serious trouble in the event of a sudden stop or an accident. He could fall off the seat and break a leg, or even become a projectile that lands in the front seat with you. Figure 13-1 shows a Beagle safely buckled into the back seat of a car using a doggy seat belt.

Doggy seat belts are available at just about any pet superstore, such as Petco or PetsMart. The devices come with detailed direc-tions on how to use them, but they're not that tough to work with after you and your dog become accustomed to them. Most doggy seat belts consist of a piece of nylon fabric that extends down the length of the dog's chest, two nylon straps that surround the dog's body, and a loop that extends from the back. First, you secure the straps around the dog, and then you run a seat belt through the loop. Voilà! Your dog is safe and secure.

Do not place your Beagle in a seat that has an airbag. If the airbag deploys, your dog could be seriously injured or even killed. Keep your Beagle out of the front seat altogether — and if your car has side airbags in the back seat, place him in the center of the back seat.

Figure 13-1: Buckle up your Beagle to keep him safe in your car.

If your vehicle of choice is an SUV or pickup truck, your Beagle still belongs in a seat away from the airbag. And under no circumstances should you let your dog ride in the truck bed or cargo area of your vehicle.

No matter where your Beagle sits, though, make sure that his entire body is in the car. That means keep the windows rolled up, or otherwise restrain him so his head's not hanging out the window. He may like feeling the wind blowing through his ears, but the price for that enjoyment could be dust or other irritants getting into his eyes.

Of course, car safety consists of much more than securing your dog with a seat belt. Other considerations include weather and whether to leave your dog alone in the car.

 Don't leave a dog in a car if the outdoor temperature is above 70 degrees. The temperature inside the car can climb to well over 100 degrees in a just a few minutes — even if you open the windows and park the car in the shade — resulting in heatstroke, which can be fatal. If you must go someplace where you can't bring your Beagle and the weather is balmy, leave your dog at home! Frankly, leaving your dog alone in a car is never a good idea.

Helping the carsick canine

Although most dogs love to go for rides in cars, a few find the experience to be nauseating — literally. If your Beagle turns out to be one of these unhappy pooches, you may be able to help him. Here are some ideas:

✔ **Run him on empty.** The dog who tosses his cookies when he's in the car may do better if he's got no cookies to toss. Try not to feed your Beagle for six hours or so before you hit the road.

✔ **Desensitize him.** Try just sitting in the car with your dog and running the engine for a few minutes at a time over the course of a few days to get him used to being in the car. After he can handle that, graduate to short rides and work up to longer trips.

✔ **Freshen the air.** Opening the windows a little bit can give your dog the fresh air he needs to quell his queasiness.

✔ **Give him some meds.** For many pets, a little bit of dimenhydrinate (Dramamine) given an hour or so before a trip can allay carsickness — although it may also make him drowsy. Consult your vet about the proper dosage.

✔ **Offer some flower power.** Some Beagles benefit from being given a few drops of Bach Rescue Remedy, a natural flower essence, several hours before a trip. These and other flower essences are available from health-food stores.

Leavin' on a jet plane

So you want to go someplace far, far away — too far to drive. Hopping on a plane seems to be the best way to get there. And you're wondering whether you can take your beloved Beagle with you.

Maybe you can — but that doesn't mean that you should.

Air travel can be incredibly stressful for Beagles and other pets. For one thing, unless your pet is small enough to fit in a carrier that can be stowed under the seat in front of you, your four-legged friend has to ride with the rest of the baggage. The noise, the absence of familiar surroundings — not to mention the absence of familiar people — do not make for a relaxed traveling environment for your dog.

And that's assuming that the airlines will even accept your Beagle. During the summer months, when temperatures are high, they won't. Airlines have a good reason for that policy: Temperatures on the airport tarmac and in the baggage compartment get extremely hot — hot enough to cause heatstroke and even kill your dog.

For that reason, I recommend not traveling by air with your Beagle unless you absolutely have to. Either choose a vacation site that's within easy driving distance, suck it up and drive the longer distance that you'd planned to fly, or leave your dog at home.

That said, however, a time may come when you have to ship your Beagle by air — for example, if you're moving overseas and want to bring your little hound with you. If that's your situation, keep the following suggestions in mind:

- ✔ **Start planning early.** A prudent owner plans her Beagle's trip well in advance — say, six months before departure. That's because most countries require owners to show that pets are healthy enough to cross their borders. Some countries merely require current rabies' vaccinations, while others demand that the owner complete numerous forms and certifications before allowing a dog to enter. Still other countries require that entering pets be quarantined in a commercial kennel for days, weeks, or even months before allowing them to join their owners. Find out, too, how long these certifications last. By starting the planning process early, you'll have plenty of time to fulfill the requirements of your destination, and also get the flight and/or kennel space that you need.

- ✔ **Do your homework.** As soon as possible, find out the animal transport regulations of the place you're moving to. The U.S. Department of Agriculture's Animal and Plant Health Inspection Service (APHIS) maintains listings of U.S. and foreign countries' animal transport regulations at www.aphis.usda.gov/ac/pettravel.html. The same site also includes some tips for traveling by air with pets. For information on airlines' requirements — particularly with respect to crates and carriers — contact individual carriers.

- ✔ **Get help from your vet.** Your veterinarian can help you obtain any health certificates you need for your Beagle and can also suggest ways to make him feel more comfortable while traveling.

- ✔ **Limit stops.** Book the most direct flight possible, even if it costs more than a flight with one or more layovers. The fewer stops you make, the fewer chances you have that something will go wrong during the trip.

✔ **Call a pro.** Professional animal transporters can maximize your Beagle's chances of arriving safely at your destination, and minimize the hassles that arise when you try to arrange such transportation yourself. For a list of professional animal transporters, contact the Independent Pet and Animal Transportation Association International Inc. The organization's Web site, www.ipata.com, has a searchable database that enables you to locate an animal transporting company in your area.

Picking pet-friendly lodging

No matter how you and your Beagle travel, you need to a place to stay after you reach your destination. These days, though, finding Beagle-friendly accommodations isn't all that difficult. That's because the hospitality business has seen the light when it comes to welcoming man's (and woman's) best friend. Many establishments that once barred the door to canine guests now realize that putting up those dogs can lead to big bucks and return visits from the dogs' grateful owners. As a result, more hotels, motels, and even bed-and-breakfasts are rolling out the red carpet for you and your Beagle than ever before.

So how do you find these pet-friendly lodgings? Start by picking up some guidebooks and magazines aimed at the dog-owning traveler. Such publications abound in this era of bringing the canine member of the family along with everyone else. Among the magazines and Web sites available are *Fido Friendly* (a one-year subscription to the print magazine is $12; more info at www.fidofriendly.com); Pets on the Go ($15 per year for premium membership; more info at www.petsonthego.com); and Dog Friendly (a free e-mail newsletter you can order at www.dogfriendly.com).

Wanna go by the book? Check out these tomes: *Traveling with Your Pet — The AAA PetBook: 8th Edition* by the American Automobile Club (AAA); *Pets on the Go: The Definitive Pet Accommodation and Vacation Guide* by Dawn and Robert Habgood (Dawbert Press); and *Fodor's Road Guide USA: Where to Stay with Your Pet, 1st Edition* by Andrea Arden (Fodor's).

After you identify a place to stay, however, don't just breeze into the reception area with your Beagle in tow. Call first to make sure an establishment's pet-friendly policy remains in effect; to learn the rules for staying with a pet at the facility; and to find out in advance whether the facility requires a pet deposit and/or an extra fee for nonhuman guests (many do).

Packing your Beagle's suitcase

Just as you pack your own suitcase when you travel, so should you pack one for your Snoopy-dog. Of course, the suitcase need not literally be a suitcase; a tote bag or old backpack is just as good. Whatever you choose, though, plan on bringing the following:

- ✔ **Your Beagle's crate:** That way he'll have a cozy, familiar place to stay when you're not in the room — and you'll prevent the room from being damaged. In fact, many hotels require that dogs be crated when owners aren't in the room with them.

- ✔ **Dog food:** A trip is no time to change your Beagle's diet. Pack enough of his regular food to keep his tummy comfy for the duration of the trip — or know whether you can buy his food in the area where you're traveling. And don't forget his treats!

- ✔ **A couple of toys:** Pack your dog's two or three favorite toys along with all of his other gear. He'll enjoy being able to play with familiar objects, especially when he's in unfamiliar surroundings.

- ✔ **Collar and leash:** Duh! Don't leave home without these!

- ✔ **Immunization record:** If your dog becomes sick on the road and needs a veterinarian's care, you'll need to furnish proof of immunizations. Your vet can provide this record easily.

- ✔ **Something with your scent:** A T-shirt or other object with your scent on it can provide considerable comfort to your Beagle when he's left alone.

- ✔ **Plastic bags:** Be a good dog owner: Bring a bunch of plastic bags so you can clean up your Beagle's bathroom deposits.

Going visiting?

Just because you're visiting your parents, your cousin Judy, or your best friend from high school, don't assume that your Beagle is as welcome as you are. Not everyone is thrilled with the prospect of hosting a canine guest — and as the human guest, you need to respect this perspective, no matter how incomprehensible it is to you. Always, always ask your host or hostess whether your Beagle is welcome in his or her home. If the answer is yes, pack your Beagle's bag just as you would if you were staying in a hotel — and show the same consideration for a host's property that you would at a five-star commercial establishment. And if the answer is no — well, make other arrangements for your dog, or stay home with him.

Leaving Your Beagle Home

Sometimes bringing your Beagle with you isn't a good idea. Maybe you're flying, or maybe you won't be able to spend much time with your Snoopy-dog while you're on the road, or perhaps your little hound isn't welcome at your destination. Whatever the reason, you need to find someplace else for your four-legged friend to stay while you're away. One option may be your home.

The friend option

If you have a dog-loving friend, consider asking her to stay in your home as a housesitter/Beagle companion while you're gone. That way, you know that your home won't be left vacant while you're gone, and you can relax knowing that your Beagle has some company. This is a great option to consider if you're going to be away for more than a couple of days. Make sure, though, that your friend has the info she needs to take proper care of your Beagle; the section "What your pet sitter needs to know" suggests what to tell your friend.

Picking a pet sitter

If you'll only be away for two or three days, a professional pet sitter who visits your home two or three times a day may be just who you need to keep your Beagle happy and set your mind at rest while you're away.

How do you find this lifesaver? Start by asking your veterinarian. He may be able to refer you to a trustworthy individual or company. Failing that, you can consult one or both of the following pet-sitting organizations: the National Association of Professional Pet Sitters (www.petsitters.org) or Pet Sitters International (www.petsit.com). Both organizations' Web sites allow you to search by zipcode for a pet-sitting company or individual who's located near you. When you contact a person or company, find out the following:

✔ **Has the person who will come to your home had a criminal background check?** You want to be sure that whoever comes into your home to take care of your beloved Beagle has no criminal history, particularly of animal abuse. If the company or person can't or won't provide this information, walk away.

✔ **Do you have references?** Get at least three, and call them. Make sure, too, that these references are clients, not personal friends of the pet sitter. Ask the client how long the pet sitter cared for the pet and how he or she views the experience.

✔ **Do you offer a service contract?** A savvy sitter will specify in writing the services that he or she will perform while you're away. Make sure you see a service contract and agree to the terms before you depart.

✔ **What's your backup plan?** If the sitter becomes ill or otherwise can't visit your home, what will happen to your Beagle? This question is especially important if you're interviewing an individual rather than a company — although in both instances, they should give you a detailed backup plan ensuring that your dog will be cared for no matter what happens.

✔ **Can you come for a visit?** An understanding sitter will realize that your Beagle needs to meet his substitute caregiver before you employ her. That way, you can see how the sitter interacts with your dog, and the sitter can see the layout of your home and ask any specific questions she may have.

What your pet sitter needs to know

If you want your Beagle to have optimum care from a pet sitter or housesitter, you need to provide the sitter with detailed information about your trip and your dog's needs. Here's the written information you should provide when you give her your key:

✔ **Location of all supplies:** Make sure your sitter knows where you keep your Beagle's food, leash, collar, toys, medications, and anything else she'll need to care for your four-legged friend.

✔ **Your itinerary:** Give your sitter information on when you're leaving, when you'll return, and a phone number to reach you.

✔ **Contact information:** Your sitter should have the telephone number of your regular veterinarian and, if available, an emergency veterinary clinic.

Boarding Your Beagle

If you plan to be away for more than a few days and you can't take your Beagle along, consider taking him to a place where he's welcome. By going to a boarding kennel or even to the home of a dog-loving friend, you can be sure that your pooch is getting the best of care at a home away from home.

A little help from a friend

My family and I recently took a Caribbean cruise — obviously, an excursion upon which our dog could not join us. But we had no worries. We took our beloved Allie to stay with someone who was thrilled to spend time with our girl: her breeder. If you bought your Beagle from a reputable breeder who lives near you, you may be able to do the same thing. In other instances, we've taken our dogs to stay with dog-loving friends of ours. Every time we've exercised these options, we've enjoyed our vacations more, knowing that our dogs were having nice vacations, too.

A friend is much more likely to agree to take care of your dog while you're away if you make clear your eagerness to return the favor!

Make sure that anyone who cares for your Beagle is an experienced owner and is someone your dog knows and trusts. A few practice sessions — say, a few afternoons or even an overnight stay at your breeder's or friend's home — can help put your dog at ease and can help you and your friend deal with any questions that may arise.

Finding a boarding kennel

If you don't have a friend who can care for your Beagle, you can pay to have experts take care of him. Plenty of places specialize in boarding dogs, and the offerings range from somewhat spartan to positively luxurious.

On the spartan-but-still-OK side may be your own vet. Many veterinary clinics offer boarding services for their clients. The staff will feed your dog, let him exercise in a kennel run, and check on him periodically. You may also be able to arrange to have him groomed during his stay. The big plus to this option is that it's probably the cheapest; the possible minus is that your dog won't be living in the lap of luxury.

At the other end of the spectrum are what can only be called dog resorts. If Zagat's, Michelin, or the American Automobile Association (AAA) rated boarding kennels, these facilities would draw the maximum number of diamonds, stars, or other rating symbols available. One such resort in my area of northern Virginia offers swimming, spa services such as massage, agility training, and a cyber-cam so you can watch your dog if you have Internet access at your vacation destination. The huge plus to this alternative is that your Beagle will enjoy his vacation as much as you enjoy your trip, if not more. The equally big disadvantage is that you may pay more for your dog's vacation than you will for your own.

In between these two extremes, of course, are facilities that contain some luxuries, but not a lot, and are moderate in price.

Depending on your budget and other preferences, you can start your search for a kennel by asking your vet whether his clinic boards dogs. Another option is to log onto the Web site of the American Boarding Kennels Association at www.abka.com. There you'll find a searchable database that will locate kennels near you.

Be sure to pay a visit to the kennel — preferably unannounced — before you agree to board your Beagle there. Leave your Beagle home so you can concentrate on checking for the following:

- **Cleanliness:** The facility should be clean, with little or no odor. Doggy accidents should not be in evidence.

- **Security:** The facility should be escape-proof. Make sure that the outdoor areas have high fences around them and that the staff keeps the dogs on leash in any public areas, such as the reception area.

- **Attentiveness:** Those who interact with your dog should love your dog, or show a liking for the canine species in general.

- **24/7 presence:** If possible, board your dog at a facility that is staffed by people around the clock.

More information on finding and checking out a kennel is available from the American Boarding Kennel Association Web site.

Part IV
Training Your Beagle

The 5th Wave   By Rich Tennant

"You know, you're never going to get that dog to do his business in your remote-controlled dump truck."

In this part . . .

You and your Beagle will be much happier together if he learns how to get along in a human household. Part IV shows you how to teach your little hound basic good manners, proper bathroom behavior, and elementary commands that make both your lives easier. This part also explains what to do if your dog has behavioral issues.

Chapter 14

Housetraining Your Beagle

. . . .

. . . .

*W*ho can help falling in love with a Beagle? Certainly not you. Your sweet Snoopy-dog's winsome eyes, long floppy ears, and soft expression had you smitten the moment you first saw her. When you brought her home, you were sure that your love for her would only grow and that nothing, absolutely nothing, could get in the way of that love.

Then she took a whiz in the middle of your white Berber carpet, which is now graced with a big yellow stain. Understandably, you are not happy. After a few more similar doggy downloads, you may not be thinking of your Beagle with a great deal of love. Instead, you may be wondering whether your little hound is anything more than a four-legged pooping and peeing machine.

I'm here to assure you that she's not. Your Beagle is still the same lovable creature that you believed her to be a couple of days or weeks ago. However, the fact that she's adorable doesn't give her the knowledge of where and when you want her to do her business. You must give her that knowledge through the process that's known as *housetraining*.

Simply put, housetraining is the procedure you employ to teach your Beagle exactly where and when you want her to poop and pee. When your dog is truly housetrained, she will do just about anything to avoid making a bathroom boo-boo. Impossible, you say? *Au contraire!* This chapter shows you how to teach your Beagle impeccable bathroom manners.

Going Indoors or Out?

Before you begin to teach proper potty protocol to your Beagle, you need to make a very important decision: whether that potty will be located indoors or outdoors.

The ideal indoor potty operates the same way a kitty bathroom does: You place several layers of newspaper or an open box of specially prepared dog litter in a laundry room, seldom-used human bathroom, or anyplace else that's away from the main living areas of your home. The ideal outdoor potty is located somewhere in your backyard or elsewhere in the outdoors, so your home's interior isn't exposed to dog waste after the dog is housetrained.

Each method has advantages and disadvantages. In the next sections, I outline the pro's and con's of each.

Indoor potty pro's and con's

Indoor training can be ideal for the owner who's away from home all day. Instead of having to wait until her person comes home, the dog can take herself to her newspapers or litter box and relieve herself there. With either a litter box or papers, indoor training helps ensure that the returning owner isn't greeted by a puddle or pile deposited in an inappropriate place in the house.

The mobility-impaired owner may find the indoor potty to be advantageous, too. By keeping the doggy bathroom indoors, the owner need not walk the dog to a potty outside. The dog can take care of her bathroom business on her own.

High-rise apartment dwellers with small dogs also may prefer to train their dogs to do their business inside. Far better to let the dog do her business in a designated indoor area than to make a mad dash to the elevator and outdoors to a proper potty spot.

And of course, indoor training seems like a great idea on those dark and stormy nights when the last thing you want to do is to take your Beagle out for a bathroom break. The indoor bathroom allows you both to stay warm and dry whenever your dog needs to take care of business.

But lest you think that indoor training is a great idea, consider the disadvantages.

The big minus that indoor training carries for the Beagle owner is that the Beagle's puddles and deposits may be a little too large, unwieldy, and gross for the owner to handle inside. That's because many Beagles are just a little too large to use the indoor potty — especially if it's a litter box. Confining your Beagle's business to an indoor location may seem convenient at first, but having to clean up that business from within your home day in and day out is likely to get very old very fast. And let's not forget the smell of Beagle poop and pee: Both stink and are a major downside to indoor training.

Outdoor potty pluses and minuses

The outdoor potty is probably better for most Beagles. When you take your dog outdoors, you don't have to worry about dealing with the indoor canine bathroom, or that your dog will outgrow her litter box or newspapers. In addition, opting for the outdoor bathroom enables you to multitask: You can exercise your Beagle outdoors during the same excursion in which you take her to do her business.

Still not convinced? Choosing to have your dog go outside frees you from having to keep oodles of newspapers on hand or make innumerable trips to the store to buy dog litter. And when you travel, your dog can poop or pee anywhere outdoors; you don't need to tote the litter box and dog litter wherever you go.

Of course, snowy days and stormy nights (and vice versa) can cause the most devoted Beagle owner to question the wisdom of locating the canine bathroom outdoors — but proper clothing for you and, perhaps, your Beagle (which you can find at any major pet supply retailer) can mitigate some of that disadvantage. And if you work all day, you can't expect your full-grown, housetrained dog to hold her water or other stuff for more than eight or nine hours or so. However, hiring a dog walker or enrolling your Beagle in doggy day care can forestall accidents that result from your little hound having to "hold it" for too long.

You gotta choose

If you've read the previous two sections and you're thinking that I'm solidly aligned with those who housetrain their Beagles outdoors, you're right. I think that keeping dog doo outdoors, even when the weather is less than hospitable to human and canine exercise, ultimately is more convenient and sanitary under most circumstances than doing that business indoors.

Still, you may think it would be great to teach your Beagle to potty outdoors on nice days and spread some newspapers on the ground so your dog can do her business indoors when the weather isn't to your liking. Unfortunately, though, what's convenient for you will only confuse your dog — and the result of that confusion will be decidedly inconvenient. (In other words, you'll be cleaning up accidents.)

For these reasons, I strongly suggest that you choose to teach your Beagle to do her business outdoors. If your heart is set on having her do the doo inside, though, check out my own book, *Housetraining For Dummies* (Wiley), which contains extensive information on indoor training.

Getting in Gear

You wouldn't put on a pair of stilettos before running a mile around the local track, would you? Of course not. Instead, you'd probably don a pair of sturdy athletic shoes. Your decision would be based on the understanding that using the right equipment is crucial to succeeding at whatever you're trying to do.

That understanding also applies to housetraining. Your Beagle will learn proper potty protocol much faster if you gather the right gear together before you try to teach her bathroom basics.

Don't hate the crate

First, last, and foremost, you need a crate. It doesn't matter which kind of crate you use (Chapter 5 outlines your options) — but without a crate, you'll have a much harder time teaching your Beagle where and when to potty. But with a crate, housetraining can be relatively easy. That's because a crate takes advantage of a basic canine instinct — a reluctance to dirty the den — and helps your little hound learn to hold her poop and pee until you can get her to the designated potty place.

And before you start to fret about what other doggy parents may think, proper use of the crate is not cruel to the dog. In fact, many dogs enjoy their crates because they know they can beat a retreat to their own inner sanctums whenever they feel the need to chill. My own dog, Allie, is taking her afternoon nap in her open crate even as I type this housetraining primer. She often chooses to go into her crate on her own. Your Beagle can learn to do the same. To understand the role a crate plays in housetraining, see the "Following Five Steps" section later in this chapter.

Keeping things clean

No matter how diligent you are in your housetraining efforts, your Beagle will make some mistakes during the learning process. Such mistakes aren't a big deal, unless you fail to clean up those mistakes quickly and completely.

Why is proper cleanup so important? Because the smell of poop or pee residue is an aromatic come-hither to your Beagle. If you fail to get rid of the odor as well as the stain from your little hound's bathroom transgression, she'll feel compelled to go right back to the scene of her earlier crime and become a repeat offender. However, the right cleanup equipment can help your Beagle make far fewer mistakes than would otherwise be the case.

 To determine whether a cleanup product will do the job, check to see whether the product contains *enzymes*. An enzymatic cleaner not only obliterates any stains that result from doggy bathroom mishaps, it also eliminates the odors that such mishaps produce. Examples of such cleaners are Petastic, Nature's Miracle, Urine Off, Equalizer, and the oh-so-wonderfully named Anti-Icky-Poo. You can order the latter from www.AntiIckyPoo.com; the others are available from pet supply retailers. No matter what you buy, though, just follow the instructions on the bottle to get the cleanup done.

 Don't use ammonia to clean up your Beagle's bathroom mistakes. Ammonia may get rid of the stain, but the smell is almost identical to the smell of dog pee. That odor will almost certainly prompt your pooch to return to the scene of his earlier anointing and do an encore. Ditto for club soda, which also gets rid of the stain but not the smell.

Let someone else doo it

If you truly can't stand to pick up your dog's poop (even after you follow the directions in Chapter 11), never fear — you can hire someone else to scoop it. In many major metropolitan areas and their suburbs, companies dedicated to the removal of canine waste will dispatch technicians to your home on a regular basis to doo their thing. The costs of these pooper-scooper services vary depending on your local area, the size of your property, the number of dogs you have, and how often the company visits.

To find a pooper-scooper service in your area, check out the International Directory of Dog Waste Removal Services at www.pooper-scooper.com/scoopers.htm.

Other helpful items

A few other items that can help you teach bathroom basics to your Beagle include:

- ✔ **Paper towels:** These not only soak up bathroom boo-boos, but create a scent cloth that tells your Snoopy-dog exactly where she should do her business.

- ✔ **Lots of plastic bags:** Cleaning up after your dog makes a deposit is a basic component of responsible dog ownership.

- ✔ **A urine detector:** If your Beagle keeps anointing the same spot in your home, even though you think you've cleaned it up, plunking down $20 or so for a urine detector can be a worthwhile investment. Among the products available are Simple Solution's Spot Spotter, which uses ultraviolet light to reveal urine spots that you can't see.

What you absolutely don't need

Pet supply companies offer a plethora of products designed to aid the housetraining process. In reality, though, a lot of these products really aren't necessary. Some of the stuff you don't need includes

- ✔ **A housebreaking aid:** This is a fancy name for a bottle of drops that show your Beagle where to do the doo. A scent cloth is a heck of a lot cheaper (see the "Step 2: Pick a potty place" section later in this chapter for more about scent cloths).

- ✔ **A pooper-scooper:** You really don't need this item. It's unwieldy and tough to use precisely. Why bother? Use plastic bags instead (Chapter 11 tells you how).

- ✔ **Training pads:** These are designed for indoor training, which generally isn't a good housetraining option for a Beagle. And even if you do decide to go the indoor route, using newspapers is cheaper and using dog litter is neater.

- ✔ **Doggy diapers:** Diapers can help an incontinent dog, but they do nothing to help your Beagle learn her bathroom basics.

Following Five Steps

To housetrain your Beagle, you need to take advantage of her desire to have her own den; her equally strong desire to refrain from dirtying that den; and her awesome sense of smell. The task is easy when you break it down into five steps.

Step 1: Create the den

Before you do anything else, get a properly sized crate and make sure your Beagle is accustomed to it. Chapter 5 gives you the low-down on how to buy a proper crate; Chapter 6 tells you all you need to know about introducing the crate to your four-legged friend.

The benefit of using a crate in housetraining is that your Beagle will do everything she can to avoid dirtying her den, which is how she views the crate. She'll hold her poo and pee, just waiting for the instant that you open up her crate and usher her to the spot where she can relieve herself. See "Step 4: Follow a schedule" for a timeline of when to put your dog in her crate and how long she can wait for the next potty break.

Step 2: Pick a potty place

Find a spot in your backyard or elsewhere on your property where you can take your Beagle whenever she needs a bathroom break. Then, show your dog where she should do the doo by creating a scent cloth and place that cloth on the designated potty place when you take her out for a pit stop.

As Chapter 6 explains, a scent cloth is a piece of cloth or paper towel that you use to wipe your Beagle's urinary area immediately after she's peed. Because dogs are drawn to the smell of their own urine, any place you put that cloth will lure your Beagle there, at which point she will almost certainly proceed to open her floodgates.

Step 3: Be vigilant

Yes, your Beagle will mess up (literally) during the housetraining process, but your objective is to keep those mess-ups to a minimum. The only way to achieve that objective is to watch your Beagle like a hawk — in other words, do not take your eyes off her — when she is out of her crate. If you can't watch her that carefully, put her back into the crate until you can.

Why such vigilance? Because you want to make sure that if she shows signs of needing to go, you can whisk her outdoors to the potty spot to unload.

Common signs of needing to use the little Beagle's room are:

✔ Pacing back and forth

✔ Trotting around in circles

✔ Suddenly sniffing the ground intently

✔ Suddenly stopping whatever she's been doing

If your dog performs any of those maneuvers, get her to her potty spot pronto — and praise her lavishly when she poops or pees there.

If she starts to unload while she's still in the house, distract her. Try saying "No!" in a loud voice. The sound may startle her and cause her to stop her bathroom operation. That's your cue; scoop her up and get her out to the potty spot immediately. If she completes her offload there, praise her to the skies for doing a good potty and tell her what a good girl she is.

Step 4: Follow a schedule

The whole housetraining process goes a lot easier when you and your Beagle follow a schedule. That's because dogs thrive on predictability — and when you create a potty schedule for your little friend, she'll learn to expect a bathroom break and hold it the rest of the time.

The number of potty breaks you take depends on your dog's age and degree of housetraining prowess. A very young puppy may need to go out hourly. A slightly older pup needs bathroom breaks when she first wakes up, after every meal, after every playtime, after every nap, and just before bedtime. A housetrained adult generally needs no more than three or four breaks each day.

Table 14-1 shows a possible schedule for a 3-month-old puppy.

Table 14-1	Training Schedule for 3-Month-Old Puppy
Time	*Tasks*
7:00 a.m.	Get up.
	Take puppy outside.
	Put puppy in crate.

Time	*Tasks*
7:30 a.m.	Feed puppy.
	Offer water.
	Take puppy outside.
	Play with puppy for 15 minutes.
	Put puppy in crate.
Midmorning	Offer water.
	Take puppy outside.
	Play with puppy for 15 minutes.
	Put puppy in crate.
Noon	Feed puppy.
	Offer water.
	Take puppy outside.
	Play with puppy for 30 minutes.
	Put puppy in crate.
Midafternoon	Offer water.
	Take puppy outside.
	Play with puppy for 15 minutes.
	Put puppy in crate.
5:30 p.m.	Feed puppy.
	Offer water.
	Take puppy outside.
	Play with puppy for up to 1 hour and/or let puppy hang out with family in the kitchen.
7:00 p.m.	Take puppy outside.
	Play with puppy for 15 minutes.
	Put puppy in crate.
Before bed	Take puppy outside.
	Put puppy in crate.
During the night	Take puppy outside if necessary.

For an adult Beagle, you can skip the midmorning break, the midday meal, and the midafternoon break. Then you do what's left: the 7:00 a.m., 7:30 a.m., noon (minus the meal), 5:30 p.m., 7:00 p.m. and before-bed breaks.

The housetraining schedule for a 3-month-old puppy or even for an adult Beagle assumes that someone will be home during the day to provide the frequent potty breaks the canine housetrainee needs. If you're not home during the day, though, you need to provide alternative arrangements.

If your Beagle is less than 4 or 5 months of age, you'll need to do one of two things: arrange for someone to come to your home during the day to take your little one out, or temporarily allow her to potty on newspapers during the day. If you choose to allow your Beagle to use newspapers in the early stages of housetraining, you train her to go indoors, all the while keeping an eye on the calendar.

Start by spreading out several thicknesses of newspapers in a corner of your kitchen or laundry room. Place a scent cloth on the papers so your puppy knows that's where she's supposed to potty. Then, start counting the days until she's 6 months old. At that point — or when you come home to dry newspapers for at least a week, you can switch to the outdoor potty.

Keep your puppy in the room where her newspapers are while you're out, and make sure that the room is enclosed by a door or baby gate so she can't wander elsewhere in the house.

For the adult housetrainee, have her stay in her crate during the morning, and have someone come to your home at noon to give her a potty break and some playtime. She should then stay in her crate until you come home. And until your dog is completely housetrained, don't work late or go out for some after-work drinks with your colleagues. Your Beagle needs you to come home and give her that potty break!

Step 5: Be patient

Time's on your side when you housetrain your Beagle, but you still need to be patient. You're asking her to learn something that's not easy to learn: to not poop or pee except when she knows she's allowed to. A healthy dose of patience, humane use of the crate, constant vigilance, and a consistent schedule will all help your Beagle become a housetraining ace.

How do you know when your dog is fully housetrained? Check out the "Declaring Victory" section later in this chapter.

Addressing Accidents

No matter how hard you try, your Beagle housetrainee will have at least a couple of accidents while you're teaching her basic potty protocol. Those accidents won't necessarily be a bad thing, though — if you use those occasions to show your Beagle what not to do and to improve your skills as a bathroom manners instructor.

Catch her in the act

You may have the good luck to catch your Beagle in the middle of a bathroom transgression. If you see your dog start to squat, distract her any way you can. A loud "No!" or clap of the hands are just two ways to interrupt the offload. After you've got her attention, pick her up and get her to the potty spot as fast as you can. If she completes the offload there, praise her for going in the right place — and vow to keep a closer eye on her next time so you'll get her outside before she starts her potty maneuvers.

Clean up without comment

You've just come home to find a puddle or pile in your hallway. Then you see your Beagle: ears back, tail between her legs, looking away from you. You think, "She knows what she did, and now she feels guilty." But you're wrong.

Beagles, like all dogs, have short memories. She has no idea that you are unhappy about the little present she left you; she doesn't even remember creating it. What she does see is your tension and your expression and she hears your loud voice. She knows you're angry. She's nervous, even scared — but she feels no guilt at all.

The lesson here: Don't scold your dog or otherwise attempt to discipline her for having made a bathroom mistake. If you come upon the mistake, you're too late to do anything other than clean it up. Do just that: Lay on the enzymatic cleaner and say nothing to your Beagle. Your bad temper will only frighten her, and a frightened student isn't likely to learn as much as a student who likes her teacher. Plus, you're getting angry at the wrong individual: If your Beagle has an accident, it's your fault, not hers.

Troubleshoot the accident

Your Beagle's misplaced puddle or pile should prompt you to conduct a thorough investigation at the scene of the "crime" to figure out why that "crime" occurred — and how you can prevent a recurrence. But you need not be a work-obsessed criminologist like William Petersen's character on *CSI* to conduct an effective housetraining crime scene investigation. Just examine what you were doing when your Beagle goofed. Here are some housetraining boo-boos, and possible explanations as to why they occurred:

✔ **Did she pee when your back was turned?** Never let her out of her crate unless you can watch her every second.

✔ **Did she eliminate in her crate?** Make sure that your puppy's crate is just large enough for her to stand, turn around, and lie down comfortably. And don't leave your housetrainee for more than two or three hours if she's a young puppy, and no more than four hours if she's an older pup or young adult.

✔ **Did she pee or poop without warning?** Start watching your puppy to see what she does just before she unloads. You'll probably see that she does the same thing almost every time she does the doo (see the "Step 3: Be vigilant" section earlier in this chapter for a list of behaviors your Beagle is likely to perform when she needs to go). If she behaves that way in the house, that's your cue to get her out to her potty spot — fast.

✔ **Does she have an accident on the same place every day?** If so, you need to do a better clean-up job. Use a cleaner formulated especially for pet stains. See the "Keeping things clean" section earlier in this chapter for more details.

Declaring Victory

Housetraining a Beagle can seem like a tedious process. You may wish you could bag the whole business of schedules, cleanups, and vigilance. You'll wonder when you can consider your Snoopy-dog fully housetrained. Here's how to know when your little hound has mastered Housetraining 101:

✔ **She's at least 6 months old.** I don't care how much of a housetraining prodigy you consider your Beagle to be — the fact is, most dogs can't hold their poop or pee for an appreciable length of time until they reach this milestone.

✔ **She hasn't goofed for at least a month.** If your Beagle hasn't made a bathroom boo-boo for a month or more, you can be pretty sure she's got the housetraining thing down pat.

✔ **She asks to go out.** If your dog finds a way to tell you that she needs to do the doo (for example, going to the door and whining, tapping her leash with her nose), consider yourself to be a successful housetrainer. (If you want to teach your dog to tell you that she needs to go, see the "You can ring my bell . . ." sidebar.)

You can ring my bell . . .

Wouldn't it be wonderful if your Beagle could tell you when she needs to go potty? Guess what: She can! Some dogs figure this out on their own — I once had a dog who would tap his leash with his nose and stare at me when he needed a bathroom break. But if your Beagle isn't telling you when she needs to go out, you can teach her how. Here's what to do:

1. **Get something she can communicate with.**

   Find something that you can hang from a doorknob and that your Snoopy-dog can reach with her paws or nose. A good choice would be a set of Christmas bells, because they make a pleasant noise with just a slight touch.

2. **Show her what to do.**

   Each time you take your dog out for a potty break, ring the bells. That way, she'll associate the ringing bells with going out to do her business.

3. **Let her try.**

   Sooner or later, your Beagle will want to investigate the bells herself. Encourage her to do just that: If she even sniffs the bells, praise her lavishly and give her a treat.

4. **Heed her call.**

   The first time your dog actually taps the bells with her nose, paws at them, or otherwise causes them to ring, respond immediately: Take her out to her potty spot. If she goes, praise her lavishly — and pat yourself on the back for teaching her how to communicate with you.

Addressing Bathroom Issues

Some dogs ace their housetraining lessons, only to develop problems later. Often, such issues have nothing to do with housetraining, but reflect another problem. Here are some examples.

She pees on her back

The Beagle who rolls over onto her back and dribbles some urine when you approach doesn't have a housetraining problem. Instead, she's telling you that you're the most wonderful being on earth. This behavior is *submissive urination,* and it's easy to fix.

Start by ignoring your deferential doggy when you enter a room. After a few minutes, get down to her level by squatting or sitting on the floor. And don't look directly at her, because she may feel intimidated by a direct stare, and she'll piddle some more. Finally, speak to her softly. Don't hug or kiss her, because she'll get excited and pee.

By making yourself less intimidating to your Beagle, she'll become more confident and the behavior will stop.

He christens everything

If your male Beagle is lifting his leg and spraying vertical objects, he doesn't have housetraining problems. He's got turf issues. Dogs of both genders use their urine to mark their territory, but the problem is more prevalent among males than females.

The best way to end a dog's attempts at marksmanship is to neuter him. A neutered male is much less turf-conscious than his intact counterpart. Expect to do some follow-up housetraining after the neutering, though, just to make sure he breaks his bad habit.

Make sure, too, that you clean up any canine christening thoroughly with an enzymatic cleaner. Failure to clean up completely will bring your dog back for encores.

She strains to pee

The dog who tries to pee, only to produce a wee bit of wee-wee, may have stones in her urinary tract. Take her to your vet pronto. Untreated urinary stones can be fatal.

She pees all the time

The housetrained dog who suddenly starts peeing all the time in all the wrong places probably doesn't have housetraining amnesia. Instead, she may have a urinary tract infection or other medical condition. Get her to her vet as soon as possible. The vet may do urine tests, blood work, and/or X-rays to determine the cause and appropriate treatment. Regardless of the cause, it's a good idea to take your Beagle out as often as she needs to go, and encourage her to drink lots of water so she can flush out her system.

Chapter 15

Schooling Your Beagle

*A*n educated Beagle — that is, a Beagle who's had some basic training — is almost always happier than a Beagle who's not had the benefit of such schooling. Why? Because when the educated Beagle knows and uses that training, the humans in his household are happy with him. And when the humans are happy, the Beagle is happy!

Conversely, when the humans are unhappy because the Beagle isn't educated, the Beagle almost always is the one who suffers. That's because behavioral problems are the overwhelming reason that people surrender their dogs to animal shelters. The dog who is destructive, hyperactive, or fails to master bathroom basics can drive his people to distraction. No one wants to live with a Beagle who makes life tougher rather than easier — and all too often, the people beset with such Beagles choose to get rid of those dogs.

Thus, taking the time to teach your little hound some basic manners is really an investment in your future with him. And yes, you can train him yourself; this chapter explains how. If you'd rather have someone help you out, though, I also explain how to choose an obedience class for yourself and your Beagle. If you need to address behaviors that put a damper on your relationship with your Beagle, such as biting, barking, or shyness, go directly to Chapter 16.

Decoding Your Beagle's SOP

Before you can teach your Beagle anything effectively, you need to understand how he learns — in other words, you need to decode his standard operating procedure, or SOP for short. Knowing how your dog's mind works and how he views his world gives you a leg up, so to speak, on teaching him what he needs to know to live happily ever after with you. Here are some basic principles to keep in mind as you contemplate schooling your Snoopy-dog.

He lives by his nose

Your Beagle's number-one tool for learning about the world is his nose, which is far more sensitive than yours.

The Snoopy-dog sniffer differs from your schnoz in many ways, meaning that your Beagle not only can detect scents that you can't, but also any odor is far more intense to your dog than to you. Check out these facts:

- ✔ The Beagle nose has more than 200 million scent receptors — cells designed specifically to detect scents — while you've got only around 5 million.

- ✔ Even better is the fact that the moisture on your little hound's nose enables him to collect large numbers of scent molecules that together heighten the smell of whatever he's sniffing.

- ✔ Even the Beagle brain is superior to the human brain — at least when it comes to smells. The area of your Beagle's brain that identifies scents is far larger than the corresponding area in your noggin.

We humans benefit greatly from the superior canine nose. We employ dogs to sniff out bombs, contraband, disaster victims, and termites (see Chapter 19). Some especially talented dogs detect cancerous moles and alert people to imminent epileptic seizures. But the same nose that can lead a dog to great accomplishments can also literally lead that dog astray — especially if that dog is a Beagle. The Beagle is more likely than many other breeds to follow his nose wherever it takes him, regardless of how much he loves you and how much danger he puts himself in.

He never feels guilty

The Beagle has mastered the art of looking woebegone, but woe to the human who thinks that those soulful looks reflect canine guilt. Your little hound doesn't connect any of your expressions of displeasure with any mistakes he's made — and if he can't make the connection, he's not going to feel guilty.

That's why scolding your Beagle for something he did awhile ago does nothing to change his behavior. Better to catch him doing something right and reward him for doing so in a way that allows him to connect the reward for performing the behavior.

He loves you, but . . .

Beagles, like all dogs, are social creatures, and love to be with their people. Your pooch is a pack animal who's hard-wired to look for canine or other company. Because you are his companion, not to mention the source of his food, shelter, and safety, he's predisposed to love you. He's happy to bestow doggy kisses on you and cuddle up for some couch-potato time while you both watch TV. And when he's unsure of something, he looks to you for guidance and direction.

But, as much as he loves you, your dog's got his own agenda. His love for you may not be enough to overcome his need to investigate that interesting smell in the yard next door. His desire to please you may not keep him from raiding the garbage can and scattering the contents all over the floor. His realization that you aren't pleased with what he's doing won't prompt him to drop whatever he's confiscated from the clothes hamper.

You're an important priority in your Beagle's life, but he's got other priorities, too. Your job as a trainer is to teach him that you need to be his number-one priority as often as possible.

He needs consistency

Dogs are incredibly astute observers of behavior. For example, my own dog suspects that I'm about to leave the house whenever she sees me put on lipstick. When Allie sees me open up a lipstick tube and apply the stuff to my lips, she starts to pant happily and lead me toward her leash. She's surmised that I'm going to leave the house, and she wants to make sure that she comes along (alas, sometimes her efforts are for naught).

How does Allie know what I'm going to do before I actually do it? Simple: I have a consistent routine, and that consistency enables my four-legged friend to anticipate my behavior.

Your Beagle thrives on consistency just as much as my dog does. Doing the same thing at the same time each day helps him to predict what happens next and to adjust his behavior accordingly. Moreover, such consistency will help him to learn the specific cues, commands, and maneuvers that you want him to learn. By using the same words and gestures to convey what you want him to do, your Beagle will learn to associate those words and gestures with a specific behavior — and, given the proper incentive, perform that behavior accordingly.

He wants to learn

A healthy Beagle is curious about the world around him. His interest in the world leads him to investigate the strange new scent in the next-door neighbor's yard, or check out that item of clothing that didn't quite make it to the laundry room. That same curiosity prompts him to study you closely for patterns in your behavior.

You can put this eagerness to work by training your little hound. Teaching him to respond to your cue or command gives him a job to do, helps him exercise his brain, and endears him to you (and vice versa).

Gearing Up for Training

Taking a positive approach to schooling your Beagle requires that you invest in a little bit of equipment — some of which you probably have already.

Accentuating the positive with the right reward

Once upon a time, not all that long ago, dog training was all about making the dog do what you wanted him to do. If he didn't comply voluntarily with your command, you'd force him to do so. A failure to sit would mean you'd push his tush to the ground. A failure to walk nicely on leash would mean that you'd yank him back to position. A failure to come when called would mean you'd go to him, grab him by the collar, and drag him back to the spot he was supposed to come to on his own.

Hamming it up

I'm way, way past high school age, but a couple of months ago, I found myself participating in a high school musical. My teenage daughter was a stage manager for a show called *Carnival,* an extravaganza that required the presence of a small dog in the opening scene. The person who was handling the dog for this show — a sweet little Beagle mix — broke her toe just four days before the show was to open, so I was asked to step in. My task: to dress up in a clown suit (hold the snickering, please), bring the dog up on the stage, and then walk with the dog offstage. The catch: The dog had to walk on his hind legs.

The dog's handler supplied me with dog treats to give the little guy an incentive to do the walking-on-hind legs maneuver. But the dog didn't seem to enjoy those little goodies, and he refused to perform as desired. Then I noticed that he was extremely interested in the backstage buffet table for the human actors, which was laden with ham, cheese, turkey, and other delectables. In a fit of inspiration, I pocketed a few pieces of ham. At the appropriate moment onstage, I held the ham aloft, just out of the dog's easy reach, and began walking. In a flash, the little dog was up on his hind legs, practically prancing his way offstage. Thunderous applause erupted, and the dog got the pieces of ham.

My point? The right reward can be incredibly persuasive. So don't get just any treat — find a goody that your Beagle really, really likes.

Not a very pleasant way to try to learn something, is it?

Fortunately, some empathetic and forward-thinking trainers realized that teaching through coercion or intimidation creates a less-than-ideal learning atmosphere. Correcting a dog for doing something wrong doesn't necessarily teach him to do something right. A better approach is to show the dog what you want him to do (or catch him doing so on his own) and then reward that behavior. Applied consistently, this approach, which trainers call *positive reinforcement,* will up the odds that your Beagle will do what you want him to do every time you want him to do it.

When you employ positive reinforcement to train your Beagle, you condition him to do what you want him to do. Just show him what you want him to do, and reward him for doing so.

Your Beagle loves you — but when it comes to training, love may not be enough to motivate your little companion to do what you want him to do. An incredibly fragrant, tasty treat can fill in the gap between your dog's desire to please you and his desire to do what he wants instead of what you want.

Click, click, click: Clicker training

Many trainers advocate the use of a clicker: a handy little gizmo that makes a "click-ing" sound when pressed. The clicker provides an instant signal to your Beagle that he's done something right, and that a reward will soon follow. Experts say that clicker-trained dogs learn new maneuvers faster than those who get simple praise to confirm that they've done what they're supposed to.

I've found clickers to be very effective in speeding up a dog's learning process. However, some individuals find the clicker to be a little cumbersome. It's one more thing they have to handle when they're also trying to juggle treats and, at times, the dog's leash. Timing is crucial, too: You need to use the clicker immediately after the dog complies with the command. That said, many trainers and students contend that once you start clicking your way to training success, you'll never go back. Give it a try, and you may find that your Snoopy-dog becomes a quicker study than you dreamed possible.

If you want to learn more about clicker training, check out *Click & Easy: Clicker Training for Dogs,* by Miriam Fields-Babineau (Wiley).

You'll probably find that your Beagle prefers soft, meaty tidbits to hard little pieces of kibble-like dog treats. Most dogs also adore hot dogs (cut up into very tiny pieces, please).

Collar quandaries

Making the right collar choice is crucial to training your Beagle successfully. To keep your training positive, opt for either a buckle collar or a tab-snap collar (see Figure 15-1) made of leather, cotton, or nylon. The collar should be nothing more than a piece of neck-wear that holds your dog's identification tag, rabies tag, local license, microchip identification number, and leash.

Steer clear of collars that purport to be training devices in and of themselves. Such collars include:

✔ **Slip collars:** Also known as training collars or choke collars, slip collars were once the canine neckwear of choice for pro-fessional dog trainers and their human students. A handler uses this metal collar to correct the dog's behavior by giving the leash a quick snap and a release immediately afterward. This snap-and-release action puts momentary pressure on a dog's neck, which hypothetically creates an incentive for the dog to cease his bad behavior. Moreover, the jingling sound of the collar is supposed to warn the dog to cease whatever he's doing.

In real life, though, slip collars aren't effective for many people, and can actually hurt the dog. If a person doesn't perform the snap-and-release action correctly, she can damage her dog's windpipe at worst, and leave him gasping for breath at best. Meanwhile, the problem behavior is all too likely to continue.

✔ **Prong collars:** This neck gear is exactly what the name says it is: a collar with prongs on it that the dog will feel if the owner needs to pull on the leash. Prong collars hurt, and they're cruel. You don't need to inflict pain or be cruel to teach your dog proper walking etiquette, bathroom manners, or anything else. Any questions?

✔ **Electronic collars:** Please. Do you really need to give your Beagle an electric shock to get him to do what you want him to do? That's what an electronic collar does. Causing pain or discomfort should not be part of any trainer's operating procedure, standard or otherwise.

Figure 15-1: Choose a buckle or snap collar for your Beagle.

Leash options

As I explain in Chapter 5, a 6-foot leather leash is the best option I know for keeping your Beagle tethered to you in comfort and safety. Longer leashes — including retractables — are difficult to handle and may violate local laws. Shorter leashes aren't practical for training.

My preference for leather has nothing to do with fashion but everything to do with comfort — your comfort. If your leashed Beagle pulls, the movement of leather across your hand is a lot less painful than the movement of nylon, which can give you a nasty scrape.

Teaching the Basics Yourself

The right equipment is crucial to teaching your Beagle basic good manners, but you also need the right atmosphere. At least in the beginning, a good training environment downplays distractions such as kids running around, TV blaring, or lots of commotion going on outdoors.

Your actual training sessions also need to be short enough to keep your dog's attention and sweet enough to keep him motivated. A training session should be five minutes — max — for puppies under 4 months of age, and no more than 10 minutes for older pups and adults. And to keep the session sweet, always end it on a positive note: Ask him to do something he already knows how to do. When he complies, lay on the praise and give him a treat.

And don't think you can't teach an old dog new tricks. Any dog can learn at any age. Older dogs may need a little more time to learn what you want them to do, but they love the attention — and the mental exercise of training can keep them healthier!

Here's how to teach basic commands that every dog should know.

His name

Training begins with teaching your Beagle his name. When your Beagle knows who he is, you can get his attention much more easily — and attention is crucial to learning. Follow these instructions to train your Beagle to recognize his name:

1. **Bring your Beagle to a place that's free from distractions.**

2. **Say his name in a cheerful voice.**

3. **As soon as he looks at you, praise him and give him a treat.**

   If he doesn't respond, don't repeat his name. Instead, change course: Eat the treat yourself (make sure it's something you both like) or leave the room for a minute or so. Then try again.

4. **Wait until he looks away from you, then repeat Steps 1 through 3.**

Sit

The Sit command is just about the easiest one that you can teach your Beagle. Here's how:

1. **Stand in front of your dog, and make sure you have his attention.**

2. **Hold a treat between your thumb and forefinger in front of him and make sure he sees it (see Figure 15-2a).**

3. **At the same time, say "Sit" and hold the treat just over his head.**

4. **With your dog's eyes on the prize, move the treat back toward his rear end (see Figure 15-2b).**

   As your dog follows your hand with his eyes, he'll automatically sit down.

5. **Praise and give the treat when his tush hits the ground.**

a

b

Figure 15-2: Use your hands, your voice, and treats to teach your Beagle to sit.

Down

Teaching the Down command follows the same principle as Sit — but make sure that your Beagle has mastered Sit before you try teaching this one. To teach the Down command:

1. **Squat, sit, or kneel down so you're close to his level.**

2. **Hold a treat in front of his face, and make sure he's looking at it.**

3. **Say "Down," in a long, drawn-out tone so you're really saying "Dooowwwwn."**

4. **Move the treat down to the ground about 6 inches in front of your Beagle (see Figure 15-3a).**

5. **Move the treat outward several more inches, so your hand is moving in an L-shaped path (see Figure 15-3b).**

   As the dog follows your hand with her eyes, he'll lie down.

6. **Praise and treat as soon as he's lying down.**

a

b

Figure 15-3: Lure your Beagle into a Down position with a treat.

Stay

The Stay command tells your dog to remain where he is. Here's how to teach it:

1. **Start by placing your dog in a Sit or Down position.**

2. **Place your open palm about 6 inches from his nose and say "Stay," in a long, drawn-out tone so you're really saying "Staaaaaay" (see Figure 15-4).**

3. **Keeping your palm up, move back one step, then return immediately.**

4. **Praise your Beagle for staying, and give him a treat.**

5. **Repeat Steps 1 through 4, moving back two steps this time.**

   Gradually increase the distance you move away from your Beagle, the length of time he must stay, and the distractions in his environment.

Figure 15-4: Your hand reinforces the Stay command.

Recall

The Recall command is probably the most important command that you can teach a dog — but for a Beagle with wanderlust (in short, probably 99.9 percent of all Snoopy-dogs), it's also just about the toughest. To teach this maneuver, arm yourself with lots of patience and plenty of treats. Then:

1. **Say your dog's name and "Come" in a happy, enthusiastic tone of voice.**

2. **Squat down and open your arms as your dog comes to you.**

3. **Welcome him enthusiastically and give him a treat when he reaches you.**

4. **Repeat the process, but gradually increase the distance between you.**

Even when your Beagle has mastered this maneuver, keep practicing it — but in a fun setting, such as hiding and calling him to come find you.

Don't practice this command outdoors unless your Beagle is on leash or in a securely fenced area!

Off

The Off command tells your Beagle to reverse course, no matter what he's doing. If he's interested in the chicken bone someone left on the sidewalk, a sharply spoken "off" will keep him from trying to eat it; if he's conducting a panty raid on your lingerie, a crisply spoken "off" will get him out of the clothes hamper or dresser drawer. To teach the Off command:

1. **Place your Beagle's favorite toy on the ground a few feet away from him.**

2. **When he heads for the toy, pick it up and say "Off!" in a loud, commanding voice that will startle him.**

3. **As he looks at you in surprise, praise him in a high, sweet-sounding voice — and then give him the toy.**

4 **Repeat Steps 1 through 3 until he instantly drops or moves away from the toy when he hears the command.**

Practice this command often — it's one that Beagles and other members of the canine persuasion tend to forget easily.

Walking on leash

Wouldn't it be nice to take your Beagle for a walk and not feel as though he's leading you in his own little reenactment of the Iditarod? News flash: You can! Just follow this plan:

1. **Leash your dog and place the leash loop around your wrist.**

2. **Grasp the leash with the looped hand just below the loop, and hold the leash about halfway down its length with the opposite hand.**

3. **Have your Beagle stand next to you on the side opposite your looped hand so the leash falls diagonally across your body.**

4. **Tell him, "Let's go!" in a cheerful but decisive voice, and start walking briskly.**

5. **As you walk, chat with your dog so he pays attention to you.**

6. **If he bolts out in front of you, let him go the full length of the leash, and then turn around suddenly — but without jerking the leash — and walk in the opposite direction.**

   Your surprised Beagle will soon learn to pay attention to you instead of whatever's causing him to run ahead.

7. **When you stop, remove your unlooped hand from the leash, and place that hand in front of your dog's face so he stops, too.**

8. **Repeat if necessary.**

Some notorious pullers acquire better walking manners when you acquire some new equipment. One option is to use a *head collar* instead of a regular collar. This device looks like a muzzle but works the same way a bridle on a horse does. If your Beagle lunges ahead while he's wearing this device, his head will be forced downward — not painfully, but enough to surprise him. Another option is a special harness that fastens at the breastbone to prevent pulling. Both are available at pet specialty stores.

Go to your place

As much as you love your Beagle, sometimes you won't want him underfoot. At such times, being able to tell him to go to a designated spot comes in very handy. Here's how to teach this maneuver:

1. **Choose a spot, such as his crate or a floor cushion in a corner of your living room, to which your dog can retreat and see all the household action.**

2. **Attach his leash, tell him "Place," and lead him to the designated spot.**

3. **Praise and give a treat.**

4. **Repeat Steps 1 through 3 until your Beagle goes to his place on command.**

Enrolling Your Beagle in Obedience Class

Although you can teach your Beagle basic good manners all by yourself, taking him to an obedience class is still a good idea. Such classes offer your little hound the chance to hang out with others of his kind, and to practice his obedience maneuvers amid more distractions. A class also allows you to compare notes with other owners and get expert help to improve your training techniques.

That said, all obedience classes are not created equal. Some are staffed by competent individuals who have made it their business to become experts on canine behavior and learning, and who make sure they keep abreast of research on dog training. Others, alas, may not have taken any training beyond what their one-gimmick franchise offers. Your job: Differentiate between the first type of trainer and the second, and make sure that you take your Beagle to the first.

Start by talking with your veterinarian and with owners of well-behaved dogs you know. Ask them where to find competent trainers in your area.

Another route to take is through cyberspace. Log onto the Web site of a training organization, such as the Association of Pet Dog Trainers at www.apdt.com. There you can search a database to find a trainer near you.

Look for trainers who have the initials CPDT after their names. This acronym stands for *Certified Pet Dog Trainer* and means that the trainer has studied for and passed a rigorous examination on positive reinforcement training.

After you've identified one or more trainers, ask them some questions. Here's what you need to know:

- ✔ **What is your training philosophy?** Most trainers are smart enough to answer "positive reinforcement" — but you need more specific information than a canned response offers. Find out how the trainer would apply that philosophy in specific situations, such as managing a dog who jumps on people. Some trainers use their knees or the leash to correct the dog's jumping; others try to divert the dog away from jumping to another, more appropriate attention-seeking action. You want a trainer who employs the latter approach.

- ✔ **What equipment do you use?** This question sheds more light on a trainer's methods. If the trainer uses slip chains, prong collars, electronic devices, or anything else that causes discomfort to the animal, walk away. Pain is not necessary to train a dog.

- ✔ **May I observe a class?** By watching a trainer in action, you can not only see for yourself whether he works the way he says he does, but also determine whether you and your Beagle would be comfortable working with him. Watch how the trainer interacts with both people and dogs, and see whether the class is too crowded (an ideal ratio is one instructor for every six dogs; a 1-to-8 ratio should be the max). Note, too, how the trainer explains and demonstrates concepts, answers owners' questions, and handles disruptive dogs. Finally, see whether the human and canine students appear to be having fun while they're learning.

- ✔ **Do you have references?** Any trainer can create a gorgeous brochure or hire a designer to build a great Web site — but neither of these marketing vehicles gives you the info you need to evaluate the trainer. That's why you should ask for references from clients and veterinarians — and why you should call at least a couple of them. Ask them what they think of the trainer, whether they found her classes effective, and how she deals with dogs who have trouble catching on.

- ✔ **Do you offer both private and group classes?** A trainer who offers both group classes and private instruction may be more versatile and flexible than a trainer who offers only group instruction. Trainers who offer both types of instruction are more likely to adapt their programs to each individual dog, and are better able to help you deal with any problems that your Beagle may have.

Chapter 16

Rehabbing the Delinquent Beagle

. . . .

In This Chapter

▶ Dealing with behavioral problems
▶ Finding expert help

. . . .

*E*very Beagle needs basic training (see Chapter 15), but some Beagles need more than the basics. These little hounds need special help to overcome special issues that trouble them — and probably trouble you, too. But you don't have to live with your Beagle's behavioral problems. This chapter helps you to deal with the problems that most often get in the way of your Beagle getting a good-conduct medal. If you can't solve the problem yourself, the chapter explains how to find an expert who can help you.

Solving Common Snoopy-dog Problems

No dog, not even your beloved Beagle, is perfect. Every little hound (heck, every member of the canine kingdom) presents her own unique set of pluses and minuses: areas where she excels and areas where she needs a little extra help. Here are some ideas on how to deal with some of the behavioral challenges that your pooch is most likely to present.

Huh? You talkin' to me?

No, I'm not saying that your Beagle is likely to imitate Robert De Niro's character in the classic film *Taxi Driver*. Unlike the melancholy Travis Bickle, the Beagle is a merry little dog who is tremendously curious about the world around her. She loves investigating new smells and sights, and is a master at living in the moment. We humans could all stand to learn from the Beagle's ability to embrace the present.

However, that ability does have a downside: Your little hound may be so interested in whatever she's doing at the moment that she fails to focus on you. Such inattention could pose a real challenge if you're trying to train her or otherwise need for her to focus on you.

The solution is to become so interesting to your Beagle that she will want to focus on you before she pays attention to anything else. The following tips will help you achieve that goal:

- ✔ **Bribe shamelessly.** The way to a Beagle's heart often passes through her stomach, so use that route to your advantage. Figure out which foods or treats your Snoopy-dog loves more than any others, and offer those tidbits as incentives for her to do what you ask.

- ✔ **Stay positive.** Never, ever ask your Beagle to do something that has a negative consequence. For example, don't ask her to come, and then scold her for an earlier transgression. (Think about it: Would *you* want to go to someone who yells at you when you get there?)

- ✔ **Avoid failure.** Don't ask your Beagle to do something she's likely to fail at. If, for example, she's having a great time playing at the dog park but it's time to go home, don't expect her to come when you call her. Go to her.

- ✔ **Be the shizzle.** The best way to get your Beagle to pay attention to you is to be the *shizzle* in her life: the most interesting, fun-loving owner that you can possibly be. Take her with you on outings, play with her when you can, and give her tasty treats when appropriate. Let her know that she's important to you, and you'll become important to her.

Putting the (play) bite on you

Dogs tend to play with their teeth. If a dog's playmate is another dog, this oral style of frolicking usually doesn't present a problem. Because they both have fur that covers their skin, and because well-socialized dogs inhibit their bites, such oral gestures generally don't hurt the two canine players. But if one of the players is a human being, everything changes. That's because bare human skin is far more tender than fur-covered dog skin, so what feels like gentle mouthing to another dog feels like a painful bite to a thin-skinned human.

But you don't have to tolerate having your Beagle put the bite on you, even if she means no harm. Try these strategies to end those toothy tactics:

- ✔ **Make like a dog.** If your Beagle plays too roughly with another dog, that dog will let her know by yelping in pain. Try doing the same thing with your Beagle: If she's using her teeth on your skin, yelp or squeal the way a puppy does. Another option: Say "Ouch!!!" in a harsh-sounding, loud voice. Either way, chances are your Beagle will look up in surprise — which means that she's no longer mouthing you.

- ✔ **Walk away.** Some dogs persist in their play biting. If your Beagle is one such dog, end the game and walk away (if she's a puppy, put her in her crate). The consistent loss of your company due to nipping may soon persuade her to find other ways to keep you around for playtime.

- ✔ **Give alternatives.** Help your rowdy little hound find other ways besides roughhousing with you to release some of the pent-up energy that can result in rough play. Toss a ball for her to fetch, do some obedience moves with her, or take her for a nice, long walk that gets her good and tired. If she's old enough, take her to a dog park to play with other pooches.

- ✔ **Teach her to stop.** A variation of the Off command, which I explain in Chapter 15, can help you teach your Beagle to keep her teeth off your person. Get out a few tasty treats, and hold one treat in your hand. Tell your Beagle "take it" and give her the treat. Now put another treat in your hand, close your fist, and say "off." Do this sequence a few times, and practice daily. Soon, you should be able to tell your Beagle "off" when she places her teeth on you.

The advice here is for juvenile and adult Beagles who engage in play-biting. If your Beagle's biting is not all in fun — in other words, if she's being aggressive — you need to read the following section.

Knocking that chip off her shoulder

Most Beagles are happy-go-lucky, all's-right-with-the-world kinds of dogs. But some unfortunate pooches, for one reason or another, have massive chips on their shoulders. They growl or bite people without apparent provocation — and they're not playing. They're belligerent and aggressive.

A person who lives with such a dog has a big problem, even with a little dog such as a Beagle. Aggressive dogs are not only dangerous to the people they come in contact with but also are financial liabilities — just try getting homeowner's insurance renewed if your dog's been deemed aggressive in a court of law.

Can the aggressive dog be saved? Maybe. If your Beagle is belligerent, follow this advice:

- ✔ **Protect others.** Until or unless you find out what's causing your dog's aggressive behavior and are able to reverse that behavior, you must protect other people from her. If you walk with her in public, make sure she wears a muzzle and a leash. (Don't walk your muzzled dog in very hot weather, and don't run with her at all.) At home, confine her to her crate if you have guests, especially if those guests are children.

- ✔ **Protect the dog.** All dogs need protection from clueless humans, but the aggressive dog needs even more safeguarding. Never leave any children alone with the dog. Do not allow children to tease the dog in any fashion, and teach your own children to refrain from running around and screaming when the dog is nearby.

- ✔ **See your vet pronto.** All too often, aggressive behavior has physical causes. For example, a dog who suffers from a specific type of epilepsy can suffer from sudden, unpredictable, and uncontrollable episodes of rage. The same may be true of a dog whose production of thyroid hormone is low — even on the low side of normal. Other physical causes of aggression include pain, trauma, certain infections such as Lyme disease, food allergies, excessive protein in the diet, and long-term exposure to toxic substances such as lead. Your vet can help you determine whether a physical problem is causing your dog's behavior problem, and he may be able to prescribe medication or another treatment to stabilize her behavior.

- ✔ **Consult a trainer.** Even if your dog's aggressive behavior has a treatable physical cause, you still need to work with a highly skilled trainer to help break the animal's habit of responding aggressively. And private lessons are essential. An aggressive dog needs one-on-one assistance from a pro to learn new behaviors, and that dog's people need help to learn how to deal with their canine companion. Make sure, though, that the trainer uses positive methods; a trainer who uses harsh, corrective methods may worsen your dog's problem.

- ✔ **Be realistic.** Sometimes, no matter how much you do to help your aggressive dog, her behavior is not reliable enough for you and others to live safely with her. In such cases, euthanasia is a humane option. Talk with your vet and your trainer if your dog doesn't seem to be responding. In the end, though, you must be prepared to do what's best not only for you and your dog, but also for those with whom the dog may come into contact.

Taming the bouncy Beagle

Who would have thought that a 13- to 15-inch dog could jump to well more than double that height? If you have a Beagle, you know the answer to that question: The little hound can morph into a canine pogo stick if the spirit moves her.

Generally, though, the spirit moves the Beagle to become airborne for one reason: She wants attention. By shooting herself upward she usually gets that attention, even if it comes in the form of, "Ouch! What are you doing to my sweater?! Don't jump on me! Get down!!" Your bouncy Beagle doesn't really care that you don't like what she's doing. She just wants a reaction — especially if she doesn't get a lot of attention in the first place. Consequently, yelling at her does nothing to stop her pogo stick behavior.

And yes, you can knee her in the chest, or grab her paws so she can't get back on all fours. However, these maneuvers call for incredibly good physical coordination on your part and, more importantly, jeopardize your Beagle's safety. A knee that lands in the chest too hard or an awkward grab of the paw can result in bruises, sprains, or even broken bones.

A better way to bring the bouncy Beagle back down to earth is to simply refuse to pay attention to her behavior. The next time she performs a doggy liftoff, walk away from her, or at least turn your back. Say nothing. Pay no attention to her at all until she's planted her four legs back on the floor and keeps them there. Then, praise her, pet her, and give her a treat. Do this consistently whenever she jumps up on you — and instruct others in your household to do the same. Pretty soon she'll realize that the way to get attention from you is to keep four on the floor.

Loving you waaaay too much

Most Beagles are reasonably independent, but a few fail to function well without their people. These sad individuals not only hate solitude but often go bonkers if left alone. They may destroy your stuff, have bathroom accidents, howl, cry, or otherwise wreak havoc when you're not around. Experts call this problem *separation anxiety,* and it can be a tough challenge for Beagle and human alike.

However, tough doesn't mean insurmountable. If prolonged solitude drives your Beagle crazy, try taking these tactics:

✔ **Wear her out.** If possible, take your Beagle for a brisk 20-minute walk or engage in a strenuous play session with her before you head out the door. Get her panting. A hearty romp may leave her too tired to miss you (and get upset) after you're gone.

✔ **Keep her busy.** Interactive toys like Kongs and Busta Cubes can give your little hound something so intriguing to do that she forgets to be lonesome. Both toys, which are available at most pet supply stores and superstores, allow you to stuff treats inside them and require your Beagle to ferret those treats out. The reward, of course, is to enjoy the goodies. If you stuff the treats tightly enough, your Snoopy-dog will have to work very hard to reap the tasty reward — which means she won't be missing you.

✔ **Change your routine.** Many dogs can anticipate when their people are about to depart because those people engage in the same predeparture routines. My own dog appears from nowhere just as I'm about to leave the house because I always put on lipstick, put on my shoes, pick up my purse, and get out my keys. Fortunately, Allie doesn't suffer from separation anxiety, but if your dog does, an unchanging departure routine can heighten that anxiety.

For that reason, you may want to prevent that anxiety-producing anticipation by varying your departure rituals. Try putting on your shoes and then going into the living room to read a book. Pick up your purse and keys, but then head into the bathroom. By breaking the chain of anxious anticipation, you can help your Beagle feel less nervous about your impending departure — simply because she won't know that you're leaving.

✔ **Downplay your departures.** Many dogs with separation anxiety have owners who make a big deal out of their departures. They rain hugs and kisses on their Beagles, who become so revved up emotionally that they have no way to discharge those emotions when the owner isn't there — except to destroy the owner's stuff. Instead, be matter-of-fact when you take your leave. A simple "Bye, I'll be back soon" or "Be a good dog and watch the house" will do.

✔ **Crate her.** For some (but not all) dogs, spending alone time in the crate can help her feel better about being all by herself — especially if she's got a Kong or Busta Cube to keep her busy.

✔ **Encourage independence.** Even when you're around, give your dog something to do on her own. That stuffed Kong or Busta Cube can keep her happy and content.

✔ **Consider day care.** If you've got the bucks, your Beagle may be a prime candidate for doggy day care. At good doggy day cares, the canine guests get to frolic with one another for most of the day. Your stuff is safe, your Beagle is happy, and you have a mellow canine companion when you pick her up and head for home.

✔ **Take her with you.** Check and see if your workplace allows you to bring your dog to work. If the answer is yes and your Beagle is generally well behaved, your problem's solved.

✔ **See your vet.** If you've tried most of the other measures and have had no luck in abating your Beagle's anxiety, see your vet. He may be able to prescribe medications that can help your dog calm down when you depart — and if she's even just a little calmer, she can benefit from other steps you take to de-traumatize your departures.

Helping the bashful Beagle

Does your Beagle run behind your legs whenever you encounter other people or pooches during your walks? Does she hide in a corner when you have guests? Does she shrink from being petted? If you've answered "yes" to any of these questions, you've got a bashful Beagle: a shy little gal who needs lots of love and attention and some help to build her confidence. Here are some ways to do just that:

✔ **Expose her.** Take your bashful Beagle out and about, and let her see what the world has to offer. Sit on an urban park bench with her, and together watch the world go by. Watch a kids' soccer game. Walk her everywhere: in your neighbor-hood, the local shopping center, a park. The more novel sights and sounds you expose her to, the better. Chapter 7 offers lots of tips for giving your Beagle a positive introduction to the joys of the world around her.

✔ **Talk to strangers.** Bring some treats with you on your jaunts, and get some approachable strangers to give those goodies to your shy Snoopy-dog. True story: Years ago I asked a local mail carrier to give my very shy dog (not a Beagle) some treats that I supplied to help Cory be less wary of strangers. The mail carrier was happy to oblige, and would offer treats to my bashful boy whenever he saw him. Within a few weeks, Cory would start dragging me down the street whenever he saw that letter carrier — and for the rest of his life he would exhibit unmistak-able excitement whenever he saw a U.S. Postal Service truck.

✔ **Teach her something new.** The dog who lacks confidence often develops amazing self-assurance when she learns a sport or new skill. Consider taking your dog to an agility or flyball class, or take her swimming. Teach her some tricks, too: *Dog Tricks For Dummies* by Sarah Hodgson (Wiley) will give you some ideas for nifty new moves that you can teach your Beagle.

✔ **Take it slow.** Don't push your bashful Beagle to do more than she's ready for, and keep your socialization sessions short.

The key here is to keep everything happy and positive, so your Beagle can build her confidence at her own pace.

✔ **Don't coddle.** If your dog starts cringing or otherwise exhibits fear or shyness, do not pick her up and start crooning, "It's okay, baaaayyyybeeeee." By doing so you reward her shy behavior — exactly what you don't want to do.

Need more help? Check out *Help for Your Shy Dog: Turning Your Terrified Dog into a Terrific Pet* by Deborah Wood (Howell Book House).

Shushing the barking Beagle

Beagles can be rather vocal individuals. They like to bark and, in true hound fashion, they like to howl. Such vocalizing will make you rather unpopular with your neighbors unless you can keep the barking to a manageable level, if not a minimum. Here's how to limit your hound's bow-wowing:

✔ **Wear her out.** A dog who's gotten plenty of exercise is less likely to have the energy to mouth off than the dog who does nothing but lie around the house.

✔ **Keep her entertained.** If your little hound's concerts start while you're away from home, give her something else to do instead. A treat-filled Kong toy or Busta cube can provide lots of tasty entertainment for your solitary Snoopy-dog, and she won't need to bark to amuse herself.

✔ **Ignore her.** Yes, it's tempting to respond to your loud-mouth Beagle by getting a little bit loud yourself — but yelling at your dog to quiet down usually has the opposite effect. Instead, walk away. Ignore her. Withdraw the attention that she seeks.

✔ **Ask why.** Sometimes dogs have a good reason for barking. For example, an intruder is nearby (the fact that said intruder is a squirrel scampering across your patio is totally irrelevant to your Beagle) or something else is amiss. Try to find out why your Bowser is barking. If the reason is understandable, thank her, give her a treat — and then give her something else to do.

Keeping the wanderer home

The Beagle is *not* a natural homebody. Like many hounds, her idea of heaven on earth is to sniff something intriguing and follow that scent to its source. If that source is beyond your property line — well, from your dog's standpoint, that's the way it (and she) goes.

What's most important to her is finding the source of that scent. She spends her life being led around by her nose.

In addition to a consuming interest in fragrant phenomena, the Beagle also is a fairly independent member of the canine kingdom. Of course she loves you — but for her, loving you and adhering to your agenda are not necessarily one and the same. She's got her own priorities, and those priorities can easily take her beyond your borders, unless you prevent her from doing so. Here's how:

✔ **Fence her in.** Either invest in secure fencing for your yard, or resolve to never, ever let your Beagle off leash unless she's in an area that's surrounded by secure fencing. Actually, do both!

✔ **Check her collar.** If your Beagle wears a buckle collar, check every few weeks to make sure that the hole for the buckle pin hasn't gotten so large that the pin comes loose. And no matter what sort of collar your Beagle wears, check periodically to make sure that the collar isn't so loose that your dog can slip her head through it and head for the hills.

✔ **Practice recalls.** Coming when called is particularly difficult for a Beagle, but practice never hurts. It's not beyond the realm of possibility that your command to come would keep your Beagle from going on the lam. See Chapter 15 for instructions on how to teach your Beagle to come when she's called.

Teaching treat-taking manners

Does your Snoopy-dog get a little too snappish when she takes the treat you offer her? If so, you can teach her better manners. Here's how:

1. **Hold the treat between your thumb and index finger.**

   Make sure that the treat is big enough for your Beagle to grab without also grabbing your fingers.

2. **Offer your Beagle the treat, saying "Take it nice" as you do so.**

3. **If she snaps or grabs at the treat, pull it back quickly and tell her "Oh, nooooooo!" in a scandalized, what-are-you-thinking tone of voice.**

4. **Wait a couple of seconds, and then repeat Step 2; if she still snaps, repeat Step 3.**

5. **Repeat Steps 2 and 3 until your Beagle takes the treat politely.**

Picking Experts' Brains

Not every Beagle responds to owner teaching or even to group obedience classes. If your Beagle is one of those dogs, don't despair: Specialized help is available. Here are some options to help the Beagle with special behavioral challenges.

Getting private lessons

Some dogs don't do well in group class settings. My own canine companion is one such animal. In any class I've taken her to, Allie performs beautifully and learns quickly — but she becomes very impatient with sitting quietly and having to wait her turn to strut her stuff. Consequently, she becomes very disruptive. She barks incessantly and tries to play with the other canine students. Needless to say, neither she nor I have been very popular with the other students or the instructors in classes we've taken.

In such cases — or if you simply can't mesh your schedule with that of a class — private instruction from a trainer could be the answer. A trainer comes to your home, works with you and your dog both indoors and out, and gives your dog concentrated one-on-one attention. The dog learns much more quickly than in a group class.

There's a downside to private lessons, of course: the price. In my area, a series of six or seven private sessions costs about $500, where a seven-session group class costs about $175. (I live in an expensive area; your mileage may vary.) But if your dog isn't likely to learn much in a group class, getting private lessons may be a good investment.

To find a trainer who does private sessions, check out the Association of Pet Dog Trainers Web site at www.apdt.com. Call a couple of the trainers you find on the site's searchable database and ask if they do private lessons. Have them come meet your dog, ask the questions suggested in Chapter 15, and take things from there.

Trying day training

Maybe you're *really* busy — so busy that you can't find the time to take your Beagle to class, schedule private lessons, or even teach her basic good manners on your own. If that's your situation, *day training* may be just the ticket for you and your little hound.

Essentially, day training means that you take your Beagle to a doggy day care or training facility and leave her there for the day. She'll get plenty of play time with other pooches, but she'll also get several one-on-one lessons from a professional trainer. When you pick your Beagle up in the evening, she'll be tired from an active day, but she also will have learned some new moves to add to her knowledge of good doggy manners.

However, you can't expect day training to work unless you're willing to do at least a little work with your dog, too. Any good trainer will do two things to ensure that your Beagle applies her new knowledge at home. First, when you pick up your Beagle, the trainer will show you what she and your dog did during the day. Second, she'll give you some written instructions on how to practice with your dog at home.

Realize, too, that day training doesn't come cheap. In my area, a program that includes a week at a doggy day care, six hours of private instruction, and a homework manual costs about $700. That said, day training can be a great investment for a busy owner who nevertheless wants a well-mannered Beagle — if the owner is willing to practice at home.

To find a day trainer, call a few local trainers and/or some local doggy day care facilities.

Finding a Beagle shrink

Some Beagles have behavioral problems that are beyond the ability of even the most knowledgeable trainer to fix. These challenges include severe separation anxiety and unprovoked aggressiveness.

But just as we can consult psychologists and psychiatrists to help us grapple with our mental health issues, Beagles (and their people) can use the services of *animal behaviorists* to help them improve their emotional well-being. Two types of behaviorists are especially well equipped to help your little hound overcome any issues she may have: an *applied animal behaviorist* and a *veterinary behaviorist*.

The applied animal behaviorist has at least a master's degree in behavioral science with an emphasis on animal behavior; many have doctoral degrees in these disciplines. They are highly qualified to diagnose and treat complex animal behavior problems; however, unless a certified applied animal behaviorist is also a veterinarian, he cannot prescribe medications. Your own vet can refer you to a certified applied animal behaviorist, or you can contact one yourself. To find an applied animal behaviorist, log onto the Animal Behavior Society (ABS) Web site at www.animalbehavior.org/ABSAppliedBehavior/caab-directory.

The veterinary behaviorist is a veterinarian who has taken postgraduate coursework in animal behavior, completed a two- or three-year residency program with another veterinary behaviorist, completed an animal behavior research project, and passed an examination. Those who complete such requirements receive certification from the American College of Veterinary Behaviorists (ACVB).

The veterinary behaviorist is particularly helpful if your dog's problem has a physical cause; for example a seizure problem that may be prompting a dog to engage in very aggressive behavior. This type of behaviorist can conduct a medical exam to determine whether physical factors are causing a behavior problem, and can prescribe medications when appropriate. Generally, your veterinarian must refer you to a veterinary behaviorist. A list is available at www.veterinarybehaviorists.org/about_us/services.

Anyone can say call himself an animal behaviorist — but applied animal behaviorists and veterinary behaviorists have the credentials to prove their expertise. If you're considering the services of a behaviorist, check to see whether he's on either the ABS or ACVB lists. If he's not — well, then for all you know, he's just hanging out his shingle, nothing more.

Reading your Beagle's mind

Many people wish that they could just understand their Snoopy-dogs a little better. They wonder what's going on in their Beagles' noggins, and are sure that a little bit of insight could help them have better relationships with their canine companions. These devoted owners may consider consulting an *animal communicator* (sometimes called a *pet psychic*).

Animal communicators claim to use mental telepathy to understand what an animal is thinking, which they then communicate to the owner. Many say that they don't need to meet the animal in person, but can get all the information they need from an interview with the owner and a photo of the animal. The interview usually takes place over the phone, although in-person interviews are not uncommon.

Animal communication and mental telepathy have plenty of detractors. Many scientists believe that the practice is just so much hokum. However, plenty of owners believe otherwise.

A long-time animal communicator, Penelope Smith, has compiled a directory of others in the profession for her Web site. Those listed in the directory must provide testimonials from past clients, pay an annual listing fee, and agree to abide by a code of ethics that Smith has developed. You can find the listing at www.animaltalk.net/consultlist.htm.

Part V
The Part of Tens

The 5th Wave
By Rich Tennant

"I don't think teaching the puppy how to help you cheat at cards was the training and bonding experience the vet had in mind."

In this part . . .

The person most responsible for ensuring that you and your Beagle have a long, happy life together is you. Part V outlines ways to make the most of life with your little hound and avoid the pitfalls that many a clueless Beagle owner finds himself enmeshed in. Also included is a final chapter that lists some unusual occupations that Beagles have engaged in to help you appreciate the many virtues of your own Snoopy-dog.

Chapter 17

Ten Ways to Keep Your Beagle Healthy and Happy

In This Chapter

▶ Keeping your Beagle in tip-top condition

▶ Helping your Beagle live longer

▶ Improving your Beagle's quality of life

*A*lthough no dog lives forever, Beagles can live a pretty long time: The average life expectancy for the Snoopy-dog ranges between 10 and 14 years. You can do a lot to increase the odds that your beloved Beagle will live out her full life span. In this chapter, I give you a list of ways to not only add months or even years to your Beagle's life, but also to keep her happy and healthy through most, if not all, of that time.

Find a Great Vet

Yes, you are your Beagle's best friend. But even you, a loving and attentive owner, can't be everything to your dog. To live her life to the max, she also needs the care of someone who has more expertise on Beagle medicine than you probably do. That individual is your veterinarian.

Throughout your Beagle's lifetime, your veterinarian will work with you as a partner in your dog's care. Regular visits to your vet will help to maintain your Beagle's good health and solve any problems that arise.

But no matter how much technical expertise a veterinarian has, you will be less likely to use his services if the two of you aren't a good match. If you don't have a vet already, Chapter 5 offers pointers on how to choose the right one for you and your beloved Beagle. Chapter 12 contains valuable tips on how to work most effectively with your vet when your dog shows signs of illness.

Give Her the Skinny

Beagles have a reputation for being insatiable chowhounds. Left to their own devices, they're likely to eat well beyond the point of stemming hunger and may turn themselves into baby blimps. A baby blimp may look cute, but looks aren't an infallible indicator of good health. Pleasingly plump isn't a plus for your Beagle (or for any other dog).

Carrying too much weight can shorten your Beagle's life. A study from Nestle Purina Pet Care showed that excessive eating can cause a dog to show signs of aging earlier than would have been the case with a normal diet — enough to reduce that dog's lifespan by two years. In addition, overweight Beagles are more likely than their slimmer counterparts to have problems with their hearts and joints because of the strain created by those extra pounds.

But if you do your part, your Beagle need not be overweight. With your vet's help, you can determine what your Beagle's ideal weight should be and work from there to get her to that point. If she needs to pare off some poundage, feed her the correct amount of the best, highest-quality diet you can afford to give her, and try to at least limit the amount of doggy treats and other high-calorie good-ies you slip her between meals. Chapter 8 gives you the skinny on how to give your Beagle the skinny.

Keep Her Moving

Any dog trainer will tell you that "a tired dog is a good dog." In other words, there's a simple secret to raising your dog to become a treasured companion who lies at your feet or across your lap, waking up from her snooze only to give you a loving lick. Moreover, any dog can become such an affectionate couch potato — even the devil-may-care, lives-to-be-active Beagle.

Ironically, the secret to creating a couch potato is to keep the couch potato moving. Make sure she gets plenty of exercise, especially when she's young. A daily session of active games, such as those described in Chapter 9, can siphon off some of the excessive energy that Beagles are notorious for. The result will be a mellower Beagle who's more likely to take to training and will be more amenable to daily love fests. A tired Beagle also is much less likely to trash your house than a Beagle who's rarin' to go but has no place to go.

Of course, calming your Beagle isn't the only benefit that regular exercise offers. Physical fitness will help keep your dog's heart and lungs in good condition and can help to forestall arthritis. In addition, the fit Beagle is likely to be a trim Beagle, because exercise consumes some of the calories packed into the food she eats.

And don't forget mental fitness! Combine exercise with games and training that will stimulate your Beagle's noggin. Problem-solving toys, such as food-stuffed Kongs and Buster Cubes (which I describe in Chapter 16), can engage your Beagle's interest and appetite — and keep her from turning into Destructo Dog when you're not home to watch her.

Do Fence Her In

More than most breeds, Beagles tend to wander far away from where they're supposed to be — and once they're wandering, they're less likely than most dogs to come back when they're called. Consequently, the person who releases an unleashed Beagle into an unfenced yard does so at his peril — and at the Beagle's peril, too. Predators, cars, and other dangers are ready to stop the merrily oblivious, scent-pursuing stray Beagle literally dead in the dog's tracks.

For that reason, you should — no, you must! — exercise your Beagle either on leash or within a securely fenced yard. And be sure that fencing is real fencing you can see; many a Beagle has withstood the shock of an underground electronic fence in the name of pursuing a bunny, squirrel, or other critter. By the same token, avoid tying your Beagle outside without your supervision. The tie-out maneuver leaves your dog at the mercy of free-roaming animals and unscrupulous humans, not to mention the ravages of her own teeth on the leash.

Chapter 5 discusses equipping your home and yard for a Beagle, and Chapter 9 discusses exercises that keep your Snoopy-dog not only fit but also safe.

Take Her to School

Chapter 15 devotes a goodly number of pages to showing you how to teach your Beagle basic good manners: to come when called, sit and lie down when told, walk nicely on leash, ask to go out, and go to a designated place when you need her to. So, why you might ask, should you also take her to obedience classes?

An obedience class gives you the benefit of real-time, face-to-face instruction with an expert: a professional dog trainer. The trainer can see any mistakes you may be making and help you refine your technique. Moreover, training amid the distractions of other puppies and people can help solidify the lessons you're trying to teach your Beagle at home, even if those distractions make the learning curve a little bit steep at first.

A class also can put you in touch with other dog people — maybe even Beagle people! — who have the same interest that you do: raising a well-trained, mannerly dog. Being able to network and brainstorm training solutions with other people can help both you and your dog to live more happily together.

Finally, a well-trained dog inevitably leads a happier life than the untrained pooch because people love to spend time with a well-behaved canine. And because just about every pooch loves to spend time with people, the Beagle who knows how to behave is happier — because she gets to spend more time with people than her unschooled counterpart.

Chapter 15 gives you pointers on what to look for in a trainer, as well as tips on how to find one.

Keep Her Pretty

A Beagle doesn't have a high-maintenance coat — which is one reason why a lot of people like this breed — but that doesn't mean these dogs don't need grooming. Grooming your Beagle not only keeps her pretty but also gives you quiet time together, which helps to build and strengthen the bond between the two of you. Another plus to grooming: The hands-on nature of the job helps you spot potential problems, such as lumps, cuts, and skin problems. Finally, certain tasks such as tooth brushing and ear cleaning help prevent other health threats such as tooth decay and ear infections.

Chapter 10 gives you all the information you need to keep your Beagle beautiful: how to give her a bath, brush her coat, clean her ears, brush her teeth, and give her a painless pedicure, among other tasks.

Be Proactive

The old maxim, "An ounce of prevention is worth a pound of cure," is as true for Beagles as it is for people. Dog-care experts such as veterinarians and trainers can do a lot to keep your dog healthy and happy — but they'll be able to do even more if you are on alert for signs of trouble between visits or classes. As you play with, train, and care for your Beagle, keep your eyes peeled for possible health and behavior problems.

On the health front, make sure your Beagle gets an annual wellness checkup until she's 8 or 9; at that point, switch to twice-yearly exams. These checkups give your vet a chance to catch possible problems early enough to up the odds of effective treatment.

 At home, keep a written record of your Beagle's health exams and other procedures. Record when she had her last checkup, and note on your calendar when you need to book her next exam. A separate notebook for this purpose can be very helpful, especially if you include copies of any results of lab tests your vet performs. Such reports, kept close at hand, can give you more information to share with your vet as you both work to maintain optimal health for your Snoopy-dog.

Chapter 11 gives tips on how to maintain your Beagle's health at home, and Chapter 12 describes diseases and conditions that are common to Beagle puppies and adults.

Trust Your Instincts

No one knows your Beagle better than you do — not your vet, your petsitter, your dog's trainer, or anyone else. Sure, they're experts in their fields and they've worked with oodles of dogs, but their knowledge is only general. They don't know your very special Beagle's individual health quirks and behavioral idiosyncrasies. And why should they? They don't live with your dog day in and day out, so they can't possibly have the knowledge you have.

That's why, if your Beagle's behavior suddenly changes, or she shows other signs of not feeling up to par, you should act on your knowledge. Call your veterinarian or dog trainer and work with them to determine what might be wrong.

 And never, ever be afraid to contact your vet or other pet professional because you think you may be making a mountain out of a molehill. Your love-driven instincts are the best tools a pet pro has for discovering problems early — and the earlier those problems are found, the more likely they are to be resolved.

If you think something's amiss with your Beagle, go with your gut. Depending on what you're observing, put in a call to your vet or other pet pro — or, at the very least, watch your four-legged friend even more closely than you usually do.

Have a Sense of Humor

Beagles are merry little dogs. They're full of curiosity and take an unabashed joy in living. For those who live with Beagles, these characteristics are a double-edged sword. On the one hand, the Beagle's happy-go-lucky nature makes her an engaging companion; on the other hand, the breed's curiosity (especially when it comes to unusual scents) can get your dog into trouble early and often. The Beagle's ability to make mischief is legendary.

As the owner of a mischief-making dog, I've learned that without a sense of humor, a dog's misguided adventures and antics can be an unbearable trial to the humans in her life. They can cause you to feel less love for her and may even prompt you to question whether you want to keep your dog. On the other hand, an ability to laugh at the mayhem your Beagle creates can go a long way toward keeping your relationship on track and keeping the two of you together.

Of course, it always helps to know that someone has gone through the same travails — or worse — than you and your Beagle have. If your sense of humor about your Beagle's behavior is lagging, try reading *What the Dog Did: Tales of a Formerly Reluctant Dog Owner* by Emily Yoffe (Bloomsbury USA, 2005). Reading about how Yoffe and her family coped with their Beagle's antics, and grew to love her nevertheless, will give you a new perspective on your own beloved Snoopy-dog.

Love, Love, Love

There's no such thing as loving a dog too much. After all, that's why you got her in the first place, right? So why hold back? Let yourself love your Beagle, even if you feel silly at first.

Go on: Get down on the floor and coo sweet nothings into the ears of your four-legged friend. Develop silly little sayings or songs just for her. Consider lightening up on some of your prohibitions such as not letting your Beagle sleep in your bedroom. Take her places: the park, the beach, the woods, the local doggy festival. In short, make your Beagle a full part of your life.

Knowing that one is loved helps anyone to live a higher-quality life, which is just as true for your Beagle as it is for you. You'll never regret making all this extra effort to please your Beagle. In giving all this love to her, you're creating a lifetime of loving memories for both of you.

Chapter 18

Ten Mistakes You Don't Need to Make with Your Beagle

In This Chapter

▶ Uncovering common Beagle ownership goofs

▶ Avoiding Beagle ownership boo-boos

*R*aising a Beagle puppy or adult dog can be a real challenge. No matter how much you want to do the job right, an unprepared owner can find plenty of ways to bungle the job. Some of these ownership goofs result from a lack of owner understanding; others are a result of owner impatience with this utterly adorable but occasionally exasperating Snoopy-dog.

Either way, many mistakes humans make with Beagles are avoidable — if the humans know ahead of time what those mistakes are likely to be. This chapter describes how and why people goof up Beagle ownership, and how you can avoid making such mistakes.

Not Doing Your Homework

The Beagle's big winsome eyes, long floppy ears, and sweet little snouts are guaranteed heart-melters. That said, you shouldn't let your heart melt to the point of buying or adopting a Beagle until you learn more about the breed first. Then you can decide whether this endearing breed really is right for you.

Chapter 2 offers much of the info you need to determine whether a Beagle is likely to be the dog of your dreams — or not. For example, if you live in an apartment, you might want to think twice about bringing a Beagle into your domicile. The reason: Beagles are vocal individuals, given to barking and other vocalizing that is likely to make you a tad unpopular with your neighbors.

Taking the time now to read up on all things Beagle will save you a ton of hassle and disappointment in the future.

Choosing Too Quickly

You've done your homework, and you've decided that a Beagle is exactly the right dog for you. You're sure you know what the next step is: getting a Beagle *now*.

Not so fast.

When you're choosing a Beagle, haste leads to heartbreak. A refusal to delay gratification can lead you to choose a less-than-healthy Beagle from a way-far-from-ideal source. Chapter 3 details those sources, such as the Internet and certain types of pet stores. The chapter also explains why other sources, such as backyard breeders and classified ads, are sources not only to question but to avoid.

 Play it safe and stick with a puppy or adult from trustworthy sources, such as a reputable breeder, an animal shelter, or a rescue group. Getting the right Beagle from a place you can trust is worth every day, week, or month you may have to wait.

Bypassing the Crate

The sight of your irrepressible Beagle running around in your fenced yard or tearing down the hallway of your house may cause you to have second thoughts about using a crate to teach him where he shouldn't run or deposit his business. You may wonder whether putting this carefree creature into a crate is cruel. You may feel that a crate is nothing more than a doggy prison. You may even fear that anyone who visits your house and sees your crated Beagle will summon a band of Animal Cops to your home to cite you for mistreating your beloved pooch.

Never fear. You're not being cruel. You're not becoming a warden for Beagle prison. And the only thing an Animal Cop would cite you for is for being a good Beagle owner.

Chapters 5 and 14 explain that a crate can be a Beagle's best friend. The crate taps into a dog's instinctive desire to live in a small den and to keep that den clean. A healthy Beagle won't pee or poop in his den if he can avoid doing so. A Beagle who's accustomed to a crate is likely to be a Beagle who's got a leg up (yes, that pun was intended!) on the uncrated Beagle when it comes to housetraining.

Here's another benefit from crate-training your Beagle: By escorting him to his little sanctuary whenever you leave the house, you can be sure that your house will be spared the ravages of Beagle mischief-making. Your furniture, carpets, and other possessions will be unmolested by Beagle claws and teeth.

Making housetraining easier, keeping your Beagle out of trouble, and sparing your stuff . . . what's not to like? Bypassing those benefits by eschewing the crate is a major mistake — a mistake that you don't need to make.

Expecting Housetraining to Be Easy

Although crates can make Beagle housetraining easier, teaching proper bathroom behavior to a Beagle still is no piece-of-cake enterprise. The reason is not that Beagles are stupid — they certainly aren't. They just have other priorities.

The ever-confident Snoopy-dog also can be stubborn, and that stubbornness may be reflected in a reluctance to do his business where and when you want him to. The Beagle also is known for his single-minded interest in following a scent to wherever that scent may take him and for his nose's ability to detect the faintest possible fragrance. Those characteristics mean that you need to be determined and consistent in teaching your dog proper potty protocol, no matter how uninterested he may act. You also must be fanatical about thoroughly cleaning up after any bathroom mistakes. The slightest trace of bodily waste residue on a carpet or floor guarantees that the Beagle will return to the scene of his crime and commit that crime again.

But like just about any dog, Beagles *can* be housetrained. As Chapter 14 explains, the keys to housetraining success are absolute consistency, abundant patience, and, yes, a good crate.

Failing to Be Vigilant

Did you fail to put one of your socks in the clothes hamper? Kiss that sock goodbye; your Beagle made off with it as soon as it hit the ground. Did you leave your ham sandwich on the coffee table while you went to answer the doorbell? The likelihood of that sandwich still being on that table when you return is zero. Did you let your Beagle puppy explore the house on his own before he was fully housetrained? Start looking for a puddle or pile now. I can safely guarantee that you *will* find at least one, maybe even both.

Until you can count on your Beagle not to use your living room as his own personal potty, don't let him wander through your house without you keeping an eagle eye on him for signs that he's planning to do his business. And *never* assume that your Beagle will stay out of your stuff. Instead, assume that he won't — and prevent any problems by keeping your stuff way beyond his reach.

Thinking That Your Beagle Is a Person

You come home from a hard day at the office and there in your vestibule is a little pile or puddle of you-know-what. Nearby, your Beagle sits, hanging his head. "Aha!" you think. He knows he's done wrong. You proceed to scold your four-legged friend, and you feel sure that his apparent guilt plus your lecture will persuade him to never, ever leave such a present for you again.

Think again.

Dogs experience many feelings, but guilt is not one of them. Your Snoopy-dog's woebegone demeanor probably results from previous homecomings in which you lectured him. He did not and will not connect your scolding with his bathroom boo-boo. Heck, he's forgotten that he even did it.

Unlike people, pooches such as Beagles do not feel guilt over that bad behavior, nor do they engage in such behavior for spite. They just do what they do unless they have the incentive to do something else. With the training tips offered in Part IV, you can provide that incentive and have a better-behaved Beagle.

Doing Things on the Cheap

Having a Beagle or any other canine companion doesn't come without plenty of expenses: the adoption fee or purchase price, vet visits, spaying/neutering, food, dishes, toys, treats. . . The list may seem endless, particularly if you're in a cash crunch. And you may be tempted to cut corners.

Maybe, for example, you think that you'll save money if you opt for generic-brand supermarket dog food over higher-quality fare. Perhaps you can't see the point of shelling out extra bucks for a stainless steel dish when plastic is so much cheaper. And if your Beagle gets yet another ear infection or another bout of diarrhea, you're understandably tempted to just let it all go or try treating it yourself, rather than schlepping him back to the vet and whipping out the plastic yet again.

The trouble is, being penny-wise is pound-foolish when you're caring for your Beagle. The recurrent ear infection or diarrhea could be a food allergy or something more serious. The plastic dish may be cheaper but also may cause a perpetual rash on your Beagle's chin. The cheap food may actually end up being more expensive than the pricey stuff because your dog needs more of the inexpensive brand to get the nutrition he needs.

Nobody is saying that you need to outfit your Beagle in a designer raincoat or rhinestone collar to give him a high-quality life. (Although if you want to and can afford to do so, that's your privilege, of course.) But investing the upfront money to take good care of your Snoopy-dog will pay off big time in good health, better behavior, and fewer visits to your vet's office in the long run. Chapter 5 and Part III explain how.

Thinking That Your Beagle Can Train Himself

Beagles are multitalented dogs. Some have excelled on the agility field or at the obedience trial. Others shine in the hospital ward as therapy dogs. Still others ferret out rabbits and other game. Even more locate illegally imported fruit and vegetables at busy airports. And even your own Snoopy-dog can learn to come when called, sit when told, and potty when and where he's supposed to.

However, he can't teach himself any of these maneuvers. He needs someone to teach him. Who better than you, his beloved human?

At the very least, take the time to teach your Beagle basic good manners — and, if all goes well, think about showing him some advanced maneuvers. Chapters 14 and 15 give you the lowdown on teaching basic Beagle etiquette, and Chapter 16 offers pointers on remedial training for the Beagle with learning issues. For the Beagle who's ready for bigger and better things, Chapter 9 describes sports that Snoopy-dogs can excel in.

Playing Doctor

The Beagle, like all other dogs, is a marvelously complicated creature. His body works because his muscular, skeletal, digestive, circulatory, nervous, and immune systems — to name just a few — work together to keep him healthy and active. When one or more of those systems goes awry, your Beagle gets sick.

Although you need to pay close attention to your Beagle's health and behavior, when he does get sick (and he will, no matter how hard you work to keep him well), you can't cure him yourself. He needs professional help from his very own doctor: your veterinarian. Tell the vet everything you know about your Beagle's condition, share your ideas, and advocate for your Beagle when necessary, but know that your vet has the training to put your pooch on the path back to wellness.

Chapters 11 and 12 give you the lowdown on how to work effectively with your vet, as well as vital information about common Beagle maladies.

Thinking That You Are More Important Than Bunnies

Your Beagle loves you. Count on it. He knows that you are the Giver of All Good Things, including great grub, tons of affection, and a warm, soft place to sleep. In his eyes, you are the most wonderful two-legged individual he has ever met. He may not always come when he's called, but that doesn't mean he is rejecting you in any way. He just has different priorities, that's all.

Those priorities are chasing rabbits, squirrels, and perhaps other interesting four-legged critters — and the drive to engage in such pursuits is hard-wired into your Beagle's psyche. As Chapter 2 explains, Beagles were developed for the express purpose of chasing down the real-life versions of Bugs Bunny and Rocket J. Squirrel. Put a fluffy- or cotton-tailed critter in front of a Beagle, and that Beagle will appear to forget that his beloved owner exists. You can't take such amnesia personally. This behavior is not about you.

To keep your Beagle safe, you need to recognize that squirrels, bunnies, and other instinct-triggering critters and smells are very likely to supercede your dog's desire to please you. Thus, you need to keep your Beagle on a leash or in a securely fenced yard, so if a local cotton-tailed burrower or fluffy-tailed tree dweller happens to amble onto the Beagle's turf, he can chase that critter without dashing into the street and into the path of a speeding car. True, the fence or leash will limit the likelihood of the Beagle actually catching the critter — but the journey, not the destination, is what counts.

Chapter 19

Ten Unique Beagle Occupations and Activities

In This Chapter

▶ Stories about real-life Beagles

▶ Beagles in literature and pop culture

▶ Other Beagle trivia

*T*his chapter won't tell you anything you absolutely, positively must know to love and care for your Beagle. It will, however, build on your love for this breed by sharing some little-known facts and stories of hard-working Beagles, chronicling a few ways that Snoopy-dogs — canine and otherwise — affect our lives.

Keeping Out Forbidden Fruit (and Other Stuff)

If you thought that winsome, big-eyed Beagles were the last dogs who could protect a nation, think again. These days, Beagles serve their country with distinction by making sure that illegally imported fruit doesn't get past U.S. Customs inspectors. These hard-working hounds were once called the Beagle Brigade and worked for the U.S. Department of Agriculture. Today, however, they are called Agriculture Detector Dogs, and they are an important part of the Department of Homeland Security's Customs and Border Protection (CBP) Canine Enforcement Program.

With the help of their human handlers, the specially trained, green-jacketed Beagles in this program patrol the customs areas at American airports and other border entry points, sniffing any luggage that crosses their paths. If a dog smells any sort of fruit, he alerts his handler by sitting down. The handler, who is a U.S. Customs officer, then asks the owner of the luggage for permission to open the bag. Much more often than not, the officer will find forbidden fruit or plants that could bear pests or diseases, which could devastate U.S. crops.

According to CBP, these dogs are responsible for about 75,000 seizures of illegal fruit, vegetables, meats, and plants every year. Nearly 150 Beagle/handler teams currently work in the United States at 24 airports, land points of entry, and major mailing facilities.

Shaming a President

Back in the mid-1960s, a Beagle demonstrated to no less than a U.S. president that a dog's ears are not designed to be handles. The Beagle's name was Him, and he belonged to President Lyndon B. Johnson. During a photo opportunity at the White House in 1964, the president attempted to show that Beagles didn't mind being picked up by their ears. American animal lovers felt otherwise, however. Even the Lyndon Baines Johnson Library and Museum acknowledges that the maneuver triggered a storm of protests. (If you want to see the picture, go to www.lbjlib.utexas.edu/ Johnson/archives.hom/FAQs/dog/pet_image_index.asp#ear. You can click on the "C311-7-64.JPEG" link to view a larger image of the photo.)

Him and his Beagle companion, Her, moved into the White House with the Johnson family in December, 1963, soon after Johnson assumed the presidency. Her died in November, 1964, after she swallowed a rock. Him died in June, 1966, after being struck by a car while racing across the White House lawn.

Inspiring Children

During a visit to Shiloh, West Virginia, children's book author Phyllis Reynolds Naylor found a frightened, abused dog — and was so haunted by the experience that she decided to write about the dog. The story became the classic children's book *Shiloh,* the story of a mistreated Beagle who finds a new home with young Marty Preston and his family. The book in turn inspired countless children to treat animals with greater kindness, to stand up for what they believed to be right, and to view fellow human beings with greater empathy than might otherwise be the case.

The book won the Newberry Medal, the most prestigious honor a book for young readers can receive, and spawned two sequels: *Shiloh Season* and *Saving Shiloh.* Two movies, *Shiloh* and *Shiloh Two: Shiloh Season,* were released in 1997 and 1999, respectively.

Nailing the Red Baron

Of all the characters in the classic Charles Schulz comic strip *Peanuts,* the most beloved may well be Snoopy, the Beagle who puts Christmas lights on his dog house, sleeps atop the same dog house, and fantasizes about being a World War I flying ace. In 1966, those fantasies inspired a singing group called the Royal Guardsmen to record "Snoopy Versus the Red Baron," a song that stayed atop the popular music charts for many weeks. A video game of the same title is available for Mac computers; you can download it from the Web at `http://snoopy2.sourceforge.net/download.html`. Not to be outdone, the U.S. Postal Service unveiled a series of postage stamps featuring Snoopy in his flying ace regalia.

Flying in (Way) Outer Space

The television show *Star Trek: Enterprise* featured a canine character named Porthos, a Beagle who belonged to *Enterprise* Captain Jonathan Archer. The backstory of Porthos notes that he and his littermates were all named after characters in the Alexandre Dumas classic *The Three Musketeers.* Porthos appeared in more than 30 episodes during the show's four-season run. A great image of Porthos with his best friend, Captain John Archer (portrayed by actor Scott Bakula), is available at `www.tvacres.com/dogs_beagles_porthos.htm`.

Comforting Other Dog Owners

Owning a dog can pose a considerable challenge to the most dedicated human. Not every dog behaves like Lassie does. Some canine miscreants steal underwear, destroy couches, and create all-around mayhem. If your Beagle fits this category, you may wonder whether you're alone in your efforts to cope with your four-legged hooligan.

Emily Yoffe, author of *What the Dog Did: Tales of a Formerly Reluctant Dog Owner* (Bloomsbury USA, 2005), assures you that life in Beagle-land can be tough for any owner. Yoffe chronicles the capers of her beloved Beagle, Sasha, and explains how, despite the havoc Sasha wreaks, Yoffe and her family come to love the dog. The story of how Sasha enabled Yoffe to evolve into a loving dog owner will comfort anyone who wonders why her Beagle isn't Lassie.

Knowing When to Mold 'Em

Mold is gross — if you can see it. When you can't see it, mold can still destroy your stuff and make you feel icky. So how do you find the mold you can see? Never fear: Mold-detecting Beagles are here! They're trained the same way Agriculture Detector Dogs are — except these doggies ignore forbidden fruit and sniff out molds instead. After you find the mold, you can take steps to get rid of it. Check out the U.S. Environmental Protection Agency's mold Web page: www.epa.gov/iaq/molds/moldcleanup.html.

Turning Out Termites

If molds suck, termites suck even more. No homeowner wants to have these obnoxious critters literally eat his house from within. Trouble is, finding the termites can be difficult, unless your house is literally falling down around you. Enter the Termite Dog — which in all probability will be a Beagle. Experts deem the Beagle the dog of choice for this specialized role, which calls for the same scent dis-crimination skills the Agriculture Detector Dogs and mold-detecting dogs employ. And because termite infestations are often hidden, Beagles can find infestations that elude human pest control specialists.

Befriending the Famous

Beagles aren't one of the most popular dogs in America for noth-ing. Their compact size, winsome good looks, and easygoing tem-peraments win them friends from countless unknown individuals, but a few persons of renown as well. Among the individuals who reportedly live with Beagles are Dr. Phil McGraw (yup, Dr. Phil); singer Barry Manilow (who has a fan club called the Beagle Bagels that raises money for various charities), and multiple members of the British royal family, past and present.

Taking Us to Our Pasts

Arguably, the most famous Beagle of all isn't a dog but a ship: the *HMS Beagle*. The *Beagle* transported naturalist Charles Darwin to the Galapagos Islands and the western coast of South America on a voyage that began in December 1831 and continued for five years. Darwin detailed his observations in his book *Voyage of the Beagle* — a book that may well contain the foundations of ideas that Darwin later developed into his theories of evolution. An image of the *Beagle* in the harbor of Sydney, Australia, is available at www. sc.edu/library/spcoll/nathist/darwin/darwin3.html.

Appendix
Wanna Know More? Additional Resources

*T*his book is designed to be the first, but by no means the last, word about finding the Beagle of your dreams and living happily ever after with her. If I've whetted your appetite for more information about making the most of life with your Snoopy-dog, you've come to the right place. This appendix contains suggestions for further reading — or, in some cases, viewing — about the joys of living with these larger-than-life little hounds, and how to make those joys yours.

Turn the Pages

A trip to your local bricks-and-mortar book superstore or its cyberspace equivalent will yield oodles of offerings on how to raise and train a dog, Beagle or otherwise. If you want more detail between two covers than is offered by the book you're currently holding, consider these titles:

✔ ***Dogs For Dummies*, 2nd Edition** by Gina Spadafori (Wiley, 2000): This is the mother of all *For Dummies* books about the canine kingdom. Spadafori has created a bible for dog-owning novices, and answers every question a wannabe dog owner could possibly ask without ever making the questioner feel stupid. A great read, and an even greater reference book.

✔ ***First Aid For Dogs: An Owner's Guide to a Happy, Healthy Pet*** by Stefanie Schwartz (Howell Book House, 1998): Every dog owner should have a compact guide to basic first aid, and this pint-sized hardcover fills the bill nicely. Schwartz is a veterinarian, but she writes in terms that lay people can understand about a wide variety of canine emergencies and mishaps that owners can treat on their own.

✔ ***The Holistic Dog Book: Canine Care for the 21st Century*** by Denise Flaim (Howell Book House, 2003): Chapter 11 of *Beagles For Dummies* touches on conventional and alternative medicine, but this book gives you all the info you could possibly need on the latter. Flaim is the pet columnist for *Newsday,* the Long Island, New York, daily newspaper, and uses all of her knowledge to create an informative guide to cutting-edge thinking in alternative dog care.

✔ ***Housetraining For Dummies*** by Susan McCullough (Wiley, 2002): Teaching proper potty protocol is a challenge for many Beagle owners. However, this little manual tells you everything you need to know about the housetraining process and then some. If Chapter 14 of *Beagles For Dummies* doesn't do it for you and your little hound, this book will fill in the gaps. I'd recommend it even if I hadn't written it!

✔ ***The Power of Positive Dog Training*** by Pat Miller (Howell Book House, 2001): Miller is one of America's best dog trainers, a passionate advocate of positive reinforcement training, and a former president of the Association of Pet Dog Trainers (APDT). In this book, she explains the science behind positive training in clear, understandable terms, and describes with equal clarity how to transform that science into a humane, effective training program for your dog. I can't recommend it enough.

✔ ***Senior Dogs For Dummies*** by Susan McCullough (Wiley, 2004): Senior dogs need special care and consideration to keep their more mature years truly golden, and this book tells you how to do just that. I also provide extensive coverage on dealing with the end of a dog's life — a subject that frightens and worries all too many owners of older dogs. And just like with *Housetraining For Dummies,* I'd recommend this book even if someone else were the author.

Divine DVDs

Plenty of trainers spread their brands of the dog behavior gospel by creating DVDs for the viewing public. Some are famous, but fame doesn't guarantee that the trainer's methods are effective or humane. For those reasons, I've limited my DVD recommendations to those by two trainers whom I've personally observed to be humane and positive in their approaches, and who get great results from both their human and canine students:

✔ *New Puppy! Now What?* by Victoria Schade (Rocket Media Group, 2006): I live with a dog who is a great adult canine companion but was a little monster when she was a puppy, especially on walks. Then I met Victoria Schade, who proceeded to take Allie and me in hand with a series of simple but highly effective at-home private sessions that helped me teach Allie some basic walking manners. With this DVD, other owners can benefit as I did from Schade's techniques. Order it from www.newpuppynowwhat.com.

✔ *Really Reliable Recall* by Leslie Nelson (Healthy Dog Productions, 2004): No trainer I've seen is more effective than Nelson in teaching a dog to come immediately. This DVD version of Nelson's renowned "Really Reliable Recall" classes includes help for challenging breeds such as Beagles. Order it from www.dogwise.com.

Peruse These Periodicals

If you want more timely information than books can offer, magazines are your ticket. Magazines about dogs and other pets come and go, but the titles listed here have stood the test of time. Unless otherwise noted, they're available on newsstands at book and pet superstores:

✔ *AKC Family Dog* (American Kennel Club): For people who love purebred dogs but aren't interested in dog shows, the AKC offers this quarterly magazine. The emphasis here is on dog care and integrating your dog successfully into your family life. The magazine is available only by subscription; log onto www.akc.org/pubs/index.cfm or call 800-490-5675.

✔ *AKC Gazette* (American Kennel Club): The bible for dog show devotees, the Gazette offers authoritative advice on dog shows, other performance events, dog care, and dog health. Each month, the magazine also profiles one of the 150-plus breeds recognized by the AKC. Available by subscription only; call 800-533-7323 or log onto www.akc.org/pubs/index.cfm.

✔ *The Bark* (The Bark Inc.): This bimonthly title lives up to its billing as "the modern dog culture magazine." Although it does include some dog care information, most of the magazine's pages focus on essays, literature, and art about dogs.

✔ *Dog Fancy* (Bowtie Inc.): This magazine is probably the most widely read dog-oriented magazine in America. Whatever you need to know about living with your Beagle, you'll find here.

✔ *Dog World* (Bowtie Inc.): While *Dog Fancy's* target is the pet-owning public, *Dog World's* demographic is owners who compete with their dogs in conformation, agility, obedience, and other performance events. If you've got a hankering to learn more about these dog sports, check out this monthly title.

✔ *Whole Dog Journal* (Belvoir Publications Inc.): This monthly newsletter reports on trends in alternative medicine for dogs and offers cutting-edge advice on positive reinforcement training. The newsletter pays special attention to nutrition and publishes a yearly evaluation of the best and worst commercial dog foods. It's available by subscription from the Web site at www.whole-dog-journal.com or by calling 800-829-9165.

✔ *Your Dog* (Tufts Media): One of the best veterinary schools in the country, Tufts University's Cummings School of Veterinary Medicine, produces this highly readable monthly newsletter that highlights the Tufts' faculty's expertise in dog health and behavior. Available only by subscription; call 800-829-5116.

Virtually Unparalleled

The World Wide Web has loads of resources for Beagle lovers and other dog devotees. Here are some of the best Web sites:

✔ *American Kennel Club*, www.akc.org: The AKC Web site has all you need to know about dog shows and other canine activities, plus info on events and breeds.

✔ *American Society for the Prevention of Cruelty to Animals,* www.aspca.org; and *The Humane Society of the United States,* www.hsus.org: Both of these sites include not only info on humane issues but also many valuable pet care tips. The ASPCA site also links to the Animal Poison Control Center.

✔ *American Veterinary Medical Association,* www.avma.org: AVMA's Web site includes a listing of veterinary specialty organizations whose members can help you deal with special problems your Beagle may have.

✔ *Association of Pet Dog Trainers,* www.apdt.com: This site has a searchable database to help you find a trainer in your area.

✔ *Healthypet.com,* www.healthypet.com: The American Animal Hospital Association created this Web site especially for pet owners. The site includes information about nutrition, common health problems, preventive care, training tips, and a searchable database to help you find an animal hospital near you.

✔ *National Beagle Club of America,* clubs.akc.org/NBC: This Web site tells you everything you may want to know about showing and competing with Beagles and then some.

Index

BUSINESS, CAREERS & PERSONAL FINANCE

0-7645-5307-0

0-7645-5331-3 *†

Also available:

✔Accounting For Dummies †
0-7645-5314-3
✔Business Plans Kit For Dummies †
0-7645-5365-8
✔Cover Letters For Dummies
0-7645-5224-4
✔Frugal Living For Dummies
0-7645-5403-4
✔Leadership For Dummies
0-7645-5176-0
✔Managing For Dummies
0-7645-1771-6

✔Marketing For Dummies
0-7645-5600-2
✔Personal Finance For Dummies *
0-7645-2590-5
✔Project Management
For Dummies
0-7645-5283-X
✔Resumes For Dummies †
0-7645-5471-9
✔Selling For Dummies
0-7645-5363-1
✔Small Business Kit For Dummies *†
0-7645-5093-4

HOME & BUSINESS COMPUTER BASICS

0-7645-4074-2

0-7645-3758-X

Also available:

✔ACT! 6 For Dummies
0-7645-2645-6
✔iLife '04 All-in-One Desk Reference
For Dummies
0-7645-7347-0
✔iPAQ For Dummies
0-7645-6769-1
✔Mac OS X Panther Timesaving
Techniques For Dummies
0-7645-5812-9
✔Macs For Dummies
0-7645-5656-8
✔Microsoft Money 2004 For Dummies
0-7645-4195-1

✔Office 2003 All-in-One Desk
Reference For Dummies
0-7645-3883-7
✔Outlook 2003 For Dummies
0-7645-3759-8
✔PCs For Dummies
0-7645-4074-2
✔TiVo For Dummies
0-7645-6923-6
✔Upgrading and Fixing PCs
For Dummies
0-7645-1665-5
✔Windows XP Timesaving
Techniques For Dummies
0-7645-3748-2

FOOD, HOME, GARDEN, HOBBIES, MUSIC & PETS

0-7645-5295-3

0-7645-5232-5

Also available:

✔Bass Guitar For Dummies
0-7645-2487-9
✔Diabetes Cookbook For Dummies
0-7645-5230-9
✔Gardening For Dummies *
0-7645-5130-2
✔Guitar For Dummies
0-7645-5106-X
✔Holiday Decorating For Dummies
0-7645-2570-0
✔Home Improvement All-in-One
For Dummies
0-7645-5680-0

✔Knitting For Dummies
0-7645-5395-X
✔Piano For Dummies
0-7645-5105-1
✔Puppies For Dummies
0-7645-5255-4
✔Scrapbooking For Dummies
0-7645-7208-3
✔Senior Dogs For Dummies
0-7645-5818-8
✔Singing For Dummies
0-7645-2475-5
✔30-Minute Meals For Dummies
0-7645-2589-1

INTERNET & DIGITAL MEDIA

0-7645-1664-7

0-7645-6924-4

Also available:

✔2005 Online Shopping Directory
For Dummies
0-7645-7495-7
✔CD & DVD Recording For Dummies
0-7645-5956-7
✔eBay For Dummies
0-7645-5654-1
✔Fighting Spam For Dummies
0-7645-5965-6
✔Genealogy Online For Dummies
0-7645-5964-8
✔Google For Dummies
0-7645-4420-9

✔Home Recording For Musicians
For Dummies
0-7645-1634-5
✔The Internet For Dummies
0-7645-4173-0
✔iPod & iTunes For Dummies
0-7645-7772-7
✔Preventing Identity Theft
For Dummies
0-7645-7336-5
✔Pro Tools All-in-One Desk
Reference For Dummies
0-7645-5714-9
✔Roxio Easy Media Creator
For Dummies
0-7645-7131-1

* Separate Canadian edition also available
† Separate U.K. edition also available

Available wherever books are sold. For more information or to order direct: U.S. customers
visit www.dummies.com or call 1-877-762-2974.
U.K. customers visit www.wileyeurope.com or call 0800 243407. Canadian customers visit
www.wiley.ca or call 1-800-567-4797.

SPORTS, FITNESS, PARENTING, RELIGION & SPIRITUALITY

0-7645-5146-9   0-7645-5418-2

Also available:
✔Adoption For Dummies
 0-7645-5488-3
✔Basketball For Dummies
 0-7645-5248-1
✔The Bible For Dummies
 0-7645-5296-1
✔Buddhism For Dummies
 0-7645-5359-3
✔Catholicism For Dummies
 0-7645-5391-7
✔Hockey For Dummies
 0-7645-5228-7

✔Judaism For Dummies
 0-7645-5299-6
✔Martial Arts For Dummies
 0-7645-5358-5
✔Pilates For Dummies
 0-7645-5397-6
✔Religion For Dummies
 0-7645-5264-3
✔Teaching Kids to Read
 For Dummies
 0-7645-4043-2
✔Weight Training For Dummies
 0-7645-5168-X
✔Yoga For Dummies
 0-7645-5117-5

TRAVEL

0-7645-5438-7   0-7645-5453-0

Also available:
✔Alaska For Dummies
 0-7645-1761-9
✔Arizona For Dummies
 0-7645-6938-4
✔Cancún and the Yucatán
 For Dummies
 0-7645-2437-2
✔Cruise Vacations For Dummies
 0-7645-6941-4
✔Europe For Dummies
 0-7645-5456-5
✔Ireland For Dummies
 0-7645-5455-7

✔Las Vegas For Dummies
 0-7645-5448-4
✔London For Dummies
 0-7645-4277-X
✔New York City For Dummies
 0-7645-6945-7
✔Paris For Dummies
 0-7645-5494-8
✔RV Vacations For Dummies
 0-7645-5443-3
✔Walt Disney World & Orlando
 For Dummies
 0-7645-6943-0

GRAPHICS, DESIGN & WEB DEVELOPMENT

0-7645-4345-8   0-7645-5589-8

Also available:
✔Adobe Acrobat 6 PDF
 For Dummies
 0-7645-3760-1
✔Building a Web Site For Dummies
 0-7645-7144-3
✔Dreamweaver MX 2004
 For Dummies
 0-7645-4342-3
✔FrontPage 2003 For Dummies
 0-7645-3882-9
✔HTML 4 For Dummies
 0-7645-1995-6
✔Illustrator CS For Dummies
 0-7645-4084-X

✔Macromedia Flash MX 2004
 For Dummies
 0-7645-4358-X
✔Photoshop 7 All-in-One Desk
 Reference For Dummies
 0-7645-1667-1
✔Photoshop CS Timesaving
 Techniques For Dummies
 0-7645-6782-9
✔PHP 5 For Dummies
 0-7645-4166-8
✔PowerPoint 2003 For Dummies
 0-7645-3908-6
✔QuarkXPress 6 For Dummies
 0-7645-2593-X

NETWORKING, SECURITY, PROGRAMMING & DATABASES

0-7645-6852-3   0-7645-5784-X

Also available:
✔A+ Certification For Dummies
 0-7645-4187-0
✔Access 2003 All-in-One Desk
 Reference For Dummies
 0-7645-3988-4
✔Beginning Programming
 For Dummies
 0-7645-4997-9
✔C For Dummies
 0-7645-7068-4
✔Firewalls For Dummies
 0-7645-4048-3
✔Home Networking For Dummies
 0-7645-42796

✔Network Security For Dummies
 0-7645-1679-5
✔Networking For Dummies
 0-7645-1677-9
✔TCP/IP For Dummies
 0-7645-1760-0
✔VBA For Dummies
 0-7645-3989-2
✔Wireless All-in-One Desk Reference
 For Dummies
 0-7645-7496-5
✔Wireless Home Networking
 For Dummies
 0-7645-3910-8